*Habits of
Highly Effective*
MARITIME
STRATEGISTS

*Habits of
Highly Effective*
MARITIME
STRATEGISTS

JAMES R. HOLMES

Naval Institute Press
Annapolis, Maryland

Naval Institute Press
291 Wood Road
Annapolis, MD 21402

© 2021 by James R. Holmes
All rights reserved. No part of this book may be reproduced or utilized in any form or by any means, electronic or mechanical, including photocopying and recording, or by any information storage and retrieval system, without permission in writing from the publisher.

Library of Congress Cataloging-in-Publication Data
Names: Holmes, James R., 1965– author.
Title: Habits of highly effective maritime strategists / James R. Holmes.
Description: Annapolis, Maryland : Naval Institute Press, [2021] | Includes bibliographical references and index.
Identifiers: LCCN 2021027757 (print) | LCCN 2021027758 (ebook) | ISBN 9781682477052 (paperback) | ISBN 9781682477106 (ebook) | ISBN 9781682477106 (pdf)
Subjects: LCSH: Naval strategy.
Classification: LCC V163 .H654 2021 (print) | LCC V163 (ebook) | DDC 359.4—dc23
LC record available at https://lccn.loc.gov/2021027757
LC ebook record available at https://lccn.loc.gov/2021027758

♾ Print editions meet the requirements of ANSI/NISO z39.48-1992 (Permanence of Paper).
Printed in the United States of America.

29 28 27 26 25 24 23 22 21   9 8 7 6 5 4 3 2 1
First printing

CONTENTS

Preface: An Undisciplined Study vii

Chapter 1	Pursue the Good Life in Strategy	1
Chapter 2	In Peace, Prepare for War	23
Chapter 3	In Peace, Win Friends and Overawe Opponents	81
Chapter 4	In War, Fight for a Better State of Peace	112

Notes 151

Index 173

PREFACE

AN UNDISCIPLINED STUDY

American physicist Richard P. Feynman once counseled an Australian youngster to "study hard what interests you the most in the most undisciplined, irreverent, and original manner possible."[1]

Feynman wryly complimented his correspondent, J. M. Szabados, on never having studied physics in any regimented way, wisecracking that because of her indiscipline there was "some chance that you may be successful."[2] Feynman's varied and often madcap career—which careened from working on the Manhattan Project that built the atomic bomb to winning the Nobel Prize in physics (for fundamental research on quantum electrodynamics) to translating Mayan hieroglyphics—testifies to the worth of a freeform approach to intellectual life and practical exploits.

Feynman's outlook on life worked well for him. He was a physicist with range. This book represents a deliberately short, Feynmanesque foray into a topic of grave importance: strategic leadership. The emphasis falls more heavily on leadership in the maritime realm, but it also should be of value to practitioners of ground and air combat. It is aimed at American readers, but those outside the United States should be able to adapt it for their purposes as well. In brief, the volume postulates that while sheer brilliance primes a fortunate few to excel at strategy, most aspirants do so not through inborn gifts but through conscious effort. Those who are set on becoming proficient at devising and executing strategy usually learn habits of mind, heart, and deed that enable them to put resources to work attaining larger ends that are entrusted to them by senior military or political leaders. Even the gifted can put a finer edge on their skills by making excellence their workaday routine. Eventually the skill becomes second nature.

Why is this book Feynmanesque? Because it is undisciplined. This is a personal document, and these are my views. They derive from my favorite sources of enlightenment. Others may draw insight from elsewhere; that is fitting and even desirable. Heterodoxy is good. Productive discord fosters fruitful debate and makes any team or alliance smarter. For instance, Indians might plumb Brahmin minister Kautilya's *Arthashastra*, the classic manual of statecraft from the ancient subcontinent, while also consulting the biographies of great figures from Indian history for both positive and negative lessons. Japanese leaders could comb swordsman-philosopher Miyamoto Musashi's *Book of Five Rings*, a treatise that is ostensibly about tactics for swordplay but covers far, far more; Japan has its own pantheon of biographies for students of strategy to review. And so forth. Sources of insight and inspiration are virtually inexhaustible.

This book, then, makes no pretense to have canvassed all the world's traditions. Nor do I pretend to have scoured "the literature" on leadership, as scholars say, reviewing current debates among specialists on this issue or that, looking for ways to improve the state of the scholarly consensus, or ranking all strategic leaders throughout history. I plunder philosophy, history, biography, and strategic theory for wisdom that is relevant for practitioners. Even pop culture puts in an appearance or two. Readers will look in vain for encyclopedic treatment of any of these disciplines.

My central goal is to apply a catalyst that helps strategic leaders think about the profession of arms without imparting predigested wisdom to them. Practitioners should ponder the ideas and examples put forward here, decide which selections speak to them most and least forcefully in light of their own experience, and then reach their own judgments.

In other words, this book is intended to be a *starting point* for the reader's journey, not the destination. The strategic canon—from classical Greek and Roman history and philosophy to tomes about strategic theory and beyond—furnishes a platform from which to begin investigating the habits that make strategic leaders great. The canon itself furnishes no set answers. Some insights from the sages prove perishable when put to the test of experience across decades and centuries. Writers had different agendas. They took different perspectives on their chosen subject, stressing everything from battlefield operations orchestrated by field commanders to "grand strategy" practiced by political grandees, diplomats, and supreme commanders. None of the masters was omniscient.

Accordingly, I take a synthetic approach, mixing and matching concepts from great books that have stood the test of time and can be put to work despite their occasional flaws. The result, I hope, is an original work of which Richard Feynman would approve and from which practitioners will profit.

WHAT IS STRATEGY?

Even freewheeling study of the kind that Feynman prescribes demands *some* modicum of structure. It was orthodoxy that Feynman disdained, not the laws of physics or the common vocabulary that is necessary for scientific discovery. Similarly, a shared definition of "strategy" is pivotal for those who practice it. Many thinkers and practitioners have put forward definitions of the term. To Prussian soldier and philosopher Carl von Clausewitz, a veteran of the French Revolutionary and Napoleonic Wars, strategy chiefly meant a framework for orchestrating battlefield operations such as that used by Frederick the Great or Napoleon Bonaparte—the martial icons who constitute his main points of reference—on European battlegrounds of old. In this understanding strategy equates to using tactical engagements to advance the larger purposes of the war.[3]

For the British military historian Basil H. Liddell Hart, a World War I veteran who wrote a century after Clausewitz and became the forefather of the concept of grand strategy, strategy meant wielding all implements of national power—not just the big stick of armed force, but diplomacy, information, and economic incentives and disincentives as well—in a concerted way to bolster the "state of peace" for a society and its friends.[4] To Liddell Hart, strategists should be reluctant warriors, laboring to fulfill their aims without actual recourse to arms. He beseeched statesmen and supreme commanders to take a long view that spans decades or even centuries and regards war as a last resort.[5]

In other words, a field commander inhabits a different milieu and needs a perspective and skills that differ somewhat from those of a supreme commander or cabinet official who lives in the capital city. The field commander oversees the use of arms for tactical and operational gain. The top-level leaders alloy different types of power into a single keen-edged implement for strategic and political gain, working to transmute battlefield results into a beneficial, long-lasting postwar settlement.

All of these definitions hold value, and we shall encounter them from time to time as this volume unspools. But simplicity is a virtue. For our purposes we turn to the late American Rear Adm. Joseph C. Wylie, another leading thinker of the twentieth century. J. C. Wylie, as he is best known, puts forward a deliberately generic definition of strategy. For him it is a "plan of action designed in order to achieve some end; a purpose together with a system of measures for its accomplishment."[6] Parse his words:

- *End*, a.k.a. *purpose*. In the politico-military arena every strategy aspires to fulfill some political end. Political leaders craft their goals while consulting with military leaders on how to use available "means"—armed might in the case of military strategy—to enable the government to achieve the outcomes that it desires more fully and rapidly. In other words, military strategy is about using armed force to help achieve larger national purposes.
- *Plan of action*. The strategist devises a theory that specifies how deploying available means in a particular way can produce desired operational and ultimately strategic effects. Such a plan, often called the "ways" of strategy, could involve anything from succoring a stricken populace after a natural disaster, to mounting a show of force to deter aggression, to dispatching forces into combat to defeat an antagonist. A plan of action is a theory that posits causes and effects, such as: taking course of action X will bring about operational or strategic effect Y. Like a scientific experiment in which researchers test their hypotheses against real-world data, any politico-military scheme is subject to revision as results from the field come in.

- *Measures.* The word *measures* can refer not just to courses of action, but also to *measurements* for gauging success or failure. Wylie does not specifically draw that distinction, but he strongly implies that strategic overseers must track progress toward desired ends. They cannot simply draw up a plan of action, set it in motion, and then trust that it will lead inexorably to a favorable outcome. Such an approach would invite underperformance or defeat. Manifold factors can confound any plan of action. Antagonists have every incentive to ruin it and possess the ingenuity to do so. Wise strategists therefore set benchmarks, monitor progress, and retune the effort periodically to ensure that they are progressing toward the goal.

Note that Wylie does not confine his workmanlike concept to handling fighting forces in times of war. In fact, strategy need not involve martial or foreign policy enterprises at all. Any endeavor in which a contestant charts a pathway toward some goal in a competitive environment, harnesses resources to achieve it, and adjusts or aborts the plan as circumstances warrant qualifies as strategy. That may be why books that are grounded in the military classics are popular among business executives.[7]

All of that said, I prefer an even simpler definition than Wylie's. For the purposes of this volume, I define strategy as the art and science of using power to fulfill purposes. Defining it that way has several virtues. It encompasses all of the usual elements—ends, ways, and means. It is also succinct—no small advantage when trying to communicate a concept to readers who may not be steeped in the arcane world of martial affairs. It conveys the dual character of strategy, which is at once a science that is susceptible to quantitative methods and an art that is grounded in the virtuosity of individual commanders or civilian officials. And it applies to all levels, from the nation's top military chief down to the commander leading troops against a foe on some battleground or distant sea. The nautical derivative, maritime strategy, is the art and science of using power to fulfill purposes relating to the sea. These are definitions for all seasons.

Two qualifiers and disclaimers: first, strategy is an undertaking with expansive range—a characteristic that enables practitioners to apply its precepts to many fields. Because this book is aimed mainly at military readers, however, it concentrates on strategic affairs in which armed might plays a key part. As noted before, the accent here is on saltwater, the domain where seagoing and shore-based forces attempt to command sea and sky in order to shape events on land. My background, interests, and professional appointment lie with the oceans, so nautical history and strategy make up my principal stockpile of strategic concepts and historical references. Others might tap different sources yet reach satisfactory findings.

Second, I take a casual approach to "levels" of strategy and war in this volume. Strategy unfolds on multiple levels, from grand strategy down to military strategy down to Clausewitzian battlefield strategy. But for strategy to be the supple concept that J. C. Wylie says it is, it must be accessible to everyone, from top political leaders to generals overseeing armies on dusty battlefields, air commanders launching squadrons into the wild blue, or admirals choreographing fleet movements on the high seas.

Some scholars and practitioners insist on defining strictly what political scientists call the "levels of analysis" on which human affairs take their course.[8] It is true that there is merit to precision. Many of the ideas distilled here, however, pertain to more than one plane within the politico-military hierarchy. The imperative to match goals with assigned resources is universal, for example. Otherwise senior leaders may demand more than tacticians can accomplish, or tacticians may waste effort and resources because they do not understand exactly what top leadership wants to accomplish. Mastering one's passions is another universal-trait underlying strategic excellence. It keeps rational decision-making in charge of martial enterprises.

Other ideas advanced here are narrower in scope. Accordingly, I telegraph when I believe that some habit of mind, feeling, or deed belongs more to one level of analysis than others, or more to a certain place along the continuum from peacetime strategic competition to armed conflict and back to peace. Nevertheless, I concur heartily with British military historian John

Keegan, who pronounced the distinction between strategy and tactics to be "as elusive as it is artificial."[9] What applies to strategy and tactics applies in large part to efforts to differentiate among the tactical, operational, strategic, and grand-strategic levels. One level blurs into the next. Too much precision may obscure worthwhile insights.

THE APPROACH

Wylie's discourse on "sequential" and "cumulative" operations is a recurring theme in this volume. In brief, he maintains that some endeavors follow a linear trajectory in which each tactical action comes after its predecessor in time and space. Actions take place in sequence, one leading to the next, until a force reaches its goal or something happens to break the sequence. For Wylie, sequential strategy represents the dominant pattern in open war.

But sequential strategy is not the only pattern. Submarine warfare, naval blockade operations, air warfare, and insurgent or counterinsurgent warfare yield strategic effects through many individual, often small-scale actions that are not connected to one another in time or space. In such cases, one tactical action does not necessarily lead to the next; many actions can take place all over the map, adding up to effects that are cumulative. This is a scattershot approach. Torpedoing a lone enemy freighter or downing a single enemy fighter plane makes little difference in itself to the outcome of an operation or campaign. Yet, demolishing many enemy aircraft can add up to major strategic impact, even if a force does not hammer away in sequence from one tactical action to the next to the next until its final goal is in hand. Cumulative operations wear down the foe little by little.

Wylie's distinction ranks among the most important in strategic theory, but he applies it too narrowly and understates its significance. What are such peacetime pursuits as diplomacy, economic policy, and force design and construction if not cumulative undertakings? They proceed by increments and in disparate fashion. Governments try to advance national well-being through a host of individual activities that do not usually take place in linear sequence aiming toward some definite end. Armed conflict departs from the cumulative pattern by adding a sequential component to the policy mix. War makes possible linear operations or campaigns culminating in victory. International relations reverts to its cumulative state when the guns fall silent and victors and vanquished together try to fashion a settlement with which everyone can live. Peace is cumulative; war is cumulative and sequential.

With these thoughts in mind, chapter 1 lays out the philosophical groundwork for this book. It looks to classical antiquity—the philosophical writings of Aristotle in particular—to make the case that strategists should groom themselves with "virtues" related to strategy, and that building sound habits blazes the surest route to strategic excellence. Students of strategy achieve excellence by emulating the virtues that successful strategists have displayed across the ages, while avoiding the vices of failed strategists. Chapter 2 explores the virtues and habits most valuable in the cumulative realm of peacetime competition, when strategic actors construct armed forces to fight should it become necessary. Chapter 3 returns to peacetime strategic competition, exploring the habits most useful for opponents who are trying to deter, coerce, or reassure one another without fighting. Finally, chapter 4 delves into habits useful in wartime—when both cumulative and sequential campaigns coexist—before reviewing the habits that are most relevant for peacemakers when the shooting stops, and when foreign policy reverts to its cumulative state.

A warning: by no means is this a how-to book or an algorithm offering foolproof methods for making oneself into a strategist of repute. Rather, it elucidates habits that are useful throughout the origins, conduct, and aftermath of war. It is designed to help readers study their profession in the kind of undisciplined, irreverent, and original—yet determined— manner that Feynman prescribed, and to discern the pathway to self-betterment for themselves. Remaining on the lookout for that path may be the most important habit of them all. With constant commitment, seekers may excel over the course of a career at arms.

1

PURSUE THE GOOD LIFE IN STRATEGY

Strategy is a habit. Or rather, it is a family of habits that accustoms practitioners of statecraft to mustering resources and putting them to work to help achieve goals that have been identified by top leadership. Successful practitioners gauge progress toward assigned goals regularly and adjust the effort if progress should prove elusive or come too slowly or fitfully. Good habits help prime strategists for success, while bad habits impede their quest for results. To excel at strategy, those who aspire to excellence must first learn what strategists do. Then they must practice doing it day in and day out.

THE TREASURE HOUSE KNOWN AS BIOGRAPHY

The title of this book pays tribute to American educator Stephen R. Covey's bestselling book, *The 7 Habits of Highly Effective People*, a work that urges readers—business executives in particular—to adopt timeless principles as their own. If these leaders take his advice, Covey contends, they will acquire a "character ethic" invaluable for strategists in any field of endeavor. They will make a habit of being proactive, starting each project with an end already in view, and on and on.[1] Habit is a recurring theme in popular literature. For example, a recent bestseller in the genre—*Atomic Habits*, by American writer James Clear—purports to teach readers how to break bad habits and replace them with good ones, achieving steady self-improvement bit by bit.[2]

Little in this book is incompatible with the arguments put forward by Covey, Clear, and like-minded writers. Indeed, Covey frames his inquiry with a testament from Aristotle to the importance of habit.³ Unlike these other works, however, this volume probes deeply into history, biography, and philosophy in search of relevant ideas and analogies. More important, it applies insights distilled from those fields to military and maritime affairs rather than to industry or everyday life. Just as war differs from peacetime enterprises, so strategic leadership differs from other ventures in noteworthy respects. In other words, the subject matter for this volume warrants a perspective somewhat different from that taken by works aimed at a broad popular audience.

Biography constitutes a fount of wisdom for newcomers to the field of strategy and veterans alike. Biography is individual history. Transcendentalist American philosopher Ralph Waldo Emerson held that "the world exists for the education of each man," but that "there is properly no history; only biography."⁴ Or, more accurately, history is the sum of the biographies of the human beings who make up the human race, past and present. An archetypal freethinker, Emerson implored individuals to come to grips with history and formulate their own judgments about it. "Every mind must know the whole lesson for itself—must go over the whole ground," he wrote. "What it does not see, what it does not live, it will not know."⁵

This is sage counsel for strategists. While history writ large divulges rich insights for makers and executors of strategy, acolytes who covet individual excellence can profitably study how notable strategists of the past thought, how successfully they mastered their passions, and what they did. George Washington remains an exemplar for American strategists, along with giants such as Civil War general Ulysses S. Grant and World War II admiral Raymond A. Spruance. Their virtues and vices, triumphs and debacles inform us, just as middling performances by lesser leaders do with their less-spectacular examples. To develop some worthwhile trait, strategists discover how people endowed with that trait developed it. Then they emulate these exemplars. They practice "virtue" as a matter of routine until it becomes a habit. Similarly, students of strategy study those who were prone to counterproductive traits, and then make it a practice to avoid such failings.

In a word, historical figures can provide a standard toward which to strive, examples of pitfalls to avoid, or sometimes both positive and negative examples wrapped up in a single individual. During the American Civil War, for instance, Maj. Gen. George B. McClellan fashioned the Union Army of the Potomac into a superb fighting implement. Yet, because he treasured that implement so much, he proved morbidly averse to wielding it in combat and risking seeing his handiwork damaged. As a result, the expert toolsmith made an indifferent field general—and provides mixed guidance for students of military affairs.

Novices emulate what their forbears did well, improve on it wherever possible, shun what they did poorly, and strive for continual refinement. With enough reflection and repetition, the strategic way of mind, feeling, and deed becomes second nature—a reflex or, to borrow a contemporary catchphrase, *muscle memory*. Nor is habituation a purely military thing. National Football League (NFL) quarterbacks such as Patrick Mahomes or Lamar Jackson refine their field generalship by undertaking self-criticism, studying game films, and conducting endless "reps" (meaning repetition, or practice sessions) of running and passing plays. Just as quarterbacks build physical and mental muscle memory for the gridiron, statesmen develop reflexes for politics and grand strategy, and military commanders increase their readiness for the field of conflict.

Strategists, however, get their reps in different ways. Consider the analogy to football once again. NFL teams play a self-contained game each week. Afterward they review game film and critique their performance, try to remedy shortcomings before the next contest, and study the upcoming opponent to compile a game plan. The nature of the game imparts structure and predictability to football strategy. War, the politico-military strategist's "game," is a messy, unstructured, open-ended struggle in which definitions of success and failure are fluid by contrast with tightly regulated athletic competitions. And, unlike the weekly rhythm of an NFL season, major wars occur only rarely—and never take place under the same scripted conditions. The nature of world politics limits the sample size of events and biographies for strategists to study. Even so, preparation through repetition—the same fundamental philosophy that rules the gridiron—holds for practitioners of diplomacy and military strategy as well.

THE GOOD LIFE FOR THE ANCIENTS

Just as biography furnishes data and examples to mimic or avoid, philosophy furnishes another trove of insight: it helps aspirants interpret data and examples and apply them to their own challenges. The realization that fulfilling the "good life" in any human enterprise involves habituating oneself to certain virtues or laudable traits is scarcely a novel insight.[6] It originated in the fourth century BC with Aristotle, a pupil of Plato and reputedly the tutor of the Macedonian king Alexander the Great. Aristotle was the founder of the Lyceum, a school in the city-state of Athens that, as Naval War College professor Carnes Lord puts it, was devoted to "research and teaching in every area of human knowledge."[7] Aristotle was arguably the finest thinker ever to grace the academy. For many, he was *the* philosopher. His teachings transcended boundaries between civilizations and eras, retaining their appeal from antiquity forward. Classical Arab scholars dubbed him the "first teacher," while medieval Europe knew him simply as "the philosopher."[8]

Such plaudits aside, Aristotle was an intensely practically minded philosopher. In his quest to improve human reasoning, he saw betterment of human thought and action as the purpose of philosophy. He confessed freely that much of what he wrote was sheer common sense. He simply codified everyday wisdom. Lord observes that Aristotle's writings derive less from abstract theory or universal laws that supposedly govern the course of human affairs than from his concept of "prudence," or "practical wisdom." Practical wisdom, Lord argues, parallels "the practical or prudential reasoning of the ordinary citizen, rooted as it is in everyday experience."[9] Aristotle is an inductive thinker, reasoning from what he observes about the world around him.[10] He deems the evidence of one's eyes and judgment the surest guide to action. The philosopher propounds a workmanlike vision for a trafficker in lofty ideas.

For Aristotle, politics is unlike mathematics or physics, disciplines that are ruled by universal, immutable laws. That is because people are not static quantities. They vary within and between societies. They interact in eccentric ways, and their interactions do not obey fixed principles. Because human affairs defy prediction, Aristotle admonishes his disciples never to disdain common sense, which he believes is the best substitute for universal laws of human affairs. In fact, he declares common sense to be the highest form of philosophy, a trusty guide to deliberation and action in the topsy-turvy world where people interact and ideas and interests clash.[11] And because common sense is common, the political philosophical canon—which amounts to codified common sense—is not some reliquary that is used to house arcane knowledge. It provides useful guidance. Consulting it spares practitioners of statecraft from having to rediscover the basics of their profession every time they encounter some new situation or task. They need not start from a blank slate.

This is philosophy for practitioners. Aristotle makes his pragmatic bent explicit. As Lord observes, Aristotle discerns "a fundamental difference between 'theoretical' sciences, which are pursued for the sake of knowledge, and 'practical' sciences"—politics foremost among them—"which are pursued principally for the sake of the benefits deriving from them."[12] Political science is "the 'practical' science par excellence."[13] Those aspiring to gain wisdom concern themselves less with discovering knowledge for its own sake than with improving praxis, or human action. They cultivate practical wisdom and through it boost their chances of prospering in arenas ruled by competition, dynamism, and unpredictability.[14]

Aristotle would doubtless classify strategy among the practical sciences. After all, it is a subdiscipline of political science, the premier science according to him. His paramount concern is politics within the city, or *polis*, yet war is a violent political act undertaken by the city. Peacetime strategic competition could culminate in war if the opponents took up arms—as they did incessantly in the days of Aristotle. Indeed, military affairs had to play a prominent part in any classical Greek treatise on statecraft. It was a matter of survival. The Aegean world was a warlike place riven by factional strife within Greek city-states, internecine feuding among them, and external warfare against domineering powers such as the Persian Empire.

And indeed, in his tract on *Rhetoric*, Aristotle catalogues five crucial topics for political deliberation, namely "what concerns revenues; and war and peace; and, further, what concerns the guarding of the territory; and imports and exports; and legislation."[15] Two of the five—war and peace and national defense—relate directly to martial endeavors. Two more—finance and trade—concern economics, and wealth is the substructure on which national power for warmaking and other pursuits is built.

It is no stretch, then, to appraise the art and science of strategy through an Aristotelian lens. The first teacher himself would urge strategists to equip themselves with practical wisdom that is suited to their special field of endeavor. Apprentices should learn to nurture virtue within themselves while instilling corporate virtue within institutions over which they preside. Even proficient strategists should strive ceaselessly to upgrade both their individual virtue and their custodianship over institutions. Both types of virtue are crucial to success, and both demand tending.

INDIVIDUAL VIRTUE THROUGH HABIT

Aristotle begins his investigation of virtue from first things, namely the human soul and the meaning of happiness. Happiness, he declares, "is a certain activity of soul in accord with complete virtue."[16] The soul is twofold. It pairs reason with "a certain other nature of the soul that is non-rational."[17] The not-strictly-rational element is "characterized by desire, and by longing in general."[18] It "does battle with and strains against reason."[19] So the two parts are at odds with each other. The rational faculty must tame passion through admonition, criticism, and exhortation. "In the case of the self-restrained person," Aristotle writes, the nonrational part "is obedient to the commands of reason—and perhaps it heeds those commands still more readily in the case of the moderate or courageous person, since then it is in all respects in harmony with reason."[20] Self-mastery means subduing the passionate part of the human soul while also drawing energy from it. It ranks among the foremost virtues for strategic leaders.

Virtue likewise corresponds to this distinction between the rational and the nonrational, "for we say that some of the virtues are intellectual, others moral."[21] Aristotle lists "wisdom, comprehension, and prudence" among the intellectual virtues and "liberality and moderation" among the moral virtues.[22] "Both the coming-into-being and increase of intellectual virtue," he explains, "result mostly from teaching—hence it requires experience and time—whereas moral virtue got its name [*ēthikē*] by a slight alteration of the term *habit* [*ethos*]."[23] Moral virtue is neither part of human beings by nature nor contrary to human nature, Aristotle contends. Rather, moral virtues are "present in us who are of such a nature as to receive them, and who are completed through habit."[24]

Fittingly for the founder of a school, Aristotle regarded education as critical to forming virtue. Education need not and must not stop when a pupil departs the schoolhouse. It must continue at the learner's initiative and may proceed along vectors of the learner's choosing. The important thing is that it does continue, lest intellectual growth stagnate. That is doubly true of strategic education. Students of strategy must consciously refresh and enrich their intellectual capital throughout their professional lives. They do so by investing their time and intellectual energy in reading about strategic theory, biography, military and diplomatic history, and literature of all kinds. Nor should they disdain fiction, sports, or popular culture. Wisdom is where you find it.

Other philosophers concur. In his masterwork, *On War*, Clausewitz proclaims that professional military education "is meant to educate the mind of the future commander, or, more accurately, *to guide him in his self-education* . . . just as a wise teacher guides and stimulates a young man's intellectual development, but is careful not to lead him by the hand for the rest of his life" [italics mine].[25] Self-education, he suggests, demands personal drive as well as curiosity.

In other words, commitment to intellectual self-betterment stems from a person's character. It emanates from a restless, venturesome, questing spirit—in other words, from the not-fully-rational part of the human soul. Moral rather than intellectual virtue spurs a never-ending search for new knowledge and insight and thus for keener intellectual virtue. Clausewitz seems to outdo Aristotle on this point, beseeching strategists to dedicate themselves to learning throughout their lifetimes. In Aristotelian parlance, they must habituate themselves to study and to introspection lest their faculties go barren and a turbulent strategic environment overtake them.

So much for why virtue is important, and why making virtuous deeds habitual is important. Aristotle explains how to deploy "correct reason" to nourish a virtue. "According to Aristotle's formal definition," as Professor Lord describes it, "virtue is a *disposition* involving intentional choice and directed toward observance of a 'mean' between vicious extremes" [italics mine].[26] Here again, the nonrational part of the soul provides the motive force. Desire, more than dispassionate analysis, excites an individual's search for the mean. Aristotle holds that the optimum lies somewhere along a scale between the excess and the deficiency of some particular trait. Virtues, he writes, "are destroyed through deficiency and excess, just as we see in the case of strength and health."[27] Overly strenuous gymnastic workouts—not just apathetic ones—"destroy strength," he argues, "and, similarly, both drink and food destroy health as they increase or decrease in quantity, whereas the proportionate amounts create, increase, and preserve health."[28] Vice is virtue carried to either unhealthy extreme, whereas locating the sweet spot between surplus and deficit unlocks virtue.

More to the point, Aristotle contends that "moderation and courage are indeed destroyed by excess and deficiency," but they too are "preserved by the mean" between extremes. Finding the optimum is the hard part, sustaining it a matter of repetition. Ideally speaking, virtue becomes a self-sustaining cycle. People become moderate by abstaining from seductive pleasures, and by making themselves moderate in temperament they can abstain from pleasures more easily. The same goes for courage, the quintessential martial virtue. "By being habituated to disdain frightening things and to endure them we become courageous," Aristotle writes, "and by so becoming, we will be especially able to endure frightening things."[29] In fact, the valiant among us *take pleasure in* enduring danger—or at any rate are "not pained by it"—while "he who is pained thereby is a coward."[30] Or, as President Theodore Roosevelt put it when reminiscing about his adventures ranching in the American West: "There were all kinds of things I was afraid of at first, ranging from grizzly bears to 'mean' horses and gunfighters; but by acting as if I was not afraid I gradually ceased to be afraid."[31] The virtuous enjoy exercising virtue, while noble deeds pain those given to vice.

That said, it is worth elaborating on Aristotle's discourse on how to strike the golden mean between excess and deficiency. He never says so clearly, but finding the mean cannot be a simple matter of determining the exact midway point between excess and deficiency. The optimum may lie closer to one extreme or the other, depending on the virtue. It need not be equidistant between the vicious extremes.

Like Aristotle, American mathematician Jordan S. Ellenberg postulates that human qualities fall along a continuum between the extremes, but he maintains that the continuum need not be linear. The amount of some quality may be unevenly distributed between the extremes, perhaps along a bell curve that bulges toward one end of the scale or the other.[32] Ellenberg is being precise, and a touch of mathematical precision is worthwhile here. Statisticians point out that the "median" need not be the same as the mean, and oftentimes is not. The median is the middle value in some set of things, whether the things be objects, data, or whatever. Half of the set lies above the median, and half lies below. The mean, by contrast, is the average value of the items comprising a set. Outliers can drag the mean above or below the median—sometimes well above or below.

If Amazon entrepreneur Jeff Bezos moves to a small rustbelt town with all his billions, for example, he will tug the town's mean wealth far higher while making little difference to its median wealth. His fortune is a huge sum in absolute terms, but at the same time it represents just one more data point among hundreds or thousands of residents of the town.

The same goes for virtue. If the desirable amount of some characteristic skews toward the excess or deficiency, the person searching to become virtuous rightly skews toward it as well. For Aristotle, as for modern statisticians, finding the mean is not a mechanical process of splitting the difference between extremes. Living the good life takes discernment.

Take courage again. If cowardice and foolhardiness are the extreme forms of courage, it is reasonable to posit that military leaders should incline somewhat toward the excess. After all, striding onto the battlefield in full knowledge that wounds or sudden death may await demands *some* measure of foolhardiness. The reckless *might* achieve their goals in close action; the fainthearted never give themselves the chance. It seems better for warriors to err on the side of disregarding personal safety.

Where does all of this leave us with regard to individual virtue for the strategist? There is a range of traits or characteristics that have made great strategists great throughout the annals of military history. Both the newcomer to the field and the oldtimer seeking further enlightenment should make a habit of studying the lives of great and not-so-great strategists in order to identify those characteristics, detect the Aristotelian mean for each, and strike it. Students of strategy should acclimate themselves to thinking critically about lists of virtues, vices, and habits compiled by others—including the list put forward in this book. As Aristotle reminds us, people vary. There is no substitute for thinking for yourself and exercising individual judgment.

Candidates for strategic leadership must pursue insights from history, political science, literature, and even sports or pop culture. The process will help them fortify existing strengths, offset their frailties, and meet their distinctive needs. Pursued with zest, the journey will prove fruitful and even pleasant. Succeeding chapters of this book unearth specific habits useful for strategists as individuals who crave intellectual and moral excellence. Some historical figures struck the golden mean, while others succumbed to the excess or deficiency of some quality. They all provide a service to posterity, supplying examples to emulate or shun.

POLITICAL REGIMES AND COLLECTIVE HABITS

Even so, excellence and virtue are not just for individuals. Aristotle's teachings on political regimes help handlers of statecraft discharge two all-important functions: he helps strategists know the polity they serve, and he helps their political masters manage that polity in stressful times such as strategic competition, war, and postwar peacemaking. An inscription at the Temple of Apollo at Delphi, in classical Greece, once admonished visitors to *know thyself*.[33] Doubtless the oracle aimed this injunction principally at individual supplicants, yet the word *thyself* could plausibly refer to a body of people working toward some common purpose. Indeed, even a casual survey of Herodotus' *Histories*, to name one venerable text, reveals that Greek city-states habitually dispatched emissaries to solicit advice from oracles before making public decisions.[34] Greeks afforded divine counsel the utmost respect.

The ancients, then, were comfortable extrapolating ideas about individual virtue and wisdom beyond the individual. And this makes perfect sense. After all, a society or organization is nothing more than a group of human beings, all of whom are prone to virtue or vice. Foreign policy institutions such as armed forces are an arm of politics and must abide by rules, procedures, and strictures encoded in the government they serve. Military commanders must know their own armed services as well as those with which they operate jointly. They must also acquaint themselves with the political authorities, diplomatic corps, financial agencies, and so on. Comprehending the workings of government and society is part of self-knowledge—not to mention acquaintanceship with the strategic environment within which warlike exploits take place.

Aristotle almost certainly would agree. He dwells on individual virtue, but, true to his political-science leanings, he also contemplates a corporate form of virtue centered on the *polis*. He regards collective virtue as a buttress for the "regime" that oversees and permeates the city. It is worth noting that by *regime* Aristotle means a city's way of life, not simply how it governs itself. Nowadays commentators tend to use the word *regime* interchangeably with *government*. Doing so impoverishes Aristotle's rich concept. For him, the regime encompasses far more, including economics, social classes, customs, and folkways—the entire culture.[35] In short, the regime that is implanted in a city is made up not just of governing arrangements but of its basic character.

The regime relates intimately to virtue. At its most elemental, Aristotle contends, a city is a partnership knit together by "fellow-feeling," or friendship, among members of the body politic.[36] Sage rulers shape and invigorate individual virtue to enrich collective virtue. They deepen and broaden the sense of kinship that unites the citizenry. The city coheres and endures under wise leadership. At the same time, cities exhibit virtues and vices, just as individual citizens do. They, too, are amenable to habit. In fact, Aristotle distinguishes a good from a base regime in that lawgivers enact measures that habituate citizens to be virtuous.[37] Habit, tended by beneficent rulers, equips the multitude for "living well."[38] Conversely, lawgivers in a debased regime issue mandates that degrade or corrupt the society.

Virtue perpetuated through habit, then, is not just relevant but central to good governance. Regimes vary in how effectively they foster the good life, but the strategist must work within the regime as it exists, blemishes and all. That is, properly classifying one's home regime helps the strategist discern the opportunities its governing arrangements, economics, and culture present while compensating for its limits, defects, and quirks. Aristotle postulates that there are six basic kinds of regime. Or, more accurately, he sees three regime types, each of which can assume an upright or an "errant and deviant" form:[39] "[S]ince it is necessary that the authoritative element be either one or a few or the many, when the one or the few or the many rule with a view to the common advantage, these regimes are necessarily correct, while those with a view to the private advantage of the one or the few or the multitude are deviations."[40]

As Aristotle defines them, "kingship" is rule by one ruler for the common good; "tyranny" is rule by the one for the benefit of the one; "aristocracy" is rule by the few for the common good; "oligarchy" is rule by the few for the benefit of the few; "polity" is rule by the multitude for the common good; and "democracy" is rule by the many for the advantage of the many. Aristotle seems to see oligarchy chiefly as rule by a well-to-do minority, although he also mentions the potential for a military oligarchy—the form of rule that held sway in ancient Sparta.[41] In other words, which regimes qualify as praiseworthy and which are blameworthy depends on whether the ruling class or individual ruler governs in the public interest or merely to advance selfish interests.

Public-spiritedness, then, is public virtue. Aristotle posits that there exists one "best regime" that spans historical epochs, peoples, and civilizations. Coming close to achieving the best regime ranks among the foremost tasks of statecraft. Aristotle is sympathetic to aristocracy—that is, rule by the leisured and public-spirited few who have time to contemplate larger things—but he seems to consider the best regime to be a mixture that combines elements of all of the upstanding regimes. At the same time, he concedes that the best regime might not fit all circumstances.[42] Societies vary, and culture stubbornly resists change. If the regime is a way of life, its political keepers may find it extraordinarily difficult to modify some aspects of it—even when doing so would benefit the public interest.

Customs are deep-seated within individuals and society. They have a way of slowing, deforming, or defying efforts to realign them. Herodotus proclaims culture to be "king of all."[43] Or as French philosopher Charles-Louis de Secondat, the baron of Montesquieu, puts it in *The Spirit of the Laws*: "Men care prodigiously for their laws and their customs; these make the felicity of every nation; it is rare for them to be changed without great upsets and great shedding of blood."[44] In modern parlance, Montesquieu believes political leaders might be better off "satisficing" in some cases.[45] That is, they might be better off erecting a less-than-ideal but achievable regime here and now instead of pursuing an optimal regime that might not be worth the time, costs, or hardships that fashioning it would demand (or that might elude them altogether). Political magnates of an Aristotelian bent should refuse to let the perfect become the enemy of the good—or the good-enough.

Understanding the regime clearly is important. It constitutes a crucial part of the setting within which strategy and operations unfold. Serving an oligarchy differs from serving a beneficent single ruler or a direct democracy. Generally speaking, comprehending the political system and working within its constraints is a passive function for military leaders. Domestic politics is part of the terrain.

Sometimes, though, generalship involves playing an active part in management and upkeep of the regime. Clausewitz approaches the nature of regimes and societies from an angle radically different from that taken by Aristotle. Clausewitz maintains that societies consist of three "dominant tendencies," or components: passions, which reside mainly with the populace; chance and creativity, chiefly the dominion of the field commander; and rational subordination of strategy to policy, mostly the province of government.[46] Senior leaders must adjust these elements during times of latent or actual strife, keeping them in balance to burnish prospects for strategic and political success. Chapter 4 returns to this topic.

Calibrating such intangibles as passion, chance, and rationality precisely is seldom easy. Statesmen must kindle popular passions for competitive ventures, but they must not fire them too hot lest the people demand too much from an undertaking and push the leadership into rash actions. Field commanders need sufficient latitude to carry out their missions, but their efforts must advance political aims. What might make tactical sense—say, leveling a city, complete with its inhabitants—may make no sense at all for the political purposes of the war. Political chieftains must keep strategy subservient to policy, but at the same time they must not suffocate the military effort or ask more from the army than it can deliver.

Senior-most military commanders are statesmen in fact, if not in name.[47] They help their political superiors achieve some semblance of societal balance, managing this Clausewitzian "paradoxical trinity" in the interest of attaining the leadership's political aims.[48] Here again, knowing one's home regime is critical. Aristotle helps strategists fathom how the people, the armed forces, and the government interact, as well as how statecraft, deftly wielded, can manage the basic forces that make up society.

Aristotle has a great deal to say about regimes and how they relate to virtue. A city is a partnership founded to promote collective well-being. Lawmakers enact laws that touch practical matters, such as finance and defense. Beyond that, they mold the society's character over time, enhancing or degrading virtue. Legislators should avoid constant tinkering with the laws, however, for as Aristotle notes, "law has no strength with respect to obedience apart from habit, and this is not created except over a period of time."[49] Strategists and the institutions they superintend contribute to regime maintenance in times of uneasy peace and times of war alike. And they do so in part by helping instill the proper habits among the populace, the government, and the military.

ORGANIZATIONAL REGIMES

Forging, sustaining, and retooling implements of strategy is part of strategy. Think of top military leaders and their political masters as toolmakers and maintainers. It is their job to establish, nurture, and oversee institutions as well as field physical implements such as ships or aircraft. Here, too, Aristotle is of help. While he concentrated his intellect primarily on individuals and city-states, his insights apply in large measure to stewardship over large organizations. Organizations are societies, and, like the Greek city of antiquity, they search for self-sufficiency. They have governing arrangements, usually tending toward rule by the few or the one. They have founders. They have distinct histories, traditions, customs, and mores. Microsoft Corporation is a society with its own regime; so is the aircraft carrier USS *Gerald R. Ford*. Aristotle would be comfortable with using his writings to illumine the inner workings of these societies.

Aristotle's appraisal of political regimes, in other words, applies to any sort of institution—including the martial institution over which a strategist presides. Just as a city is a partnership geared to attaining the good life, an organization is a partnership aimed at some common purpose. Its leadership should likewise inculcate virtues that help the institution fulfill its purpose, attaining the good life as the leadership defines it. Aristotle alludes to this when discussing smaller partnerships within the city. He lists household management as one endeavor that is subject to varying types of governing arrangements, but he also mentions everyday disciplines such as medicine, gymnastics, and seafaring.[50] Maintaining warlike institutions such as navies also must number among these pursuits, for woe soon befell the classical Greek city-state that neglected its defenses.

In this way, regimes also pervade bureaucratic institutions, not just cities or countries. For the first teacher, it bears repeating, a regime is not merely a set of governing arrangements; it is a way of life. It embraces formal governance, but also far more. Part of strategy is establishing, managing, and reforming organizations so that they perform smoothly once set in motion. Wise strategists attune themselves to the nature of the regime permeating a bureaucracy. They must also manage change. After all, Aristotle points out that over time incremental change can transform a regime for the better or for the worse. The leadership must enact beneficial reforms while making a kind of strategic Hippocratic Oath its credo. The leadership must foresee and forsake changes, both major and minor, that do the regime cumulative harm over time.

Aristotelian thinking, then, offers insight into everyday bureaucratic leadership as well as into politics. Ensuing chapters probe the rigors of institutional stewardship in greater depth. Summoning up the breadth of Aristotle's body of work shows that, as in other human enterprises, living the good life in strategy is a matter of intellectual and moral virtue, and that virtue comes from conscious effort to develop sound habits. Practicing collective virtue as a matter of routine makes a military institution proficient at arms.

HABIT FOR MODERNS

Turn-of-the-twentieth-century American psychologist-philosopher William James builds on the groundwork laid by Aristotle. Aristotle reveals why habits are important; James agrees on their paramountcy in human endeavors and shows how to develop them. In his 1890 treatise, *Principles of Psychology*, James explains how individuals go about training their reflexes. He also expands on the function habit plays for institutions and societies. While he takes an interest mainly in the physiology of habit—for example, how a novice becomes a virtuoso pianist or craftsman—he also holds forth on the "philosophy of habit."[51] His discourse on the philosophy of habit bears directly on the study of strategic leadership.

People are "bundles of habits," James writes.[52] Some habits come from instinct, others from education. It is easiest to implant habits while people remain young and their character and intellect remain "plastic."[53] By *plastic* James means "a structure weak enough to yield to an influence, but strong enough not to yield all at once."[54] He likens the process to water cutting ruts in soil: "Water, in flowing, hollows out for itself a channel, which grows broader and deeper; and, after having ceased to flow, it resumes, when it flows again, the path traced by itself before."[55] Young people are not yet set in their ways, in other words, while plasticity calcifies in middle age. Hence, James maintains, "the period between twenty and thirty is the critical one in the formation of intellectual and professional habits."[56] Before twenty is optimal "for the fixing of personal habits."[57]

The philosophy of habit yields important implications. For one, James writes, habit "simplifies the movements required to achieve a given result, makes them more accurate, and diminishes fatigue."[58] For another, habit "diminishes the conscious attention with which our acts are performed."[59] Reflex is automatic. It demands little deliberate effort, accelerates individuals' handling of routine chores, and thus frees up body and intellect for other undertakings. "The more of the details of our daily life we can hand over to the effortless custody of automatism," he says, "the more our higher powers of mind will be set free for their own proper work."[60]

American historian William Manchester makes much the same point in his biography of H. L. Mencken, an essayist and polemicist for the *Baltimore Sun* a century ago. Manchester reports that Mencken "wore the same blue suit, smoked the same cigars—fragrant specimens known to Baltimoreans as 'Uncle Willies'—and met the same friends each evening after work. It was this establishment of a definite pattern which permitted complete freedom in the abstract."[61] Mencken never had to make minor choices about such matters. He thus liberated his mental faculties for other things.

William James celebrates the role of habit in the profession of arms, at one point quoting the Duke of Wellington, the victor at the Battle of Waterloo, as having exclaimed, "Habit a second nature! Habit is ten times nature." The degree to which this is true "no one can probably appreciate as well as one who is a veteran soldier himself," James comments. "The daily drill and the years of discipline end by fashioning a man completely over again."[62] It is easy to understand this. Armed forces induct young people at a time in their lives when their character remains malleable; in effect the youngsters undergo a rebirth as fighting men and women through constant practice.

Yes, habit has its disadvantages as well as advantages, James says. It is "the enormous flywheel of society," its "most precious conservative agent. It alone is what keeps us all within the bounds of ordinance" and predisposes people to do hard, thankless labor that civilized society needs done.[63] In that sense, it renders invaluable service to the group.

But habit has its drawbacks for individuals, James writes. It can stultify: "It dooms us all to fight out the battle of life upon the lines of our nurture or our early choice, and to make the best of a pursuit that disagrees, because there is no other for which we are fitted, and it is too late to begin again."[64] By age twenty-five, "you see the professional mannerism settling down" on people.[65] "Little lines of cleavage" run through their character, including "the tricks of thought, the prejudices, the ways of the 'shop.'"[66] Ingrained habits verge on inescapable, James suggests. They reinforce established ways of thinking, feeling, and acting while deadening heterodoxy. James' lament conforms to Florentine philosopher-statesman Niccolò Machiavelli's observation that individuals find it nigh on impossible to change to keep up with changing times (to be reviewed in chapter 2), regardless of how crucial it may be to adapt to new circumstances.

What about the mechanics of forming or discarding habits? James pays homage to the work of Scottish philosopher Alexander Bain, one of the founders of the field of psychology. "Two great maxims" stand out in Bain's writings on "moral habit,"

James says.[67] First, after resolving to inculcate a new habit or shed an old, "we must take care to launch ourselves with as strong and decided an initiative as possible."[68] The aspirant should set incentives that encourage the new habit while discouraging the old: "In short, envelop your resolution with every aid you know."[69] And second, "never suffer an exception to occur till the new habit is securely rooted in your life."[70] As Bain maintains, instilling a new habit involves the "presence of two hostile powers," namely the old and the new trait, "one to be gradually raised into the ascendant over the other."[71] The new habit must achieve an unbroken string of victories over the old to solidify its standing as habit. Exceptions hamper self-training.

James adds a third and fourth precept to the two that Bain propounds. For the third, he urges readers to "seize the very first possible opportunity to act on every resolution you make."[72] In other words, take practical action to reinforce the new habit. And do so early and often. Otherwise the person intent on self-improvement risks paying lip-service to the new characteristic rather than actually putting it into practice. And fourth, to steel the will to act on the new habit, "keep the faculty of effort alive in you by a little gratuitous exercise every day. That is, be systematically ascetic or heroic in little unnecessary points, do every day or two something for no other reason than that you would rather not do it, so that when the hour of dire need draws nigh, it may find you not unnerved and untrained to stand the test."[73] Habit begets acceptable performance amid stress.

In short, William James, Alexander Bain, and Aristotle together prescribe a regimen for conditioning the intellect, the passions, and the body in healthful ways. Repetition makes exercise easy, in professional life as in the gym or the music conservatory. In combination, these thinkers show how to live the good life in strategy—advancing the national weal.

PHASED APPROACH TO THE INQUIRY

Aristotle observes that to everything there is a beginning, a middle, and an end. Accordingly, the remaining three chapters in this volume take the question of strategic habits in phases.

Clausewitz also helps inspire this sequential arrangement. Clausewitz consciously refrains from holding forth about peacetime diplomacy, and has still less to say about postwar peacemaking apart from stressing the supremacy of policy at all times. He avers that "the activities characteristic of war may be split into two main categories: *those that are merely preparations for war*, and *war proper*."[74] The Prussian scribe continues:

> The knowledge and skills involved in the preparations will be concerned with the creation, training and maintenance of the fighting forces. It is immaterial what label we give them, but they obviously must include such matters as artillery, fortification, so-called elementary tactics, as well as all the organization and administration of the fighting forces and the like. The theory of war proper, on the other hand, is concerned with the use of these means, once they have been developed, for the purposes of the war.[75]

Clausewitz wrote for the field general bestriding the battleground after the outbreak of armed conflict, and so he confines his inquiry to the war proper, after combatants submit some quarrel to the verdict of arms. He does not denigrate the importance of preparations for war, as some commentators hold. Why would he? A society that neglects warlike preparations in peacetime effectively hands the wielder of the military instrument—that is, the field commander—a faulty tool for chiseling out strategic gain. Clausewitz, who fought against Napoleon, witnessed firsthand the wages of deficient peacetime preparations; he simply had a different agenda and audience in mind for his own writings. What happened in contact on the battlefield was what interested him, rather than how governments raised, supplied, or maneuvered armies.

While this book adopts Clausewitz's phased approach, it takes a broader perspective than his. This is not a book exclusively about war strategy, although warfare comprises a major part of it—as it must. After all, as the classical Chinese general Sun Tzu warned, war is "a matter of vital importance to the

State; the province of life or death; the road to survival or ruin. It is mandatory that it be thoroughly studied."[76] Aristotle could only applaud. Still, strategy is not solely about fighting. The British military historian B. H. Liddell Hart, the forefather of the concept of grand strategy, notes correctly that strategy is about orchestrating a "better state of peace," a peace that benefits the state's and society's interests and purposes.[77] Statesmen and commanders should fix their eyes on a better state of peace throughout the cycle from peace to war and back again. In fact, Liddell Hart, echoing Sun Tzu, exhorts them to do their best to get their way *without* fighting—avoiding the costs, perils, hardships, and reversals of fortune endemic to warfare.

Liddell Hart's grand-strategic perspective—the perspective of political and military leaders who fuse not just military but diplomatic and economic instruments into a single weapon for political gain—shapes and permeates this inquiry into the habits that are most precious for strategists. As Clausewitz observes, top commanders act concurrently as soldiers and statesmen. In fact, he intimates that the supreme commander should join the political cabinet, embodying the interface between policy and strategy. The portfolio of strategic habits that befits top leaders differs from the portfolio that is best for the commander in charge of an army corps, a naval task force, or an expeditionary air force—in other words, for the purely military overseer of an armed contingent.[78] This book aspires to help strategists operating on each of these levels refine their professional acumen.

Chapter 2 covers the phase before the outbreak of armed conflict, when competitors gird for war should it come. Chapter 3 inquires into how peacetime strategists manipulate armed forces to influence opinion among friends, potential foes, and bystanders, and so try to get their way without actual resort to arms. Chapter 4 investigates the war proper, when those who wield force attempt to compel their antagonist to do their bidding, and closes by reviewing habits that help the victor consolidate its political gains—founding a durable postwar order that gladdens the hearts of the citizenry while being acceptable to the defeated.

The good life in strategy, then, involves taking the long view and keeping one's eyes riveted on peace, even amid the clangor of combat. It involves amassing strategically relevant resources in peacetime and handling them to good effect in peacetime strategic competition and wartime alike. And perhaps most important, it involves setting priorities and enforcing them ruthlessly lest a combatant take on too much and exhaust its stock of resources. Strategic leaders thrive when they develop a repertoire of habits that make these higher-order functions second nature.

2

IN PEACE, PREPARE FOR WAR

Strategic leaders who crave excellence must school themselves in a variety of warlike endeavors that range far beyond frontal engagements on the battlefield. As an old martial truism puts it, there is more to war than warfare. In fact, there are no successful frontal engagements without diligent peacetime preparation for full-scale war. Political and military leaders must ready implements of war before the shots ring out, and they must consolidate a mutually acceptable peace once the guns fall silent. Nor is war preordained—let alone desirable—in any event. From antiquity forward, the greats of military history and theory have counseled political and military grandees to avoid violence whenever possible; instead, they argue, bloodless victory should be their paramount goal. Chinese general Sun Tzu, to name one, declared winning without fighting to be "the acme of skill."[1]

It is important to note that Sun Tzu was not some cuddly peacenik or devotee of nonviolent conflict resolution. Soldiers are servants; advancing the sovereign's interests or desires in the face of intransigent foes constitutes the core task of generalship. Indeed, *winning* outranks *without fighting* in Sun Tzu's formula. Nevertheless, Sun lists pragmatic reasons for seeking victory without bloodshed. First, winning without actual recourse to arms preserves the sovereign's forces and the national treasury, not to mention the resources and manpower found within the territory that the sovereign covets. Indeed, it is military prudence, rather than moral qualms or goodwill toward the adversary, that obliges rulers and commanders to devote ample forethought to a matter of dispute before unsheathing the sword.

Western strategic thinkers have agreed, albeit not in such stark terms. To be sure, Prussian soldier-philosopher Carl von Clausewitz devotes most of his treatise, *On War*, to instructing field commanders on how to use armies in action to impose the sovereign's will on an unwilling foe. His operational perspective shapes his discourses. But when Clausewitz explains how to *win* a war, transmuting tactical success into strategic and political results, only one of the three methods that he identifies involves actual battle. True, crushing the enemy and imposing terms offers the swiftest, surest route to victory, Clausewitz says. But rendering a foe unable to carry on the struggle "can, in practice, be replaced by two other grounds for making peace: the first is the improbability of victory; the second is its unacceptable cost."[2] Wielders of armed force can dishearten their opponents—in other words, convince them that the fight borders on unwinnable. Or they can convince their opponents that victory will cost more than it is worth to them or even exceeds their means altogether. Either way, by Clausewitzian reasoning a rational protagonist should lay down arms and come to terms rather than offer fruitless battle.

Similar logic animates American naval officer and historian Alfred Thayer Mahan. Reputed to be a prophet of apocalyptic naval battles, Mahan in fact deplored armed force as an "alien element" in economic and diplomatic intercourse.[3] War is bad for trade, and thus for prosperity, he maintained. Consequently, he warned against using arms unless forced to it by some aggressor. Mahan also noted that maritime strategy, unlike other types of military strategy, operates in peacetime and wartime alike. It has "for its end to found, support, and increase, as well in peace as in war, the sea power of a country."[4] Handlers of maritime strategy are entrepreneurs, he argued. The best of them remain forever on the lookout for opportunities to augment national sea power, whether by upgrading naval forces or by seeking well-placed sites for militarily relevant facilities such as naval bases overseas. But they should refrain from picking a fight whenever possible.

Judging from the canon, strategic leaders confront two main challenges in peacetime: building military and naval forces sufficient to deter or defeat opponents in wartime, and brandishing those forces in nonviolent fashion to deter or coerce opponents while giving heart to allies and friends. Strategic leaders, then, act as toolmakers while at the same time carrying on what I call an "armed conversation" or "armed debate" with rival contenders about who is stronger, who is weaker, and who is more resolute. This chapter explores strategic leaders' role as builders, and chapter 3 investigates their role as warrior diplomats. The more adroitly strategic leaders perform as constructors and conversationalists, the more imposing the nation's armed forces will seem—and the greater their power to impress and sway others will be.

Few prospective foes choose an unwinnable fight, so strategic overseers have a duty to field formidable forces, and to draw on those forces to project a convincing image of power and resolve. The right habits will help them discharge their duty with aplomb.

FASHION IMPLEMENTS OF WAR

Because of contemporary circumstances, superintendents of strategy and force design must cast the necessary armaments in peacetime. In an industrial age there is no improvising fleets or other implements of maritime might after war breaks out. Fitting out ships and planes simply takes too long. Think about World War II. The United States got a head start on preparations for war, thanks to farsighted leaders such as Rep. Carl Vinson (D-Ga.), the influential chairman of the House Armed Services Committee. Starting in 1934, Vinson shepherded three modest naval expansion bills through Congress, despite lingering economic hardships from the Great Depression. That made an auspicious beginning.

Then, in June 1940, France fell to Hitler's army. The next month, spurred by the prospect that events soon would compel America to join the war, lawmakers rushed the "Two-Ocean Navy Act" into law. The measure authorized the construction of 257 warships and 15,000 combat aircraft, increasing the Navy's aggregate tonnage by 70 percent.[5] In effect, the United States built a second navy under this prescient legislation. As a result, the nation commenced gathering sinews of military power long before finally joining the fighting in December 1941.

Even so, it took almost three years from the passage of the Two-Ocean Navy Act for those ships to be built and start arriving on station. Until mid-1943, U.S. naval commanders had to make do with the remnants of the armada that had been shattered at Pearl Harbor. The delay granted the enemy time. Strategically offensive operations remained nigh on unthinkable. Fleet sailors and aviators did well with what they had, especially at the Battle of Midway in June 1942. But fortune might not have smiled on American arms in the way it did. No practitioner of statecraft worth the name knowingly courts risks of the magnitude that the United States faced during World War II. Future policymakers and commanders must ensure that the force in being today is sufficient to discharge its combat purposes today. Allowing a foe to run amok for months or years before reversing its aggression is a mark of imprudent strategy.

Foresight, then, is at a premium in modern strategic competition. Most of the battle panoply must already exist at the onset of fighting. That is because prospective opponents are intent on winning short, sharp wars in their immediate environs rather than protracted, wide-ranging conflicts such as the Pacific War. They will refuse to give America time to arm. So again: although the Navy is steeped in the lore of World War II, no one should regard that as a template for future U.S. strategy. Better to foster the intuition, prudence, and sense of urgency of a Carl Vinson than to permit antagonists time to fulfill their purposes before U.S. forces can build up strength, reach the scene of battle, and turn them back. The war could be over—and lost—before then.

In a sense, then, it is the job of peacetime strategists to peer into the future as best they can, divine which weapons and platforms will be handiest in future combat, and build them in sufficient numbers ahead of time. But there is more to the force-design process than budgeting, managing programs, or dreaming up ingenious technology—the kind of endeavors that dominate daily life in the Pentagon and the operating forces.

These tasks are necessary, but far from sufficient. To fashion the implements for sea warfare, statesmen and commanders must nurture the supply chain for maritime commerce and naval power, developing policies and enacting laws that foster militarily relevant industries and guarantee that there will be a sufficient supply of recruits to handle vessels, aircraft, and weaponry in both peacetime and wartime maneuvers.

Few of the classics discuss how to raise a force. Sun Tzu concerns himself mainly with how to maneuver an already existing army to achieve strategic effects. Likewise, Clausewitz pays scant attention to peacetime preparations for war—and that is by deliberate choice. As chapter 1 noted, Clausewitz was chiefly interested in what happened during active fighting—the bloodstained interlude that he terms the "war proper."[6] He makes perfunctory obeisance to "preparations for war," saying that they are "concerned with the creation, training, and maintenance of the fighting forces."[7] The war proper, on the other hand, "is concerned with the use of these means, once they have been developed, for the purposes of the war."[8] Chapter 4 looks into the open-war phase of strategic competition.

By contrast, Alfred Thayer Mahan lavishes attention on peacetime preparations for war. In his landmark work, *The Influence of Sea Power upon History, 1660–1783*, he spends the first ninety pages or so pondering which nations have the right stuff to take to the sea and how political and military leaders can tap that potential. Mahan believed that America did have the right stuff to go to sea, but he fretted that Americans might not exercise their seaward option because circumstances did not force them to do so. The United States was less like the British Isles or the Netherlands—countries that were not well-endowed with natural resources were obliged to trade with other countries if they wanted to become rich—than like France, a pleasant land that could satisfy its own needs and wants without the bother of overseas commerce. French society could prosper on land; so could America's.

In that sense, North America's natural bounty was a curse. Nature had lashed previous oceangoing hegemons—such as Spain, Portugal, Holland, and Britain—to the sea in search of wealth. Their inhabitants confronted a bleak choice: they could take up seafaring or resign themselves to a life of poverty. But nature had made that unnecessary for America. Sea power was an option for the United States, not a must. Americans might make the conscious political choice to stay home rather than venture out to sea in any sustained way.

Mahan dreaded that possibility and set out to keep it from coming true. He had a cause, and he wrote with an agenda. Despite his reputation, he was no mere chronicler of sea fights in the age of sail, and no mere advocate of battleships. He wanted Americans to take up mercantile seafaring in the age of steam, and he insisted that they construct their first oceangoing battle fleet to protect American coastlines and merchant shipping. He took a broad view of sea power and maritime strategy, depicting the naval profession in grand-strategic terms of which British military historian B. H. Liddell Hart could only approve. "The necessity of a navy," Mahan wrote, "springs . . . from the existence of a peaceful shipping, and disappears with it, except in the case of a nation which has aggressive tendencies, and keeps up a navy merely as a branch of the military establishment."[9]

And Mahan, as a sea-power evangelist, wielded clout.[10] British historian John Keegan, himself one of the greats in the field, later anointed Mahan "the most important American strategist of the nineteenth century."[11] Mahan's writings prodded the United States to look outward in search of prosperity, diplomatic influence, and naval might. Such was the imperative of sea power.

How did the Mahanian project work? Mahan describes a "chain of sea power" connecting the homeland to foreign harbors.[12] Though an avowed Anglophile, he celebrates a French statesman, Jean-Baptiste Colbert, for building up French sea power during the reign of the "Sun King," Louis XIV (1638–1715). Under Colbert's "wise and provident administration" as navy minister, Mahan writes, French officialdom orchestrated domestic agriculture and manufacturing; "internal trade routes and regulations" facilitating movement of goods between the French interior and coasts; laws and regulations encouraging construction of shipping to carry French wares across the sea;

and treaties opening freer market access than France's imperial competitors enjoyed.[13] Colbert instituted countless measures to encourage production at home, lay down shipping to carry on trade and wage war, and pry open foreign markets. Mahan lauds Colbert for showing how building up sea power—defined as production, shipping, and markets—should be done.[14]

The trio of commerce, ships, and seaports makes a handy way to think about the seaward enterprise. Yet Mahan casts Colbert not just as a visionary but as the protagonist in a cautionary tale. In an autocratic society, Mahan notes, the will—even the whims—of the autocrat are all-important. Because Colbert "was not king," his maritime project thrived only until he fell from royal favor—as he eventually did.[15] As it had in the past, the French crown proved inconstant. In 1672 King Louis turned his energies from the sea to land warfare against the Netherlands. Once royal attention wandered, French sea power languished. The Sun King did not have the seafaring habit of mind. As Mahan laments, all the "wonderful growth" that Colbert had nourished "withered away like Jonah's gourd when the government's favor was withdrawn."[16]

French maritime culture wilted as well. "Time was not allowed" for sea power to put down roots "deep into the life of the nation," Mahan maintains.[17] Continental war struck at "the agricultural classes, manufactures, commerce," and markets.[18] "Louis steadily turned his back upon the sea interests of France, except the fighting ships, and either could not or would not see that the latter were of little use and uncertain life" if the marine industry and the merchant fleet were to perish.[19] People are policy. Dismissing the architect of French sea power undid the maritime project that he had fostered.

While Mahan sifts through the age of sail for lessons, he frames sea power in strikingly modern terms. In effect he regards maritime strategy as a matter of building parallel supply chains—one for seagoing trade and commerce, the other for naval power. Mahan depicts industry at home, commercial and naval fleets, and markets and bases abroad as three inseparable components of sea power. He does not put it this way, but, judging from his formula, sea power must be a product of *multiplication* of the three variables—not addition. If any determinant of sea power—commerce, ships, bases—is zero, the total is zero; a would-be seafaring people has few prospects. For example, if industry produces nothing worth selling, the government has little need for merchantmen to carry cargo. It also has little need for a navy to protect nonexistent commerce, and, without sufficient tax revenue, it has few means to pay for a navy in any event. Nor does it need foreign marketplaces or naval stations, since producers have little merchandise to sell and scant need for overseas access. The seagoing enterprise founders.

Strategists of Mahanian leanings, then, operate a foundry for sea power. They make a habit of thinking in terms of economics as well as diplomacy and warfare and are singleminded about augmenting sea power. They also devote themselves to ensuring the long-term upkeep of sea power, making every effort to prevent the links in the twin supply chains from corroding. Constancy is their watchword; their key habits are maritime consciousness and passion for the sea.

Mahan alighted on the concept of the supply chain long before economists coined the phrase. For economists, three clusters of economic activity make up the commercial supply chain—production, distribution, and consumption. The supply chain connects industrial production at home; distribution from domestic points of departure through air, sea, or land transport; and markets overseas, which enable consumers to procure goods to satisfy their needs and wants. Maritime trade and commerce constitute a subset of the supply chain in which goods travel by water. Bulk goods typically go by ship, because waterborne transport costs less. This is a purely peacetime construct. Hofstra University professor Jean-Paul Rodrigue, a leading economic geographer, says little about geopolitics and still less about furnishing a naval protector for seaborne trade and commerce.[20]

Still, what Rodrigue calls "the geography of production, distribution, and consumption" provides waypoints to any aspirant to mercantile and military sea power.[21] Mahanian sea power is little more than the bluewater global supply chain endowed with a guardian in the form of a navy. Domestic industry produces both the goods and the merchantmen needed to transport them to foreign commercial harbors. Naval power is the product of a supply chain that comprises naval shipbuilders and munitions makers; the combat fleet itself; and naval stations established to support operations far from home. Distinguishing between the commercial and naval supply chains reveals how symbiotic they are. The government harvests revenue from trade and commerce (often, nowadays, through income taxes) in order to fund pursuits that officialdom deems worthwhile—including a navy to safeguard trade and commerce. The navy, then, safeguards the stream of tax revenue that helps pay for ships of war.

To Mahan, starting up this virtuous cycle of sea power and keeping it turning into the indefinite future is one of the foremost acts of statecraft. To help U.S. political and military leaders estimate the United States' potential and manage its maritime quest prudently, he postulates six "elements of sea power" that provide a rough and ready way to gauge any country's fitness for seaborne pursuits.[22]

The first three attributes are geophysical, and so are more or less fixed. For instance, the United States' "geographic position" is immutable.[23] Mahan implores maritime thinkers and practitioners to cultivate the geographic habit of mind and infuses geography into all of his works. Oceans adjoining each coast help insulate the republic from Eurasian geopolitics, but at the same time they make it hard to wage a forward strategy in what American geopolitics scholar Nicholas Spykman calls the "rimlands"—the borderlands between a continent's deep interior and the sea. (Chapter 3 has much more to say about Spykman's rimlands strategy.) North America not only lies thousands of miles from the rimlands, but shifting forces from one U.S. seacoast to another posed a daunting challenge in Mahan's day. North and South America formed a supercontinent joined by the narrow isthmus of Central America. Ships could cross from Atlantic to Pacific or back only by journeying around Cape Horn, traversing storm-wracked waters at the southern tip of South America. Geography imposed strategic quandaries on Americans until the Panama Canal was completed in 1914, providing shipping traffic a shortcut between the oceans.

Similarly, Mahan writes, a country's "physical conformation" and "extent of territory" are largely set.[24] Short of acquiring new lands or devising new ways to exploit natural resources, its inhabitants must content themselves with the resource endowment nature has granted them. The length of its shorelines and the number of harbors are mostly fixed as well. It is possible to modify physical attributes, sometimes dramatically so. Harbors can be dredged and new infrastructure built. Mahan alludes to the possibility of improving Gulf of Mexico seaports such as Pensacola and Key West to help the U.S. Navy control the Gulf and Caribbean Sea.[25]

Moreover, Mahan showed how digging a canal across the Central American isthmus would transform the Caribbean and Gulf from a backwater into one of the world's great marine thoroughfares.[26] Together they would become a true middle sea, much like the Mediterranean Sea after the Suez Canal went into service in the 1860s. The Panama Canal made possible a drastic increase in maritime movement between the Atlantic and Pacific. It ameliorated the strategic plight that beset a bicoastal United States, much as the Suez Canal opened a sea route from the Mediterranean Sea, which separates the European and African land masses, to the Red Sea and Indian Ocean. Seldom does an opportunity come along to initiate engineering works with such sweeping strategic import. Still, it behooves strategic leaders to remain watchful should such an opportunity beckon. Singlemindedness and steadfastness are useful habits for them.

Mahan's three other elements of sea power are malleable to one degree or another, and so are subject to strategic leadership. First, consider demographics. For Mahan, the "number of population" refers both to the total population and the makeup of that population.[27] Population density constitutes part of this determinant of sea power. Mahan claims that the Confederacy could have broken the Union Navy blockade and defended its internal waterways during the American Civil War if the South had had a greater population density. Instead, the federal blockade held. Union gunboats penetrated the Mississippi River, roaming freely in the Confederate interior. In effect, Mahan declares, Dixie's rivers "turned against" Southerners, admitting "their enemies to their hearts."[28] Never had history witnessed such a decisive use of maritime power, he concludes, and the riverine campaign owed its success as much to sparse Southern demographics as to Northern naval heroics.[29]

But basic population figures tell only part of the story. To thrive, a populace must produce a critical mass of specialists in marine-oriented trades. Mahan asserts that "a great population following callings related to the sea is . . . a great element of sea power."[30] During the age of sail Great Britain generally prevailed over a more populous France because Britain had more sailors, shipfitters, and so forth. As an early mover in industrialization, Britain also benefited from having more people than France working in industries that were not oriented toward the sea but were compatible with seafaring. Mahan relates the tale of Sir Edward Pellew, a Royal Navy captain who recruited Cornish miners for his frigate crew at the outbreak of war against revolutionary France in 1793. Trained sailors were in short supply, so Pellew sought crewmen where he might—and won the war's first frigate action against a veteran French crew.[31]

So, while having a bigger total population than your likely foes is helpful, it is just as important to have a population that is endowed with the skills and talents that matter most in sea war. Should strategic leaders try to field overpowering forces in peacetime? Not necessarily, Mahan says. A business-oriented republic such the United States needs to maintain enough strength in peacetime to forestall defeat in wartime. Staving off disaster buys time to bulk up the armed forces and win. He observes:

> If time be . . . a supreme factor in war, it behooves countries whose genius is essentially not military, whose people, like all free people, object to pay for large military establishments, to see to it that they are at least strong enough to gain the time necessary to turn the spirit and capacity of their subjects into the new activities which war calls for. If the existing force by land or sea is strong enough so to hold out, even

though at a disadvantage, the country may rely upon its natural resources and strength coming into play for whatever they are worth—its numbers, its wealth, its capacities of every kind.[32]

To be sure, Mahan was thinking of major wars in the ages of sail and steam, when combatants had some leisure to augment their forces at the onset of war. His observation may still hold for big, protracted wars. But combat operations tend to be brief in an era like today, when antagonists mostly resort to arms to obtain limited aims around their own geographic peripheries. They want to win before powerful outsiders can intercede. Countering their ambitions makes it imperative to invest in military strength sufficient to win short wars, and to make the investment in peacetime. Mahan is correct: America is a republic not given to offensive warmaking. It should not maintain surplus military forces. Yet, estimating how much is enough to meet strategic demands remains a matter of prudential judgment for strategic leaders.

Mahan also is right about how "national character" shapes peacetime strategy and force-building.[33] It opens up some strategic vistas, forecloses others, and steers foreign policy in certain directions. National character, or culture, is irrepressible if not intractable. Popular will, traditions, and customs mold even authoritarian regimes that appear indifferent to the sea, and in turn government laws and policies help mold the national character. As a result, Mahan, like Aristotle, perceived an interactive relationship between national character and the character of government. The Spanish imperial regime, he maintained, was prone to "cramp and blight" the entrepreneurial spirit, but at the same time "the character of a great people breaks through or shapes the character of its government."[34] Had Spaniards' national bent favored oceanic trade, "the action of government would have been drawn into the same current," he writes.[35]

If even absolute rulers have to accommodate themselves to culture, managing it vexes leaders of liberal governments even more. Predictably, since Mahan considers commerce to be the prime mover impelling the quest for sea power, he urges political and military leaders to encourage their society's propensity to trade. He assigns commerce top priority. To him, not high-seas swashbuckling but "the tendency to trade, involving of necessity the production to trade with" is "the national characteristic most important to the development of sea power."[36] Trade sweeps peoples to the sea in search of prosperity. Once there, they clamor for naval protection. Accordingly, Mahan seems to believe that naval excellence lies downstream from vibrant seaborne commerce and flows naturally from it. Sustaining an existing culture of marine trade or implanting one where it does not exist constitutes a leadership challenge of a high order.

National character thus demands care and tending. Senior political and sea-service leaders must make an ingrained saltwater culture their goal. Wolfgang Wegener, a World War I German admiral, attests to the fervor that coursed through British nautical culture during the ages of sail and steam. Britons exhibited unshakeable "strategic will" to the sea, Wegener maintains.[37] Seawater flowed through their veins. They combined the nautical habit of mind with passion for the sea. Great Britain in its imperial heyday is an example worth replicating. To follow the British example, officialdom must nurture maritime culture in peacetime. Or, as Mahan puts it, the "government by its policy can favor the natural growth of a people's industries and such seagoing bent, when they do not naturally exist; or, on the other hand, the government may by mistaken action check and fetter."[38]

The "character of the government" seems to occupy pride of place among Mahan's six sea-power determinants.[39] It is the main repository of strategic leadership. Mahan proclaims that "according as it is wise, energetic and persevering, or the reverse," the exercise of "intelligent willpower" on the part of strategic and political leaders begets "success or failure in . . . a nation's history."[40] Liberal governments fare best when they act in tune with the national character:

> a government in full accord with the natural bias of
> its people would most successfully advance its growth

in every respect; and, in the matter of sea power, the most brilliant successes have followed where there has been intelligent direction by a government fully imbued with the spirit of the people and conscious of its true general bent.[41]

Like Aristotle, Mahan regards the type of regime as crucial to national destiny. Mahan seems to think that liberal governments hold the advantage over illiberal ones, but that need not always be the case, he writes. "Free governments have sometimes fallen short, while on the other hand despotic power, wielded with judgment and consistency, has created at times a great sea commerce and a brilliant navy with greater directness than can be reached by the slower processes of a free people."[42] An autocrat such as Louis XIV can issue mandates and see them obeyed. The advantage in energy and decisiveness goes to authoritarian regimes.

The disadvantage is that the entire enterprise hinges on the wishes of the ruler. If the ruler's enthusiasm flags, as the Sun King's did, the seaward project may come to grief. But even if one ruler remains committed to high-seas endeavors, the ruler's successor may evince little passion for them. In that case, sea power faces a grim fate. The result is that seafaring tends to embed itself more deeply in liberal societies, even though authoritarian societies can outrace them to the oceans if led wisely, decisively, and consistently.

Even so, while Mahan believes that instilling a national character that favors commerce comes first, he also beseeches strategic leaders to take an active hand in designing and maintaining diplomatic and military institutions—especially the navy. Again, singlemindedness is paramount. The leadership must imbue the navy with cultural traits that are conducive to battle success. Or, to borrow from the observations of Royal Navy Fleet Adm. Andrew Browne Cunningham, it takes three years to build a ship but three centuries to build a tradition.[43] A navy is far more than matériel alone. It is also human beings and their habits. One generation bequeaths to the next the proper ways of looking at the naval profession, along with bureaucratic procedures stipulating how the institution will conduct its affairs. Fostering a healthy new culture or refreshing an existing culture gone stale demands care.

Mahan visits the age of Franco-British sea warfare once again to punctuate his claims about culture. He catches sight of a cultural mismatch between the rivals. He contends that the Royal Navy was always on the attack. For him, the offensive spirit manifested itself most visibly in Lord Horatio Nelson, the victor of the Battle of Trafalgar in 1805. Indeed, Mahan wrote a biography of Nelson touting him as "the embodiment of the sea power of Great Britain."[44] Against this aggressive force Mahan juxtaposes the French navy, a force sometimes better than its British foe by material measures such as numbers or quality. He nonetheless condemns French conservatism, risk aversion, and overall defensive-mindedness for nullifying French advantages at sea. British mariners fought to win; French mariners sought to preserve their ships from destruction. The French way, he attests, is no way to run a navy. Offensive-mindedness is the trait to hone.

Nor is offensive-mindedness for wartime combatants alone. Mahan commends an energetic spirit to grand strategists as well. In 1902, while weighing the merits of trade reciprocity against those of protection, he contended that "protection is essentially a defensive measure, and in all struggles, *in commerce as in war*, it is not defensive action but offensive ... which ultimately wins" [italics mine].[45] Enterprise was an American virtue for him. "It is in truth this factor of offense, shown in the activity of the American mind, in the energy with which it carries ideas into practice and in the flexibility which readily embraces improvement, that has won the superiority which enables us latterly to invade the markets of the world," Mahan wrote.[46] Not just sailors and soldiers, but lawmakers, captains of industry, and diplomats should stay forever on the offensive, vigilant for new opportunities for national betterment.

For Mahan, it seems, little falls beyond the purview of maritime strategic leaders. They must shape not just implements of war but individuals, institutions, and society itself in the interests of seagoing commerce and warfare.

HABITS OF MIND FOR TOOLMAKERS

In peacetime, then, toolsmiths fire a Mahanian forge for sea power, nurturing commerce, seeking out access to foreign seaports, and upgrading the inventory of merchantmen and ships of war. They should take an Aristotelian approach to their work, ridding themselves of unhelpful habits while replacing them with provident ones. Which habits are worth discarding and which cultivating? Philosophers have sparred with one another for centuries about what constitutes virtue, what virtues are relevant to this endeavor or that, and how to inculcate them, not just within individuals but within fellowships of all types. To pick an example at random of how arcane these quarrels can become, look at Roman biographer Diogenes Laertius' *Lives and Opinions of Eminent Philosophers*. His chapter on Zeno of Citium chronicles the views of a single philosophical school called the Stoics.[47] Stoics have flung point and counterpoint at one another across the decades and centuries. Debates between schools of thought only add to the intellectual clutter.

In this volume I take a practical and actionable approach rather than risk becoming bogged down in arcane exchanges with master philosophers. As Aristotle contends, virtues worth making second nature fall into two broad categories—those of intellect and those of temperament. Prudence comes from mastering both types. In turn, prudent strategic leaders undertake prudent actions, seeking out worthwhile goals while taking heed of their limits. Accordingly, I catalog habits of mind and habits of temperament useful for strategists in each arena of strategic endeavor. Excellence in making, executing, and revising strategy is a product of excellence in these qualities. The quest to become a virtuoso yields better force design and more creative uses of the tools forged in peacetime.

KEEP ENDS, WAYS, AND MEANS IN ALIGNMENT

First consider habits of mind. As strategy is the art and science of putting power to work to achieve some purpose, so keeping ways and means in alignment with ends—and vice versa—is the elemental skill. This takes firm self-discipline. There is little point in pursuing goals that the society cannot afford out of its resource base or for which citizens or their leaders are unwilling to pay the requisite price. And yet strategic leaders can expect some constituency or another to advocate for virtually any national commitment conceivable, and to do so with fierce conviction. Strategic leaders must steel themselves to say no. Thinking in these terms is an essential habit.

Strategic leaders must be choosy, discriminating between vital and nonvital goals. There are many ways to classify and rank interests, problems, and tasks. Hans Morgenthau, one of the grand masters of academic international relations, implores practitioners and students of foreign policy to draw a "sharp distinction between the desirable and the possible—between what is desirable everywhere and at all times and what is possible under the concrete circumstances of time and place."[48] If something is desirable yet impossible, Morgenthau would counsel against pursuing it. Conversely, it would be wasteful to pursue something undesirable simply because it is attainable. Strategic agents should confine themselves to seeking what is desirable and possible to obtain. Morgenthau's analytical tool is simple, yet deceptively powerful.

Dwight D. Eisenhower was a quintessential problem-solver, first as supreme allied commander in Europe during World War II and then as president. Eisenhower took a bracing approach to setting priorities. He distinguished among types of problems and formulated a hierarchy of courses of action. On one occasion he approvingly quoted Dr. J. Roscoe Miller, former president of Northwestern University, as having said, "I have two kinds of problems, the urgent and the important. The urgent are not important, and the important are never urgent"—an adage that later became known as the "Eisenhower Principle."[49] The meaning of *important* is self-evident, albeit hard to quantify. Something important must be done. *Urgent* invokes the factor of time. Something urgent must be done as soon as possible. President Eisenhower advised leaders to take personal charge of tasks that are important and urgent; to plan ahead for tasks that are important but not urgent; to delegate urgent tasks that are of little importance; and not to bother attacking problems that are neither important nor urgent.[50] Where Morgenthau devised an either-or tool for deliberating about interests and goals, Eisenhower sketched a decision matrix.

Clausewitz has his own ideas about how to assess priorities. He preaches the need to keep goals as few as possible while concentrating effort and resources on obtaining those few. Lesser goals are dispensable. He beseeches commanders to aim their efforts at the enemy's "center of gravity," which he defines nebulously as "the hub of all power and movement, on which everything depends."[51] They should forgo peripheral endeavors unless they meet a stringent three-part test. First, to qualify for consideration, a secondary undertaking must be "exceptionally rewarding," promising enough strategic gain to merit the effort. Second, it must not place what matters most—the main theater or effort—in jeopardy. And third, commanders should therefore reject a secondary endeavor unless the force that they superintend enjoys "decisive superiority" in the primary theater. A force commanding a sizable surplus of resources in the primary theater has a large enough margin to cope with unexpected setbacks there. It may be able to spare a contingent for a subsidiary undertaking without running undue risk.[52]

Reward, risk, resources: I have taken to calling these "Clausewitz's Three Rs." For Clausewitz it makes no sense to hazard top priorities by diverting effort into some lesser venture. Secondary ventures should proceed only when they do not interfere with the primary effort. He intends for this rule to help manage priorities in wartime campaigning, but it applies to peacetime force-building as well. In peacetime, too, wise strategists debate which purposes and theaters matter most and then apportion resources to them. Strategic indiscipline—that is, trying to do it all out of a finite reservoir of national resources—is a prelude to disappointment, if not disaster. It attenuates the resources available for any one venture and risks shortchanging all of them.

Only after they have their priorities straight can strategists begin evaluating courses of action to fulfill the most pressing goals.[53] At its most primal, strategy is about maintaining self-discipline while taking purposeful action to fulfill some end. Setting and enforcing priorities keeps a strategic actor's purposes from outstripping its resources. A sense of direction is pivotal.

In Peace, Prepare for

The strategic leader's inward compass must be matched w~~ the fortitude to steer toward the destination even when adverse winds buffet the ship of state. Strategy, in other words, combines farsightedness with moral courage. As the Roman philosopher Seneca once counseled a young friend,

> Whenever you want to know what is to be avoided or what is to be sought, look to the highest good. . . . Only someone who has before him a general purpose for his whole life will put individual things in order. No matter how ready one's paints might be, no one will produce a likeness unless he has a clear notion of what he wants to paint. So we make mistakes because we deliberate about the parts of life; no one deliberates about the whole. . . . *If you don't know what harbor you sail for, no wind is favorable.* [italics mine][54]

Seneca admonishes individuals to take a global perspective while navigating toward well-defined goals. So it is for individual helmsmen; so it is for armed forces and societies. Developing a broad attitude toward the profession of arms and the statecraft it serves constitutes an essential habit. Like Seneca, Britain's Liddell Hart urges senior strategists to take an all-encompassing perspective and a long view. Tacticians occupy themselves with winning battles. Grand strategists think in terms of fostering national well-being along all axes, over the course of decades or longer.

Liddell Hart insists that war and preparations for war are about peace. While the "horizon" of military strategy is "bounded by the war, grand strategy looks beyond the war to the subsequent peace," he maintains.[55] Strategists should not only combine diplomatic, economic, and military instruments to accomplish strategic and political ends "but so regulate their use as to avoid damage to the future state of peace—for its security and prosperity." Strategists strive to engineer "a better state of peace—even if only from your own point of view."[56]

For the masters of strategy, the habits of taking the correct perspective while remaining mindful of power and its limits help leaders to set, enforce, and balance and rebalance among priorities. Their logic is straightforward. Diplomatic, economic, and military resources are scarce, while national interests and purposes are many. Taking on too many commitments dilutes the resources that are available to fulfill any single one. Those who try to accomplish everything everywhere typically end up accomplishing little anywhere.

In peacetime, then, strategic leaders size and configure military forces for advantage in peacetime wars of perceptions and wartime trials of arms. For insight, consider a historical example, such as Great Britain's naval policy during the late eighteenth century. It amounts to a parable about the perils of vacillating in peacetime strategy and force design. For global sea powers such as Britain then and America now, nurturing a sizable, capable, battleworthy navy constitutes part of strategic upkeep. This remains true regardless of whether a challenger that intends to seize maritime supremacy for itself has appeared on the horizon yet or not. If all goes well, exercising foresight and husbanding political resolve in peacetime will avert war—bettering the state of peace without open resort to arms.

British policy during this era was negligent at times and prudent at others. As a result, the kingdom's maritime fortunes underwent needless ups and downs. Steady policy would have kept the troughs shallow, improving London's average strategic performance. In 1763 Britain scored a signal triumph over rivals France and Spain after years of continental and maritime warfare. Maritime historian Sir Julian Corbett exalts the peace that followed the Seven Years' War (1756–1763) as "the most triumphant we ever made."[57] According to Corbett, British success owed much to Prime Minister William Pitt the Elder, the overseer of the British war effort. Assured of "practical superiority at sea" throughout the conflict—superiority that derived from prudent force-development during the prewar era—Pitt proved to be "a true War Minister, with almost undisturbed control of army, navy, and diplomacy" and wielded Great Britain's army and navy as "the blade and hilt of one weapon."[58]

The course of events warrants such plaudits. To name one monumental achievement, British arms delivered New France into British hands in 1759–1760, when the British army conquered Quebec and then Montreal. In 1759 a Royal Navy fleet stood into Quiberon Bay, along the French Atlantic coast, and smashed its French counterpart during a hurricane. Indeed, historian Frank McLynn heralds 1759 as "the year Britain became master of the world."[59] The resounding victory, however, wrought perverse effects on the British psyche, bringing forth a combination of hubris, myopia, and parsimony in postwar London. Britons seemed to regard their victory as permanent—and to conclude that naval preparedness no longer ranked first among affairs of state.

In other words, after having spent lavishly out of the public treasury to prosecute land and sea war, Britons demanded a peace dividend. Claiming such a windfall often sends ill effects rippling into future strategy, and postwar Britain was no exception. Think about force planning. Parliament and governments traditionally provided enough hulls to make the Royal Navy equal in numbers to the French and Spanish navies put together. At the time, the Bourbon dynasty ruled both France and Spain, so the two archfoes tended to team up against Britannia in wartime. Taken as a single strategic unit, they set the standard for British sufficiency at sea. Yet Mahan takes the British leadership to task for letting the Royal Navy dwindle in numbers and capability following Britain's triumph in the Seven Years' War. He ultimately tenders an uncompromising verdict:

> It had been a maxim with the best English naval authorities of the preceding era . . . that the British navy should be kept equal in numbers to the combined fleets of the Bourbon kingdoms—a condition which, with the better quality of the *personnel* and the larger maritime population upon which it could draw, would have given a real superiority of force. This precaution, however, had not been observed during recent years.[60]

It was sound strategy for the Royal Navy to put its faith in peerless seamanship, gunnery, and élan to make the difference in fights between fleets that were kept equal in numbers as a matter of policy. The Royal Navy was renowned for these qualities. It was asking too much to expect the human factor to offset a lopsided numerical mismatch. Mahan goes further, faulting London for failing to provide a *surplus* of vessels. To keep equal numbers of vessels at sea, he implies, the Royal Navy needed *more* ships than the combined French and Spanish navies. After all, British strategy involved blockading hostile shorelines—an arduous task. Ships took a beating from the elements and needed to rotate home from patrol duty periodically to refit.[61] French and Spanish fleets were spared the rigors of enforcing maritime quarantines and so could get by with fewer hulls.

In Mahan's analysis, Britain's false economies ended up costing it dearly. The leadership had flouted time-honored policy, and so was forced onto the defensive once France and Spain entered the War of American Independence in 1778 and 1779, respectively, siding with the American colonists against the redcoats. During the war, Mahan notes, the British fleet was "habitually much inferior" to the allied fleet in European home waters. Because of the Royal Navy's debilitated inventory of fighting ships, it had to make do with an inferior fleet at home. As a result, the admiralty ended up exposing the British Isles—the homeland—to attack in order to keep adequate numbers of ships in the Americas.

That meant that the War of American Independence, a war waged to reaffirm British sovereignty in continental North America, metamorphosed into a "truly maritime war," as Mahan puts it.[62] It was folly, he insists, for London to depart from "England's traditional and true policy by committing . . . to a distant land war while powerful enemies were waiting for an opportunity to attack her at sea."[63] The conflict raged not just in the Atlantic Ocean, the aquatic highway connecting North America with the British Isles and an obvious arena for strife, but in the Caribbean and Mediterranean Seas as well. Fighting even sprawled into the Indian Ocean, where it remained uncertain which imperial power would rule the subcontinent. As new combat theaters erupted, the British leadership divided up the Royal Navy in an attempt to cover them all—even as it subdivided its forces in North America.[64]

Such was the plight of the enfeebled Royal Navy. As a rule, no force can be stronger than all likely foes in all places at all times. The onset of alliance warfare against an isolated Great Britain endangered British interests and territorial holdings outside North America while thinning out British fighting strength at any given scene of action. In fact, the competing priorities compelled British leaders to demote the campaign to reconquer the American colonies—which had been the primary cause of the war—to secondary importance in a conflict that spanned the British Empire. After France and Spain made common cause with the colonies, writes the late American military historian Russell Weigley, "the British had to treat the American mainland as a secondary theater. Since their global triumph in the Seven Years' War, they had complacently allowed their naval strength to wither so badly that the Admiralty could no longer guarantee the home islands against invasion when threatened by the combined fleets of the Bourbon monarchies."[65]

Strangely, then, America was reduced to a secondary theater in the American war. But while the British lost the colonies, both the nation and its navy rebounded from disaster—and managed to preserve the imperial holdings that the leadership cherished most. After the war formally ended in 1783, furthermore, London put British sea power on a firmer footing. Postbellum naval policy stood the Royal Navy in good stead when the French Revolutionary and Napoleonic Wars broke out starting in the 1790s. Liberal societies are resilient when adeptly led. They learn from their mistakes and stand a good chance of avoiding repeating them in the future.

Two markers help chart Britain's naval renaissance: the Battle of the Virginia Capes (1781) and the Battle of the Saintes (1782). French and British fleets dueled off the mouth of the Chesapeake Bay in August 1781, fighting to a tactical draw that yielded a strategic triumph for the Franco-American alliance. Warding off the Royal Navy from the coast enabled allied ground forces to keep up their siege of Lord Cornwallis' army at Yorktown. Denied seaborne support, Cornwallis capitulated that October—and effectively brought the War of American Independence to a close.

Britain's fortunes cratered at Yorktown. Yet the fleets met again in the Caribbean Sea the following year. The British mauled the French foe in the rematch at the Saintes, even though Mahan grouses that they might have inflicted even more damage had they pressed their tactical advantage.[66] Britain's naval performance remained on the upswing following the Saintes. But like Mahan, British naval historian Herbert Richmond points out that Britain need not have suffered the losses it did if the antebellum leadership had kept the Royal Navy fit for its missions during the interwar years. The Saintes, he writes,

> restored the [British] command of the sea in the West Indies and baffled [an] intended attack on Jamaica, accompanied by the drain upon French and Spanish commerce, [and predisposed] the enemies to abandon their designs; and peace followed in 1783. When so much was done with the inferior forces at the disposal of the sea commanders, little imagination is needed to discern how much might have been done, and what losses would have been avoided, if the statesmen of Britain had acted on principles advocated by Pitt [the Elder] . . . and had attended to the needs of the country's sea power, maintaining it on a scale adequate to the extended services it was to be called upon to perform.[67]

In other words, officialdom had strayed from sound principles since 1763. Richmond singles out successive prime minister William Pitt the Younger for accolades for putting British sea power back on a solid footing. Pitt formed a government in December 1783, after the close of the War of American Independence. Even though "the country lay under the shadow of a threatened bankruptcy and was in urgent need of economy and the rehabilitation of its finances," observes Richmond, Pitt nonetheless found money to recruit additional sailors and lay new keels.[68] Taken to task for profligacy, the prime minister

> replied that no one could wish more than he for economy, but the best economy that any country could

practice in time of peace was to keep up such a force and take such measures of defense as would be most likely to render that peace permanent and induce its duration; so long as the necessary force for the country's defense was maintained, it was the less likely that its tranquility would be disturbed.[69]

Having endured setbacks during the War of American Independence, Britain found farseeing political leadership—leadership that prepared the empire for tests to come during the wars with revolutionary and Napoleonic France. Britain stood at its peak in 1763, suffered self-inflicted setbacks during the War of American Independence, then regained its momentum in time for the French Revolutionary and Napoleonic Wars. Strategic leaders could do worse than study and mimic the habits of William Pitt the Elder and William Pitt the Younger, thinking constantly about generating maritime means sufficient to make good on the country's political ambitions.

THINK JOINTLY

Times have changed since the days of the Pitts. Technology has advanced by leaps and bounds, if often fitfully. During the age of sail, for example, the effective firing range of artillery remained short. Fleets enjoyed the liberty to roam the high seas mostly unencumbered by interference from shore. Lord Nelson rightly jested that "a ship's a fool to fight a fort," but a vessel had to steer close inshore to come within reach of the fort's guns.[70] Rudimentary weapons technology let captains skirt clear of danger zones for the most part, annulling Nelson's maxim except for local sea areas. Today high-tech armaments and sensors increasingly constrict that freedom, placing fleets in harm's way across broader and broader swaths of the world's oceans and seas.

Sea power, then, is no longer an affair strictly for navies. Nelson's quip applies with new and growing force. We inhabit an age of joint sea power. Armies, air forces, and ground-based missiles can reach out and shape events on the open sea even as navies radiate influence onto foreign seacoasts. Ground and air forces are maritime forces in the near-shore environment. The imperative to think jointly stems in large part from the state of technology. Astute observers have seen this future coming for many decades. Over a century ago, President Theodore Roosevelt, a naval historian of considerable renown, testified to the symbiosis between landward defenses and the battle fleet:

> [I]n time of war the navy is not to be used to defend harbors and seacoast cities. . . . The only efficient use for the navy is for offense. The only way in which it can efficiently protect our coast against the possible action of a foreign navy is by destroying that navy. For defense against a hostile fleet which actually attacks them, the coast cities must depend upon their forts, mines, torpedoes, submarines and torpedo boats and destroyers, . . . but [these] in no way supply the place of a thoroughly efficient navy capable of acting on the offensive. . . . But the forts and the like are necessary so that *the navy may be footloose*. [italics mine][71]

In other words, coastal artillery should operate in concert with swarms of small, short-range, super-empowered warships to deny a hostile force the use of waters and skies immediately offshore. If shore-based firepower can protect harbors and coastlines, erecting a nautical buffer zone, it relieves the battle fleet of that defensive duty. Roosevelt's footloose fleet can take to the high seas to search out its opponent for a decisive duel or to execute such missions as senior commanders or their political masters ordain. But where T. R. saw a division of labor between the fleet and shore-based defenses, technology has rendered fleets more and more interdependent with shore-based defenses. In this guided-missile age, when the reach of antiship and antiair munitions is measured not in a few miles but in scores, hundreds, or even thousands of miles, a footloose battle fleet cruising within range of friendly coasts can call in shore-based firepower to augment its own. It is a free-range fleet with vast room to maneuver, yet it can supplement its combat power by summoning aircraft and missiles from dry land to the scene of action. Hostile forces such as Communist China's have fashioned forces and doctrine that align with this expanded version of T. R.'s joint logic. American commanders must think and act along similar lines to extract operational and strategic gain from littoral campaigns.

But there is more to multiservice sea power than technology. In a historically informed theoretical brief on behalf of joint sea power, Corbett insists that the prime function of maritime strategy is to "determine the mutual relations of your army and navy in a plan of war."[72] The "right consideration" of any scheme of war, he adds, demands that the army "be regarded primarily as forming an integral part of the maritime force" that will prosecute it.[73]

Why did Corbett declaim so vehemently about the joint nature of military operations? Because, he insisted, great affairs of state are settled on land. People live on land; therefore wars are decided there through concerted action of the ground and sea arms of military might.[74] He lambasted naval enthusiasts for obsessing over decisive fleet actions that yield maritime command. Sea battle remains a fleet's supreme function, he concedes, but fleet actions seldom come along. Instead, Corbett asserts, "the function of the fleet, the object for which it was always employed, has been threefold: firstly, to support or obstruct diplomatic effort; secondly, to protect or destroy commerce; and thirdly, to further or hinder military operations ashore."[75] He broadens the field of view beyond Mahan's singleminded emphasis on seagoing trade and commerce. There is far more to maritime strategy than apocalyptic encounters reminiscent of Trafalgar, Tsushima, or Leyte Gulf. Yet, Corbett contends that the "drama" of such encounters claims an outsized share of naval thinking, obscuring valuable everyday functions of the fleet.[76] He aims to counteract that myopia.

If ships, aircraft, ground forces, and the associated weaponry now take part in battles for maritime dominion, and if there is more to warfare than the single decisive clash, then not just naval commanders but those in charge of air and ground forces must habituate themselves to thinking like maritime commanders. One imagines that Aristotle would locate the golden mean in "jointness" or "jointery" toward the upper limit of saltwater thinking. If a conflict pertains to the sea—as American wars almost invariably do—then commanders must default toward the excess of joint thinking. Only that way can they extract maximum performance from the naval and military resources afforded them—and keep ways and means in sync with strategic and political ends.

EXERCISE ANXIOUS FORESIGHT— AND KEEP PACE WITH THE TIMES

Foresight is a cardinal virtue for military and political leaders. How else can they fit forces, strategy, operations, and doctrine to potential futures? They must envision the contours of the future strategic environment and design forces, institutions, and methods—all tools of policy and strategy—so they can flourish in that environment. This is easy to say, far from easy or straightforward to do. International relations scholars sometimes bewail the "entropic" nature of world politics, pining for a world with predictable rhythms that lend themselves to fixed political aims and grand strategy.[77] Such longings aside, factors such as complexity, dynamism, and perverse twists of events are inexorable features of international interactions. Politics stubbornly refuses to comply with human wishes.

Even so, there is no escaping the effort to discern what may come. Eisenhower captured the paradox between the necessity and impossibility of foresight in a quip (in 1957) that "plans are worthless, but planning is everything."[78] In times of crisis, he declared, the first thing to do is "take all the plans off the top shelf and throw them out the window and start once more."[79] Planning is not prediction, but it nevertheless provides an intellectual platform from which to make sense of new situations. It keeps practitioners "steeped in the character of the problem" that they one day may be called upon to solve.[80] Orienting them toward likely challenges warrants all the effort that goes into planning.

Clausewitz would nod knowingly. The Prussian sage cautions that a multitude of factors deflect strategic competition and war from smooth, predictable, linear pathways—in particular the reality that competitors jostle constantly for strategic advantage while trying to frustrate one another's strategies. Discontinuities and swerves of fortune are the rule. Consequently, Clausewitz decries as a fool's errand any effort "to equip the conduct of war with principles, rules, or even systems."[81] People tend to disregard "the endless complexities involved," Clausewitz says, but this represents a fatal mistake because "the conduct of war branches out in almost all directions and has no definite limits; while any system, any model, has the finite nature of a synthesis."[82] War has a fractal nature. Clausewitz is describing the climate of open war, but strategic competition short of war is scarcely less mercurial or impassioned.

As a result, complex systems defy efforts at accurate diagnosis. This is why Clausewitz, like Eisenhower, advises commanders and their political overseers to undertake educated guesswork about the characteristics of rivals and the strategic setting while also remaining humble about their prospects for success.[83]

There is also a cognitive dimension to the challenge of foresight. American risk analyst Nassim Nicholas Taleb observes that people seem hardwired to project the past into the future.[84] They extrapolate, forecasting that past trends will continue along straight, continuous lines more or less forever. Taleb reprimands those who succumb to determinism of this sort while admonishing them to think in terms of probabilities.

In his 1902 treatise, *Retrospect & Prospect*, for example, Mahan ransacks nineteenth-century history for trends to help him glimpse the twentieth-century world that was then bearing down on him.[85] He achieves a modicum of success. But as Taleb warns, straight-line projection masks reality. Events have a way of confounding blithe predictions. Trends can plateau. Upward trendlines can flatten out, crest, or descend. Downward trendlines can bottom out and then perhaps ascend. Or some discontinuity—a "black swan," Taleb's metaphor for a highly improbable event entailing major consequences—could fracture a trendline altogether.[86] Such a rupture—such as the Pearl Harbor attack on December 7, 1941, or the World Trade Center disaster of September 11, 2001—invalidates past practices while disorienting those caught in it. That a black swan might appear is always a possibility.

And yet, because it is impossible to do more than gaze through a glass darkly into the future, people extrapolate from what came before. They must project the past into the future while remaining mindful of their incapacity to prophesy with precision. They must keep watch for intervening factors that could bend or break the trajectory of events. Journalist and geopolitics scholar Robert Kaplan implores strategic and political leaders to exercise "anxious foresight" when preparing themselves, their institutions, and their societies for the future.[87] Carl Vinson saw storm clouds gathering over Europe and Asia during the 1930s. No one could have foreseen the exact path that events would trace. But Vinson could chart broad trends, most of which boded ill. So he acted. In large measure the U.S. Navy that won World War II was Vinson's handiwork. Few politicians can rival him for nautical statesmanship.

Similar examples appear in classical antiquity. Few maritime strategists can match Themistocles, the father of the Athenian navy, for prescience and the resolve to act on what he anticipated. Ironically, it was the Athenians' success in a land engagement—the Battle of Marathon, in 490 BC—that propelled Themistocles into naval affairs. Athens' infantry had just repulsed a ground assault launched by Persia, which was then the Aegean world's dominant power. The victory was so stunning that it sowed complacency in Athens even as it stoked fury in Persia. According to the Greco-Roman biographer Plutarch, Themistocles' countrymen "thought that the defeat of the [Persian Empire] at Marathon was the end of the war; but Themistocles thought it to be only the beginning of greater contests."[88] He took it upon himself to ready his city for fresh hazards.

With that in mind, Plutarch reports, Themistocles "anointed himself . . . to be the champion of all Hellas, and put his city into training, because, while it was yet afar off, he expected the evil that was to come."[89] In other words, he judged that another Persian host would come sooner or later—and that this time Athens would need a navy of serious heft to beat back the onslaught. Recognizing that democracies seldom prepare well for distant dangers, he resorted to political guile to win over Athenians to his scheme. The democratic assembly was debating what to do with mineral riches dug out of the silver mines at Laurium, southeast of Athens along the Aegean seacoast. One faction favored dividing up the wealth among the citizenry; Themistocles prevailed on the assembly to invest in sea power. Plutarch recounts how Themistocles, "and he alone, dared to come before the people with a motion that this division be given up, and that with these moneys triremes"—the triple-decker, oar-driven galleys that were the capital ships of the classical world—"be constructed for the war against Aegina," a nearby island city-state and the preeminent Greek naval power of the day.[90]

As Plutarch describes it, Themistocles advocated lavish public expenditure "not by trying to terrify the citizens with dreadful pictures" of the Persian horde—"these were too far away and inspired no very serious fear of their coming"—but instead by dredging up "the bitter jealousy which they cherished toward Aegina in order to secure the armament he desired."[91] In other words, he invoked a clear and present, albeit limited danger to convince Athenians to build the fleet that he believed they would someday need to counter the more remote but incomparably greater menace manifest in Persia. Themistocles' brief for sea power carried the day. Shipwrights built a hundred triremes with the proceeds from Laurium. Themistocles' ships of war made up the nucleus of the allied sea force that fought the Persian fleet at the Battles of Artemisium and Salamis in 480 BC—and saved Greece from likely conquest.[92] In fact, Plutarch affirms that Themistocles was "the man most instrumental in achieving the salvation of Hellas and was foremost in leading the Athenians up to the high repute of surpassing their foes in valor and their allies in magnanimity."[93]

To be sure, Themistocles' methods are not above reproach. "Noble lies" of the kind that Aristotle's teacher, Plato, encouraged "philosopher-kings" to tell in order to help promote the common weal are still that—lies—and such tactics should give posterity pause.[94] Furthermore, Themistocles sometimes resorted to trickery at his allies' expense. On the eve of battle at Salamis, when it appeared bickering among the commanders would break up the Greek fleet, he covertly sent word to the Persian commanders to encircle the island and the allied fleet. He thus maneuvered the foe into preventing any Greek contingent from leaving the scene—and preserved the fleet's unity.

A smashing Greek triumph ensued. Plutarch leaves it to others to judge whether Themistocles besmirched "the integrity and purity of public life" through his fleet-building project and other endeavors.[95] Either way, his displays of cunning and deception do not detract from his foresight.

Think about the magnitude of Themistocles' accomplishment as a founder. Italian Renaissance philosopher Niccolò Machiavelli probes classical antiquity for insight, concluding that founding a republic or kingdom ranks among the most daunting acts of statecraft.[96] What Machiavelli says applies alike to institutions like sea services. In Aristotelian parlance, after all, institutions, like states, are partnerships formed to advance common purposes while achieving self-sufficiency. In the age of Themistocles navies existed chiefly to suppress piracy, win high-seas battles, guard against seaborne invasion, and land troops on foreign shores. These qualify as compelling reasons to raise and maintain a fleet.

And yet founding something was doubly difficult in ancient Athens. In a direct democracy like Athens no Machiavellian prince had the power to erect a new institution by fiat—even a necessary force such as a navy. The Athenian assembly made all decisions relating to public affairs. An advocate like Themistocles had to rally popular opinion behind his cause. To sway such a body a would-be founder needed not only vision but rhetorical gifts of impressive scope. These Themistocles possessed in abundance. From his youth, according to Plutarch, Themistocles deftly "stirred the people up to many novel enterprises and introduced great innovations."[97] He championed the cause of sea power out of anxious foresight, personal drive and ambition, and rhetorical dexterity. This is a rare combination of gifts. His example is one toward which maritime strategic leaders can strive while remaining wary of his ethics.

Where does the Aristotelian golden mean—that intermediate state between deficiency and excess—lie in the realm of foresight? One imagines that it lies not at the precise median between extremes, but rather that it tends toward the excess. True, the excess would be a conviction that the future can be accurately predicted, and that is a vice to avoid. Yet strategic leaders who are grievously deficient in foresight are apt to fall out of step with the times and strategic surroundings. They neither recognize nor acknowledge that change is occurring. Machiavelli deprecates individuals' capacity to adapt when circumstances change around them even as he attempts to school his readers in methods of statecraft—including, it seems, adaptive methods that hinge on foresight. And he claims that republics have an advantage in this over autocracies. If an autocrat lags behind the times, by definition no one else can intercede to correct the problem. Republics, by contrast, can draw on diverse citizens and talents. If flux leaves one statesman behind, republican leadership can appoint a replacement who is fit for the times.

Change may be an ordeal for individuals, Machiavelli says, but liberal societies have the luxury of working around human nature. He cites the examples of two Roman commanders, Fabius Maximus and Scipio Africanus, to make his point about changing personnel to align a republic with the times.[98] The Senate appointed Fabius, nicknamed "the Delayer," to command the Roman army when the Carthaginian warlord Hannibal was on the rampage through Italy. The reason: Rome could not yet defeat Hannibal, and it needed time to amass military resources. Fabius gave the city a respite by waging slow, methodical defensive actions. He denied the Carthaginians a decisive battle while harrying them in the field, and thus conserved his army until it could wrest away the strategic offensive and win.

While Machiavelli pays homage to Fabius, he also upbraids him for being unable to see when the time for offensive action had arrived. Had Fabius been king, he might well have lost the war, Machiavelli contends. In fact, the cautious commander spoke out bitterly against making the transition from defense to offense. But Rome was a republic, able to change leadership as need be. The Senate dismissed the Delayer from command and appointed the offensively minded Scipio in his stead. Scipio took the initiative, carried the fight across the Mediterranean Sea, and defeated Carthage on its own soil at the Battle of Zama (202 BC).

From his survey of Roman history Machiavelli concludes that a republic can accommodate itself to changing times through "the diversity of the citizens that are in it. For a man who is accustomed to proceed in one mode never changes," and "when the times change not in conformity with his mode, he is ruined."[99] If that happens, the city turns elsewhere for farsighted leadership—and wards off collective ruin. It's true that Machiavelli does present an absolute. He fervently hopes that gifted individual leaders *can* train themselves to calibrate their actions to the times. "For one sees that some men proceed in their works with impetuosity, some with hesitation and caution," he writes. "And because in both of these modes suitable limits are passed, since one cannot observe the true way, in both one errs. But he comes to err less and to have prosperous fortune who matches the time with his mode."[100] Anxious foresight as Machiavelli conceives of it helps individuals navigate their way between rash and overly cautious stances in politics and strategy, perceiving when to act boldly and when to hunker down.

This is why Kaplan's phrase *anxious foresight* is so well-crafted. Left unmodified, the word *foresight* could delude strategic leaders into believing it is possible to forecast events with certitude. But *anxious* strategic leaders are alert to their limits and remain humble. It is possible to take anxiety to such extremes that strategic leaders imagine hobgoblins everywhere, all equally menacing and all lodging an equal claim against national resources and leaders' time and energy. Forebodings would cloud foresight. Paralysis could result, or the strategist might conclude that it is imperative to defend every interest and meet every peril, disregarding the need to set and enforce priorities. Trying to do everything constitutes a sure way to overdraw one's finite stock of resources. It is no way to make strategy or plan forces.

Even so, kept within bounds, anxiety helps individuals and institutions avert mental fallacies commonplace in diplomacy and war. Consciousness of human frailty tempers the confidence with which people try to espy the future. Chastened forecasters are careful forecasters. For example, a measure of apprehension administers a palliative for what the ancients called "hubris"—outrageous arrogance that triggers the wrath of the gods, or Fate, or Providence. Strategic leaders guilty of bombast assume they can impose their will on their rivals as though sculpting an inert mass. They downgrade opponents' commitment and ingenuity, scripting out how the competition will unfold and expecting opponents to follow the script as though they have no alternative.

Yet, opponents do have alternatives. Most often, prideful leaders set themselves up for a fall while realism primes those conscious of their limits for success. A more salubrious attitude comes from Clausewitz: "So long as I have not overthrown my opponent I am bound to fear that he may overthrow me. Thus I am not in control: he dictates to me as much as I dictate to him."[101] In other words, it is safer to overestimate antagonists than to slight them.

Healthy foresight also tempers strategic leaders' tendency to accept established ways of doing things. As we've already shown, Machiavelli considered individuals intractable even when it was imperative to change standard practices: "Two things are causes why we are unable to change: one, that we are unable to oppose that to which nature inclines us; the other, that when one individual has prospered very much with one mode of proceeding it is not possible to persuade him that he can do well to proceed otherwise."[102] Human nature combines with a track record of success to stymie necessary change. An old U.S. Navy proverb testifies to Machiavelli's wisdom: *if it ain't broke, don't fix it*. The proverb conveys something real about the inertia built into human nature. People find it hard to see when past practice is *broke* and needs to be *fixed*—either by revising it by increments or by jettisoning it outright and replacing it with something more fitting for new times.

Or, look at the problems of foresight and adaptability through the eyes of a scientist. The Austrian-British philosopher Karl Popper articulated the classic definition of scientific progress, portraying it as an orderly process by which researchers formulate and then attempt to "falsify," or debunk, a hypothesis about some phenomenon as they gather data and observations.[103] This is how the scientific method works—or rather how it should work. Scientists put a theory to the test of reality and amend or discard it depending on how well it fares in field trials. A theory stands—provisionally—until it has been falsified.

Long ago, however, Massachusetts Institute of Technology philosopher Thomas Kuhn took issue with Popper's approach. In a 1967 book, *The Structure of Scientific Revolutions*, Kuhn argued that human knowledge progresses not through an orderly process of falsifying theories, but through a messy, disorderly, herky-jerky *political* process. Kuhn contends that keepers of an existing theory, or "paradigm," are invested in it for personal and professional reasons, and that rather than scrap an outdated paradigm they claw with all their might to preserve it—even when a new one better accounts for reality. Kuhn cites the Copernican revolution, along with many others. Church fathers sternly refused to accept a heliocentric paradigm of the solar system even though it explained the cosmos better than did the venerable Ptolemaic geocentric paradigm. But Kuhn says politics—not the scientific method—drove their opposition.

Admittedly, paradigms are important. A paradigm furnishes the axioms, or assumptions, from which individuals or groups reason. Any system of logic flows from assumptions that participants regard as self-evident and that can be neither proved nor disproved within the system. Just the same, Kuhn observes, "anomalies" may accumulate that separate observed reality from what the paradigm predicts. Once too many anomalies accumulate—or the paradigm is found to contain even a few anomalies that are too glaring to explain away—a crisis ensues. The claims of the reigning paradigm no longer comport with reality, and the assumptions underlying the orthodox view come into question. Once the anomalies become too incontrovertible to explain away, gatekeepers can no longer defend the paradigm. The way opens for gatecrashers to install a better paradigm. The fresh paradigm might someday yield to another, and still another, and on and on.

And that is how Kuhn believes human knowledge advances—fitfully and through strife rather than dispassionate argument. So it is with military and diplomatic institutions—if not more so. Think about it. A strategy is a theory about cause-and-effect. Its framers postulate how employing available means in a certain way will bring about desirable strategic and political effects. In peacetime, strategic leaders posit hypotheses about how a particular size and configuration of armed forces will help the country get its way in peacetime competition or in war, should matters come to that. Military leaders are as susceptible as scientific researchers or anyone else to orthodox paradigms and, as a result, to Kuhn's critique.

Consider the strange case of early twentieth-century American naval officer William S. Sims. The Navy of Sims' day was the custodian of a Mahanian paradigm of sea battle cemented in 1898 through victories over Spain at Santiago and Manila Bay. American gunnery did not appear broken. Quite the reverse. Yet Sims—a middle-aged bachelor and workaholic with a curmudgeonly streak and the willingness to disregard his career prospects—saw a problem and set out to shatter the old paradigm.

While serving as a lieutenant in the U.S. Asiatic Fleet, Sims got to know Captain Sir Percy M. Scott of the Royal Navy, who had pioneered a technique called "continuous-aim firing."[104] Until then gunfire was a matter of training the gun mount at a target, elevating the gun to a particular angle, waiting for the ship to roll until the target came into the sights, and then firing. Gun elevation remained more or less static. Dependence on the tactical environment and the reflexes of individual crewmen fettered both accuracy and the rate of fire. Marksmanship suffered. During the Spanish-American War, in fact, gun crews recorded a minuscule percentage of hits scored out of rounds fired. At Manila Bay only 121 of some 9,500 rounds disgorged from American ships found their mark against an anchored—and thus stationary—enemy fleet.

Scott combined newfangled telescopes with easy-to-operate gun elevating gear and other technical innovations that enabled gunners to keep the barrels on target while the ship rolled and pitched around them. Crews could make constant minute adjustments, elevating or depressing the guns to score a hit regardless of the motion of the hull. According to Sims' biographer, Elting Morison, almost overnight Scott recorded a 3,000 percent improvement in British warships' rate of accurate fire. Struck by the Briton's accomplishment, Sims inspected U.S. Navy fire-control techniques and hardware and determined they were not up to the challenge of continuous aim. The U.S. Navy could get away with slipshod fire-control against an overmatched foe such as the Spanish navy, but the Americans would find themselves at a serious if not catastrophic disadvantage if they went up against a fleet equipped with continuous aim.

Alarmed at the anomalies separating U.S. techniques from sound practices employed by the British, Sims delivered a barrage of reports to the Navy's Bureau of Ordnance detailing the fleet's gunfire inadequacies while extolling the Royal Navy system. Unfortunately, they fell largely on deaf ears. Sims was no diplomat. The substance of his entreaties was unwelcome, but it was his abrasive tone that affronted senior officers and sowed ill will—and spurred resistance to his message. As a result, as Morison tells it, the Navy bureaucracy was reduced to arguing that continuous aim was mathematically impossible. In effect, the bureaucracy denied that a revolution in naval affairs that had already happened could happen.

Thomas Kuhn would instantly recognize the symptoms of the "paradigm shift" that convulsed the U.S. Navy. Tumult—not an orderly revision of past practices and hardware—ensued. Lieutenant Sims ultimately succeeded in persuading the Navy to embrace his gunfire revolution, but only by writing directly to President Theodore Roosevelt—twice. T. R. apparently had him appointed inspector of target practice for the entire Navy, and the revolution was on. By the time he left that post Sims had earned acclaim as "the man who taught the U.S. Navy to shoot."[105] Continuous aim was standard procedure for surface combatants by the time World War I broke out. In Kuhn's parlance, the fire-control revolution qualified as a paradigm shift—complete with the turmoil that accompanies seismic change.

Adherence to a paradigm can be extraordinarily intractable, as the U.S. Navy's gunfire travails show. This is the sinister side of basing leadership on habit. Building habits is important, but habits need reform over time. Time and repetition can reduce valid precepts about the profession of arms to maxims—slogans meant to express important concepts. As a rule, though, maxims oversimplify ideas from the governing paradigm. For example, Julian Corbett took the Royal Navy's old guard to task for exalting offensive operations. He deplored orthodox concepts such as *the enemy's coast is our frontier* and *seek out and destroy the enemy fleet* at the outset of war. The conceit underlying such sloganeering was that British mariners would seize the offensive in hostile home waters at the outbreak of war and fight a decisive battle early—settling the question of who would rule the waves. For Corbett these maxims were little more than a "fetish," devoid of thought or imagination. He told one astonished audience at Portsmouth that waging war by one-liners was like singing "Rule, Britannia" to plan a campaign.[106] It smacked of hubris—and a self-congratulatory service risks paying a severe penalty in war. Sloganeering makes for poor strategy at times when original thought is at a premium—at all times, in other words.

Others agree. In his RAND Corporation treatise, *Strategy in the Missile Age*, American strategic analyst Bernard Brodie ascribes the course of World War I in large measure to the deadening effect of military maxims. Brodie reproaches statesmen and commanders across Europe for succumbing to a tyranny of maxims. "The maxim," he declares, "may be the final distillate of profound thought; but it is likely to be such only at its first use, when it is still an apt expression and not yet a slogan. When it becomes common currency it is likely already to be counterfeit."[107] For example, Europeans mistook Clausewitz's writings extolling concentrated effort for advocacy of pure violence. They are not. The cult of the offensive—the belief that sufficiently gallant troops could overcome fixed fortifications defended by machine guns and artillery—was a faulty maxim, with consequences soaked in blood.[108] Yet soldiers went back time and again to a playbook that was out of step with battlefield reality. As Brodie and Corbett attest, maxims may provide a starting point for wisdom. Seldom, if ever, do they suffice in themselves. Strategic leaders must view them with extreme skepticism and insist that subordinates do likewise. Superficial understanding begets faulty strategy.

Clearly, then, fealty to a paradigm poses dangers. A related mental blind spot, historical forgetfulness, is also worth considering. Combatants thirst to win in wartime, the more convincingly the better. But colossal victories carry baneful effects alongside their blessings. These ill effects could reverberate into postwar strategy, impairing efforts to remain battle-ready for when future contingencies arise. As pointed out before, Great Britain fell prey to complacency after the Seven Years' War. Or think about the Cold War, when a mortal antagonist, the Soviet Union, in effect committed assisted suicide after a prolonged strategic competition. The end of the Cold War set loose a peculiar and virulent form of euphoria in the United States and the West.

American political scientist Francis Fukuyama gave the zeitgeist its name, writing an article entitled "The End of History?" in 1989 and a book expanding on his thesis in 1992.[109] Fukuyama wrote to make a limited point about the future of liberal government. The Navy and Marine Corps took end-of-history reasoning much further, in effect proclaiming an end to naval history. By coincidence the sea services' first post–Cold War strategic directive, titled " . . . From the Sea," appeared at almost the same moment as Fukuyama's book. The document's framers declared, "With the demise of the Soviet Union, the free nations of the world claim preeminent control of the seas and ensure freedom of commercial maritime passage. As a result, our national maritime policies can afford to *deemphasize efforts in some naval warfare areas.* But the challenge is much more complex than simply reducing our present naval forces. We must structure a *fundamentally different naval force* to respond to strategic demands" [italics mine].[110]

In effect, service chieftains argued that the West had won the battle for maritime supremacy for all time and that the sea was now a safe sanctuary from which to project power onto foreign shores. Maritime forces could go where they would with impunity. Never again would they have to fight their way into important waters.

The services obeyed their new mandate by dismantling valuable hardware such as long-range antiship missiles and making little more than perfunctory efforts to keep up proficiency at surface, antisubmarine, and antiair warfare—specialties essential to battle for command of the sea. The problem was that standing down presented opportunities to future competitors such as Communist China, which resolved to build a great navy around the time that the U.S. Navy and Marine Corps were restructuring fleets and amphibious forces away from their primary mission. China made its debut in naval history as America was declaring it over.

The lesson from the 1990s? It is a grave blunder to believe that victory has repealed a military service's first and foremost task. There is often an interregnum after a smashing victory, but no victory is eternal. Others have succumbed to this fallacy as well. British naval historian Andrew Gordon examines the malign effects of a previous resounding triumph, the Battle of Trafalgar, on its victor, the Royal Navy. Gordon postulates that the Royal Navy found itself caught in a "long calm lee" after trouncing a superior Franco-Spanish fleet off the Atlantic coast of Spain in 1805.[111] The navy faced no peer competitor for a century after Trafalgar. It spent the balance of the nineteenth century waging imperial police actions against outclassed opponents, not battling rival fleets for maritime command.

With no adversary of comparable stature to keep the Royal Navy sharp, its leadership fell into bad habits. Senior commanders took to choreographing fleet maneuvers in minute detail, denying more junior officers the liberty to handle their ships for themselves and innovate. Flag signals from ship to ship—the primary means for issuing orders to the fleet—grew more and more elaborate, and thus cumbersome and hard to decipher. The high command became obsessed with spit and polish, and with impeccable paperwork.

Top leadership also insisted on unquestioning obedience to orders. So accustomed were officers to automatically carrying out orders that in 1893 the Mediterranean Fleet saw its flagship, the battleship HMS *Victoria*, sunk after colliding with another Royal Navy vessel during routine steaming. Vice Admiral Sir George Tryon, the fleet commander, ordered a tactical maneuver that everyone around him plainly saw would cause a collision. They executed it anyway. Gordon ascribes the Grand Fleet's subpar performance at the Battle of Jutland in 1916 in part to the Royal Navy's inability to rid itself of bad habits and practices such as these that encrusted it during the long century after Trafalgar.[112]

Gordon uses the metaphor of a lee to describe the perils implicit in winning too big. A lee is the calm behind a landmass or some large object such as a ship, but it is a false calm. The wind can change, exposing whatever was sheltering in the lee to the elements afresh. But if, perchance, a lee does last for a long time, its inhabitants may come to see it as the permanent state of things. They forget how to ride out stormy weather—and may flounder when forced to traverse rough seas once again.

Today the U.S. Navy finds itself entrapped in the long calm lee of two titanic events: the Battle of Leyte Gulf in 1944, history's last major fleet engagement to date, and the Cold War. The Navy spent the post–World War II decades projecting power ashore from safe maritime havens off war zones such as Korea and Vietnam, not vying for maritime mastery against a peer foe. The Soviet Navy concentrated minds among the naval leadership for a time in the 1970s and 1980s. But then "... From the Sea" declared that America's ability to command the sea was permanent, and the Navy no longer had to worry about maintaining it. But if history ended, it is back. Strategic leadership today means rekindling competitive fire throughout the officer corps and enlisted ranks while reequipping and retraining the sea services for combat. Molding an enterprising and historically minded culture—and avoiding a fate like the Royal Navy's a century ago—constitutes a pressing task.

The habit of anxious foresight helps strip off intellectual blinkers such as these. In that sense it is an *anti*-habit. It grounds strategic leaders in reality, reminding them of their personal limits, the limits of big bureaucratic institutions, and the limits of martial might. A compound of humility and a scientific cast of mind—doubt, in other words—clearly is the best attitude to adopt when forecasting future trends. Karl Popper, the exponent of falsification, urges scientists to entertain "bold ideas" while being "highly critical of their own ideas" and trying to "find whether their ideas are right by trying first to find whether they are not perhaps wrong."[113] The great scientists "work with bold conjectures and severe attempts at refuting their own conjectures."[114]

What applies to scientists toiling in a laboratory applies to seafarers riding the main, aviators flitting through the wild blue, or soldiers bestriding battlegrounds. Any good commander compiles a "theory of victory" to explain how to reach desired goals with the resources that he or she has been allotted.[115] Strategists, like scientific researchers, posit what effects each cause they apply will yield. But they must afford the hypothesis intimate scrutiny before subjecting it to the test of strategic competition or war, and revisit it periodically as new data come in. The hypothesis may have been false to start with and been disproved by reality. It may have been correct at the start but superseded by events. It may need partial revision at the outset or later on. Amending a theory of victory and readjusting strategy and operations is crucial to the Machiavellian project of keeping abreast of fluid times and circumstances.

The Greek philosopher Socrates protested that the unexamined life is not worth living.[116] He might have added that the unexamined life in martial affairs is downright dangerous. The best-crafted theory of victory warrants regular reexamination and updating. Proficient strategists apply the scientific habit of mind to their profession as a matter of reflex.

COMPETE THROUGH FORCE DESIGN

Fitness for the times, then, is a mark of strategic excellence. Sage strategic leaders also bring a competitive cast of mind to the job of creating implements of power. The Irish philosopher-statesman Edmund Burke saw value in facing a formidable competitor. "He that wrestles with us strengthens our nerves and sharpens our skill," Burke declares.[117] "Our antagonist is our helper. This amicable conflict with difficulty obliges us to an intimate acquaintance with our object and compels us to consider it in all its relations. It will not suffer us to be superficial."[118] Burke was thinking about matching wits with lawmakers in Parliament, where he served, or with rival authors in print. His exchange with English political activist Thomas Paine over the merits of the French Revolution remains the stuff of legend.[119] But his point applies just as well to the martial arena. In fact, Andrew Gordon might agree with Burke that a dearth of competition was the Royal Navy's problem after Trafalgar.

Armed antagonists are not potted plants, inert masses with little capacity to shape their own destiny. They are strategic agents intent on fulfilling their own goals at our expense. Paying them respect, probing their strengths and weaknesses, and learning from them represents the beginning of wisdom in strategic competition.

But there is more to force design than measuring oneself against current or potential adversaries. During the latter part of the Cold War, Andrew Marshall, the legendary director of the Defense Department's Office of Net Assessment, the Pentagon's think tank, fashioned a concept he termed "competitive strategies."[120] The adjective appears superfluous—strategy is competitive by definition—but it serves an important purpose. It shapes attitudes. In 1972 Marshall observed that the United States and Soviet Union had become embroiled in a long-term strategic competition. He worried that Moscow was competing more effectively and sustainably than Washington because it took a selective approach to hardware investments. The Soviet military deliberately procured affordable technologies that were expensive and difficult for Western rivals to counter.

Marshall wanted to reverse the trend toward ultra-high-priced armaments and steer the competition into areas of American advantage and Soviet disadvantage. Just as important, he hoped to induce the Soviet military to compete in a way that would prove more costly for itself and more manageable for the U.S. military to keep pace. Imposing opportunity costs on the Soviets promised immediate gain. After all, every ruble spent countering a technology in some competitive domain of America's choosing was a ruble that the Soviets were not able to spend on making mischief for NATO somewhere else. Over time, Marshall concluded, the smaller Soviet economy would flag, making open-ended competition unaffordable. The United States would come out ahead by dint of economic power and crafty force design.

Central as that was, however, there was more to competitive strategies than flipping the cost curve against the Soviets. Marshall outlined a cultural component in the initiative as well.

In Peace, Prepare for War • 67

The Soviet and Russian way of war was a product of Russian history and geography, just as any combatant's heritage and physical surroundings help form its national mindset. In particular, Napoleon's invasion in 1812 and Hitler's attack in 1941 had imprinted themselves on the Russian psyche. The result was a marked proclivity for defensive strategy. Marshall reasoned that the U.S. Navy and other allied forces could exploit that preference, using Western excellence at antisubmarine warfare to menace the Soviet ballistic missile submarine fleet. To safeguard this core of Soviet nuclear deterrence, Moscow would direct the navy to retreat to "bastions," marginal seas off the Soviet coast where the surface fleet and land-based air and missile forces could help protect ballistic missile submarines against Western sub hunters.

This snapshot of the late Cold War suggests a worthy habit for strategic leaders. Framers of strategy should be perpetually on the lookout for opportunities to steer great-power competition in a favorable direction. First, they should hunt for areas of competitive advantage that promise disproportionate gain at steep cost to the opponent and manageable cost to themselves. Second, they should estimate the opportunity cost to the opponent from each move they make, much as driving the Soviets into a defensive crouch close to home discouraged adventurism elsewhere on the map during the 1970s and 1980s.

Finally, they should figure out what moves will resonate most powerfully with the adversary for cultural reasons. Antisubmarine warfare resonated with Moscow back then, spurring heavy investment in nautical defense. Today, Chinese Communist leaders are acutely aware that offshore geography limits their geopolitical aspirations. Threatening to close Asia's "first island chain" to maritime movement between the China seas and the Western Pacific would have an outsized impact on Beijing.[121] In exercising long-term strategic leadership, cultural inventiveness is an asset of major proportions.

As Johns Hopkins University professor Hal Brands maintains, "what is critical is that the United States get back in the habit of imposing costs [on adversaries] rather than having costs imposed upon it."[122] Let opportunism prevail.

DESIGN AND CARE FOR INSTITUTIONS

Unlike inanimate tools, military institutions have a human dimension that requires regular tending. Armed forces are bureaucracies with all the strengths, weaknesses, and eccentricities that large government organizations entail. Stewardship of institutional culture is a crucial ingredient of strategic leadership. Leaders should make it a habit to regard themselves as cultural custodians.

The turn-of-the-twentieth-century German sociologist Max Weber—perhaps history's most astute analyst of public administration—held up the bureaucratic method of organization as a marvel of efficiency, a cornerstone of the modern administrative state. Weber viewed bureaucracy as a kind of mechanical extension of the sovereign's will, implying that these institutions would carry out directives reliably, expeditiously, and efficiently. According to Naval War College political scientist Carnes Lord, bureaucracy "vastly improved the efficiency of large-scale organizations, both public and private, rationalizing and routinizing the tasks they perform, subjecting them to fair and impartial rules, and creating specialized forms of expertise that brought scientific knowledge to bear on practice."[123]

Highly centralized bureaucracy earned special accolades from Weber, who maintained that, because it concentrates power in the hands of a few accountable officials, it is "finally superior both in intensive efficiency and in the scope of its operations."[124] It is rational in a way that more traditional modes of organization are not. Weber regards bureaucratic organizations as engineering systems, observing that "the fully developed bureaucratic apparatus compares with other organizations exactly as does the machine with the non-mechanical modes of production."[125] "The choice," Weber insists, is "only that between bureaucracy and dilettantism in the field of administration."[126]

To their credit, enthusiasts for modern public administration acknowledge—usually in a roundabout way—that bureaucratic institutions suffer from intrinsic shortcomings. First, although they are well-suited to performing routine functions, large organizations find it exceedingly difficult to shift course even when the need for change seems compelling. Bureaucracy is a machine, and machines do not readily reinvent themselves while running or when the operating environment changes around them. Weber testifies indirectly to the inflexibility of administrative institutions, admitting that, once a bureaucracy is fully established, it is "among those social structures which are the hardest to destroy."[127] The individual official is "only a small cog in a ceaselessly moving mechanism which prescribes to him an essentially fixed route of march. The official is entrusted with specialized tasks, and normally the mechanism cannot be put into motion or arrested by him, but only from the very top."[128] Only top leaders, then, can realistically hope to steer administrative organizations in a different direction.

Because of their training and career incentives, lesser officials are invariably jealous of the interests of the organization, Weber writes. "The individual bureaucrat is, above all, forged to the common interest of all the functionaries in the perpetuation of the apparatus"—sometimes at the expense of the larger national interest.[129] These elements make administrative institutions, which are built on the "settled orientation of *man* for observing the accustomed rules and regulations," extraordinarily resistant to change.[130] Indeed, Weber concludes, modern administrative organization makes real political revolution, "in the sense of the forceful creation of entirely new formations of authority," practically impossible.[131]

The literature on psychology sheds additional light on bureaucratic dysfunction. A body of ideas molds how any institution conducts its affairs. A paradigm explains in detail how the institution will put the means allocated to it to work achieving the goals assigned to it. Maxims may express parts of the paradigm in terms accessible to people at all levels of the organizational hierarchy. But machine-like bureaucracy also is vulnerable to what scientists, analysts, authors, and marketing agencies nowadays call a "meme." Merriam-Webster defines a meme as a sort of intellectual contagion, terming it an "idea, behavior, style, or usage that spreads from person to person within a culture."[132] British ethologist Richard Dawkins coined the term in *The Selfish Gene* (1976), postulating that natural selection distinguishes not only among biological organisms, as Charles Darwin maintained, but among ideas. Competition among ideas determines which are fittest—or, at any rate, which concepts or images seem fittest to the most observers.[133] Then they spread. Dawkins likens memes to "mental viruses."[134]

Memes are a mixed blessing. For example, opinionmakers hunt constantly for catchphrases likely to "go viral" among influential officials—that is, likely to be spread via the internet, social media, and other modes of communication—and ultimately help mold policy. Authors whose writings go viral boost book sales and advertising revenue while burnishing their reputations for ability and clout. Memes can also ensnare institutions, which, again, are nothing more than groups of individuals. Take a group of people, put some in authority, and suppose some meme entrances those holding authority. What impact will the meme have on institutional practices? In all likelihood the leadership will transcribe it into rules, procedures, and doctrine. The dominant idea may come to shape—or perhaps warp—how Weber's machine transacts its business.

Like the fallacies bruited before, memes inhibit the ability of institutions to adapt. Bureaucracies are mechanical organizations built to perform a standard repertoire of tasks using routine methods and procedures. Visceral experiences—major successes, catastrophic failures, big ideas thrust on the institution by senior leadership—have a way of encoding themselves within the organizational culture. Effacing them is hard once they are embedded in the bureaucratic repertoire. A fixed idea becomes an assumption from which members of the organization reason, and assumptions are taken as self-evident rather than subjected to questioning or disproof.[135] Any meme likely to beguile top leadership will probably conform, more or less, to the organization's preexisting paradigm for how it ought to do business. It will reinforce what the leadership is predisposed to believe. In that case, the viral idea will further entrench the ruling paradigm.

Examples of military memes abound. After the Battle of Bunker Hill in 1775 the Continental Army leadership forecast that the British army would keep doing what it had done in

Boston: charging fixed defenses at steep cost in redcoats' lives. Thus the American army could drain British manpower and win the Revolutionary War over time—even if it lost the contested ground in individual engagements. British commanders refused to abide by the meme, and the patriot army had to search out new tactics and operational methods. It nearly lost the war in the process. The Battle of Tsushima Strait in 1905 convinced the Imperial Japanese Navy that future foes such as the U.S. Navy would dispatch their battle fleets across transoceanic distances to fight in Japan's backyard. Japan would crush debilitated enemies the way it crushed the Russian Baltic Fleet at Tsushima. In both cases, change came slowly, and only after great costs. It took repeated defeats to induce Continental Army leaders to abandon the Bunker Hill meme. Japan's navy careened into World War II without any experiences that refuted the Tsushima meme. Cataclysm awaited.

The mass-production mentality suffusing bureaucracy seems to predispose military leaders to believe that they can replicate past successes. Once memes have been written into rules and procedures, they obstruct efforts to adapt to changing surroundings. If natural selection distinguishes among ideas, as Richard Dawkins contends, then one meme may give way to another with relative ease among individual human beings. People are known to change their minds. Memes come and go. But bureaucracy is designed *not* to be as supple or adaptable as individual minds. It is a production line designed to execute a slate of tasks again and again, the same way every time. The machinery imposes standard ways of thinking and doing on the individuals who comprise it. Written into rules and procedures, a meme can have a stultifying effect on operations and strategy.

Bureaucracy also interferes with the clash among ideas that refreshes and enlivens strategic debate, debunks ideas that prove false or outlive their usefulness, and ensures that the ideas fittest for the surroundings and the times prevail. Transcribing a meme into policy exempts it from critical scrutiny. It becomes axiomatic. In other words, a meme can sap an institution's dexterity of thought and action, impairing efforts to remake itself as circumstances change around it.

After this survey it is worth asking how paradigms, maxims, and memes relate to one another. For one thing, they all express ideas about how an institution ought to interpret its surroundings and perform its missions within those surroundings. A paradigm is a formal theory about politico-military affairs, much as schools of thought coalesce around scientific theories in Thomas Kuhn's telling. A maxim derives from the paradigm and expresses one of its key ideas in brief, blunt, easily intelligible terms. It may faithfully reflect a complex concept from the paradigm, but its very simplicity and brevity encourage members of the institution to oversimplify. People repeat the one-liner as accepted truth, with little sense of the reasoning that brought it forth. Nuance vanishes. That recalls Brodie's jibe that a maxim conveys meaning only when it is first introduced, and it is little more than a counterfeit after that. A meme is a simple idea that captures the fancy of a critical mass of people in positions of authority. It may find favor despite being little more than a gimmicky slogan that appeals to them. In other words, ideas matter in strategic affairs—and their influence may have little to do with their intellectual heft.

If martial bureaucracies are acutely susceptible to fashionable memes and orthodox paradigms, they are prone to what American social psychologist Irving Janis calls "groupthink."[136] Janis defines the term as a phenomenon in which dissenters within a group subordinate their views to the group consensus, refraining from voicing dissent in hopes of retaining the good opinion of their colleagues. He depicts it as "a mode of thinking that people engage in when they are deeply involved in a cohesive in-group, when the members' strivings for unanimity override their motivation to realistically appraise alternative courses of action."[137] Groupthink is insidious because it is not the product of tyrannical group leadership. Members are not sycophants who are afraid to speak their minds. Yet this subtle process results in "a deterioration of mental efficiency, reality testing, and moral judgment" owing to "in-group pressures."[138] An excess of cohesion keeps the group from identifying and vetting all alternative courses of action. In effect the group closes its mind.

As an antidote, Janis urges group leaders to appoint a "devil's advocate." The metaphor harks back to the medieval Catholic Church, which assigned a lawyer to argue against the credentials of any candidate for sainthood, lodging counterarguments fair or foul. Having heard the brief from the devil's advocate, church potentates believed, they could render a decision having weighed the full range of evidence and opinion. Janis updates the concept for modern secular groups. "If the leader genuinely wants the group to examine opposing arguments," he maintains, "he will have to give the devil's advocate an unambiguous assignment to present his arguments as clearly and convincingly as he can, like a good lawyer, challenging the testimony of those advocating the majority position."[139] The leader should reward the devil's advocate for playing the part with zeal—making that protagonist's performance evaluations and other career incentives contingent on a spirited, imaginative, lawyerly effort at cross-examining the group consensus.

As Dawkins contends, a meme must withstand the contest of ideas to win initial acceptance. And, as he implies, it must withstand challenge in the arena again and again as the times change and people formulate contending ideas. It might need to be amended or scrapped altogether. Yet that is hard to do once a meme is insulated by bureaucratic procedure and groupthink, as Dawkins and Janis show so well. Incumbent ideas reinforced by standard methods could prove so deadening that only some harrowing event could empower fresh ideas to oust and replace an entrenched but outdated meme. An armed service might find itself forced to flout doctrine or established wisdom in order to prevail in combat. It might suffer a crushing defeat that discredits the old meme and generates demand for new thinking. Or hardheaded uniformed or political leadership might etch new ideas on the institutional repertoire, displacing or overlaying the old. It commonly takes some trauma—if not a disaster—to jolt institutions out of obsolescent ways of doing things.

Lord prescribes a Machiavellian remedy in cases where senior leaders resolve to subdue a bureaucratic organization. They may simply need to enlist sincere support from top career officials. They may have to reeducate career officials and introduce training that instills a healthier culture in new hires. They may undertake wholesale firings or purges, replacing balky officials with individuals who are more congenial to top leadership's wishes. "This is not to say that modern leaders can or should act with the ferocity of princes of old," Lord says, "but there are many ways of slipping in the poisoned stiletto."[140]

Three themes emerge from this survey of the literature on public administration. First, bureaucratic institutions are efficient at performing routine tasks entrusted to them. Second, bureaucracy resists reform and so hampers efforts to keep a military service in tune with the times. And third, only an institution's topmost leadership stands much chance of effecting change. The U.S. sea services always have been far from immune to the numbing effects of bureaucracy. "To change anything in the Na-a-vy is like punching a feather bed," wisecracked Franklin Roosevelt, who served as President Woodrow Wilson's navy secretary. "You punch it with your right and you punch it with your left until you are finally exhausted, and then you find the damn bed just as it was before you started punching."[141] Henry Stimson, FDR's war secretary, mocked "the peculiar psychology of the Navy Department, which frequently seemed to retire from the realm of logic into a dim religious world in which Neptune was God, Mahan his prophet, and the United States Navy the only true Church."[142]

It is incumbent on geographic and fleet commanders and their advisers to fight against such tendencies with gusto, implanting a culture that goes beyond defying groupthink and is actively hospitable to innovation. How? American longshoreman-philosopher Eric Hoffer advises that creative cultures are mirthful, whimsical, even giddy. They neither punish nor discourage, but celebrate intellectual entrepreneurship. Hoffer's favorite among his own works was *The Ordeal of Change*, parts of which read like a missive to any military service intent on cultural reform.

In all likelihood Hoffer would advise the leadership of such an institution to make the climate among its members as *American* as possible. By that he meant nineteenth-century America, imbued with pioneering spirit. "Only here were the common folk of the Old World given a chance to show what they could do without a master to push and order them about," he maintains.[143] History "lifted by the nape of the neck lowly peasants, shopkeepers, laborers, paupers, jailbirds, and drunks from the midst of Europe, dumped them on a vast, virgin continent, and said: 'Go to it; it is yours!'"[144]

From that came Americans' boundless "faith in human regeneration . . . a faith founded on experience, not on some idealistic theory," Hoffer says.[145] He recalls wondering who were the pioneers' heirs in the 1930s Southwest. Not the comfortable—what incentive does someone living the good life have to shake things up? Hoffer concludes that the tramps he encountered on the road were the true pioneers. Misfits and losers tinker because they hate being weak. Tramps are the dregs of society, but they enjoy autonomy. No one pushes or orders them about, and they are possessed of a fiery desire to survive and thrive. Struggle steels character. Hoffer would advise U.S. naval and military leaders to revive the pioneering ethos. The less authoritarian and bureaucratic a service's campaign for operational excellence, the better. Top leaders should empower individual officers and enlisted folk to be themselves.

Hoffer goes further. He surveys human history, gazing back to the dawn of recorded time. His verdict is that innovative ages are exuberant ages typified by a "playful mood."[146] Worthwhile inventions start out as playthings or follies, not concerted or somber efforts to improve the private or public weal. Practical use is a byproduct of whimsy. "When we do find that a critical challenge has apparently evoked a marked creative response," he writes, "there is always the possibility that the response came not from people cornered by a challenge but from people who in an exuberance of energy went out in search of a challenge."[147]

Classical Athens, the Renaissance, Elizabethan England, and the Enlightenment all were "buoyant and even frivolous" epochs that witnessed outbursts of learning and invention, Hoffer says.[148] Conversely, dour, pedantic, anti-individualistic eras are seldom creative. Ideologues crave dull conformity to their wishes, not an enterprising counterculture. The lesson from a longshoreman? Strategic leaders should do away with orthodoxy, keep things upbeat, and liberate their subordinates' inquisitive natures in the process. Playfulness begets experimentation—and helps bolster combat effectiveness.

While Hoffer puts the accent on merriment, Feynman observes that doubt, failure, and incremental improvement are pivotal to an experimental ethos. Combining Hoffer's and Feynman's insights makes it appear that strategic leaders should foster a bureaucratic culture that makes doubt and failure . . . fun! A freethinking culture unlocks the creativity of officers, enlisted, and civilians alike. Properly shaped and nourished, it goes beyond removing obstacles to experimentation. It actively rewards innovators for formulating heterodox ideas, subjecting them to the test of reality, and amending or discarding them for the next wacky idea. There cannot be too much institutional stewardship for strategic leaders. They should incline strongly toward the excess when interpolating between the excess and the deficiency of this function.

PLAINSPOKEN ENGLISH

The last habit befitting peacetime toolmakers—not to mention strategic leadership throughout the spectrum of competition and conflict—is clear communication. Senior leaders must hone their skill at rhetoric—the art of persuasion, as the ancients defined it—with the same fervor they bring to designing fleets or drawing up budgets. Strategy is storytelling. It goes far beyond the mechanical-seeming process of devising ways to harness diplomatic, economic, and military means to secure political gain in a competitive environment. Good strategy does more than simply impart information or map out a plan of action. It lays out national purposes and explains to specialists and nonspecialists alike how its executors intend to put military and nonmilitary power to work fulfilling those purposes.

If a strategic narrative is cogently framed, it sweeps audiences along to the writer's or speaker's conclusions. That is how rhetoric works: it informs, provokes, and inspires. And it must appeal to audiences from different backgrounds and demographics. If Congress is the audience, defense spokesmen typically try to convince lawmakers to provide the armed forces with the implements they need to make the story—and its happy ending in particular—come true. If the American people are the audience, strategy should persuade ordinary citizens that spending tax dollars on armaments will advance a worthy if not righteous cause. If allies or prospective foes are the audience, the script should convince them that America can and will keep its international commitments. Allies will take heart, consoled that the United States will be there for them; opponents will be disconsolate and might postpone or abandon any malign aims. Communicators must tailor their message to the readers or listeners whose views they mean to shape—much as Aristotle counsels in his discourse on *Rhetoric*, reviewed briefly in chapter 1 and well worth studying in full.

Consider the U.S. Navy again. In many cases Navy leaders excelled as communicators during the World War II era. In November 1940, for example, the Chief of Naval Operations, Adm. Harold R. Stark, managed to evaluate the strategic situation in the Atlantic and Pacific, outline and evaluate potential U.S. courses of action, and formulate recommendations—all in a crisply written document the length of a graduate-school seminar paper. Stark's "Plan DOG" memorandum, mapping out the course of a two-ocean war, remains worth studying eighty-plus years on.[149]

Adm. Ernest J. King, who doubled as the Navy's operational and administrative chief during the war, found virtue in brevity and clarity in communications within the service. In early 1941, while serving as U.S. Atlantic Fleet commander, he distributed a circular letter to the fleet condemning the "excess of detail in orders and instructions."[150] Senior officers, he complained, cramped their subordinates' entrepreneurship by telling them precisely how to execute their orders, as opposed to instructing them *what* to do and leaving it to them to figure out *how*. King's acerbic directive is a tonic.

If strategic leaders fail to tell the story fluently, popular or elite support for some endeavor could quail. A rhetorical deficit plagued naval officialdom during the years following World War II. J. C. Wylie attended the Naval War College shortly after the war and later served on the faculty. While in Newport he voiced dismay at how fecklessly Navy brass defended their service during the "revolt of the admirals," a bureaucratic struggle between the Navy and Air Force over the two services' roles, missions, and force structures for the atomic age. There was a real danger that the Navy might survive only as a convoy force. Air Force squadrons would take over the nuclear strike mission—and much else besides.

In 1951, to stave off a dark future, Wylie collaborated with the Naval War College president, Rear Adm. Richard L. Conolly, to compose a letter to the Chief of Naval Operations, Adm. Forrest P. Sherman. They faulted the naval officer corps not for technical, tactical, or administrative failings but for inability to understand or explain sea power. "Very few of us were able to reason with the Congress or present our case convincingly to the people" that the United States still needed a Navy built to fight for high-seas mastery, they wrote. "Our understanding and our exposition of the indispensable character of our profession and the undiminished and vital nature of Sea Power have been dangerously superficial and elementary."[151] Dangerously superficial and elementary—that is quite an indictment.

To delve deeper, Conolly and Wylie proposed founding a new advanced strategy program at the Naval War College. They foresaw grounding the curriculum in analytical history. Such study goes beyond chronology, helping aspirants search out basic truths about societies, cultures, and armed forces. History, then, is one key to rhetorical fluency. Knowing the subject matter thoroughly is crucial to explaining it convincingly. Knowing what maritime forces have done across the centuries is essential to deep understanding of sea power.

Wylie also warned naval officers not to keep secrets, as members of specialist guilds typically do. He was less worried that officers would deliberately withhold information than that they might fail to realize they were using insider language, and so might miss out on the opportunity to explain themselves fully and clearly. "The basic patterns of strategic thought should not be looked on as any kind of a secret," he wrote in his treatise on *Military Strategy*. "The more people who know about and understand these patterns, the more healthy will be our democracy in its strategic decisions."[152] After all, Congress makes strategic decisions through the budget process all the time, he pointed out. "The congressman voting on a military appropriation is, in a very real sense indeed, making a fundamental strategic decision, and he does not need very many 'secrets' to lead him toward sound decision. . . . None of the really important aspects of strategy is out of the public attention."[153]

To put this bit of wisdom into practice, sea service officials should purge discourses about naval and military affairs of insider language. That means eradicating jargon, acronyms, and anything that is not immediately clear to the intended audience. It also means looking for everyday metaphors for martial matters—from literature, sports, or even pop culture—that make the subject at hand obvious to nonspecialists. For example, Mao Zedong, founding chairman of the Chinese Communist Party, described his "active defense" strategy to the Chinese peasantry in terms of boxing strategy.[154] Active defense was a strategy by which the weak overcome the strong through patience and guile—much as the lesser but smarter pugilist could beat a brawnier but foolish opponent.

In other words, strategy is not and must not be some esoteric art intelligible only to initiates. The strategic narrative will fall flat if it is couched in language that is too dense for the audience to fathom. Listeners or readers will tune out—and the effort at persuasion will fail. Style counts as well. Plain English is a must; vibrant prose helps. American author William R. Manchester describes how H. L. Mencken, one of history's greatest and most venomous wordsmiths, burst onto the literary scene in 1908: "Discrimination and poise were futile; gusto, energy, and a stallion prose were needed. These were Mencken's."[155] He "threw his first shell into the breech, and fired."[156] Mencken soon earned the sobriquet "disturber of the peace." Naval officials should take history's great communicators as their inspiration.

Feynman would agree about the merits of clear expression. According to him, you do not understand something well enough yourself if you cannot explain it to a sixth-grader. If you cannot explain it at that level, he advises you to review the material until you have a firm grip on its vagaries; clarify, simplify, and streamline how you explain it; and try again until you have convinced yourself a youngster could comprehend your explanation.[157] Feynman worked on the Manhattan Project and went on to pioneer quantum electrodynamics. If scientists such as Feynman can explain intricate subjects like theoretical physics to neophytes to the field, U.S. military officers and their political masters can explain strategy to laymen.

Take it from a physicist and from the greats from many other fields: defense officials must alert themselves to the dangers of abstruse language, maintain intimate acquaintanceship with their subject matter, nurture the habit of speaking and writing clearly, and be ruthlessly critical of their rhetorical work. Plainspoken language works best. This is an Aristotelian habit of singular importance to strategy.

Preparing for war is plainly a demanding business. It sprawls far beyond the mechanics of devising weapon systems and sensors, administering programs and budgets, and discharging the multitude of other tasks that consume daily life in defense circles. It demands that strategic leaders refine their foresight, manage the culture within institutions entrusted to their care, and explain themselves cogently to a variety of audiences. They must equip themselves with habits that help them look beyond everyday routine—and act on what they see.

3

IN PEACE, WIN FRIENDS AND OVERAWE OPPONENTS

Chapter 2 inventoried the basic bundle of habits that are necessary for strategic leaders to acquire as they discharge their duty as peacetime builders of military and maritime might. We now survey how they can use power to fulfill objectives short of open war. It is worth restating that many of these habits span the continuum from peace to war and back again. Wartime strategy differs from peacetime strategy chiefly in the fickle dynamism of interactions among combatants. For example, keeping ends, ways, and means in alignment is paramount during both war and peacetime. So is managing institutional culture in the interest of strategic success. Governing personal and popular passions also is a timeless challenge. I have merely assigned each habit to the chapter representing the sector along that continuum where I believe it matters most. From time to time the book touches again on habits covered before, but only insofar as they vary from phase to phase.

This chapter identifies habits that are valuable in strategic competition during peacetime—that intermediate state between the relatively static realm of designing and building forces and the dynamic realm of actually using those forces in combat. Sage strategic leaders try to get their way through nonviolent diplomacy in peacetime while building up sufficient national economic and military power to outmuscle antagonists in case war comes despite their leanings. They should cultivate habits of mind, sentiment, and deed useful for deterring or coercing foreign competitors, giving heart to allies and friends, and commanding respect and support from their home society and government. A strategic competitor that husbands its strength, conveys the willpower to use force under certain circumstances, and makes influential audiences believers in its physical might and political fortitude can position itself to prosper in statecraft, peaceful and violent alike.

Peacetime strategic competition is virtual war. To borrow a slogan from former secretary of defense James N. Mattis, successful American armed diplomacy impresses upon others that they have no better friend and no worse enemy than the United States.[1] Prospective foes, friendly powers, and domestic constituents trust such a country to follow through on its threats while honoring covenants with allies and friends. Keeping its commitments earns a contender a reputation for power and steadfastness—and reputation is everything in global politics.

A SKETCH OF AMERICA'S GRAND STRATEGIC PURPOSES

This book is aimed chiefly at U.S. military readers. Before investigating the habits that American strategists should cultivate, it is worth investigating what tasks elected leaders may call on them to do during their careers. Johns Hopkins University professor Hal Brands defines grand strategy "realistically" and straightforwardly as "a set of basic principles that guide policy."[2] Such principles are grounded in national history, national character, and geopolitical circumstances. A snapshot of U.S. grand strategy is in order. The latest guidance on American strategy comes from such documents as the National Security Strategy, National Defense Strategy, National Military Strategy, and Maritime Strategy. Acquaintanceship with these statements of power and purpose is fundamental for anyone entrusted with executing them and, in turn, with fulfilling the wishes of the American people.

Strategy documents of this type vary from presidency to presidency. Peering back into diplomatic and military history nevertheless reveals five perennial tenets of U.S. foreign policy and strategy. These tenets are ideas about purpose and power that endure from decade to decade and administration to administration. They command support from both major political parties and a broad swath of the electorate, making them durable. All undergo some adjustment as circumstances change. Few, if any, seem likely to vanish from Washington's grand-strategic repertoire. Reviewing them, even in this cursory way, will help orient strategic thinkers and practitioners to the demands that they may face. Deeper study of U.S. history will enrich their understanding and insight.

First, the United States acts as keeper of the status quo when the status quo favors U.S. interests and purposes. University of Pennsylvania historian Walter McDougall depicts the early republic as a "promised land," with a society that was content to set an example for others in hopes that they would follow.[3] For a century after its founding, the United States was mainly an inward-looking society. Americans had a continent to subdue after winning independence from Great Britain. Like all rising powers, the new republic busied itself building infrastructure and developing a vibrant economy that could generate wealth.

Even during this age of introspection, however, U.S. leaders went on record pledging to uphold the regional order in the Americas. In 1823 Secretary of State John Quincy Adams and President James Monroe issued the classic statement about U.S. stewardship over the Western Hemisphere, informing Congress that the Western Hemisphere was now off-limits to fresh European colonization or proxy rule. The "Monroe Doctrine" declared that Latin American states had won their independence in a series of revolutions and would no longer be subservient to European great powers.[4] The United States would use the power at its disposal to prevent any new encroachment. Washington thus appointed itself the defender of Latin American independence—even though it would not build a navy capable of enforcing the Monroe Doctrine until the 1880s.[5]

In doing so, Adams and Monroe inaugurated and codified a custodial strain in U.S. foreign policy. Although the republic would remain introspective for decades to come, it entertained large—arguably even imperial—ambitions. Indeed, the Monroe Doctrine remained a staple of U.S. foreign policy well into the twentieth century. Even so, in 1898, McDougall writes, U.S. foreign policy underwent a revolution. The promised land metamorphosed into a "crusader state" intent on remaking the regional order—and eventually the world order—to suit itself.[6] In 1883 Congress authorized the laying of keels for the Navy's first armored, heavily gunned, steam-propelled battle fleet. In 1898 President William McKinley ordered that fleet to the Caribbean Sea and Western Pacific, where it demolished the Spanish navy, landed troops, and wrested Spain's island empire from it. Almost overnight the United States acquired its first overseas empire.

Washington kept the islands yet did not administer the nation's new holdings well, especially in the case of the Philippines. After the Spanish-American War, pundit Walter Lippmann excoriated every presidency—with the partial exception of the Theodore Roosevelt administration—for skimping on the defense of the Philippines. To Lippmann, taking on vast commitments in close proximity to a rising Japan and then failing to provide military resources to protect those commitments constituted a recipe for disillusionment at home and failure in the Pacific. Lippmann blamed Washington for "monstrous imprudence" for pursuing bold political ends with paltry means.[7] Strategic malpractice invited aggression, he warned; yet, the impulse to enforce the status quo endured.

The geopolitical revolution was hastened by an artificial modification of marine geography—the construction of the Panama Canal. The transisthmus waterway was completed in 1914, slashing thousands of miles off voyages from the U.S. east coast to the Pacific. In 1898 geography had compelled the Pacific-based U.S. battleship *Oregon* to circumnavigate all of South America to get into the fighting in the Caribbean. No more. With the canal in operation, American warships could swing between the Atlantic and Pacific Oceans with relative ease—helping the Navy manage challenges in two oceans. Commercial shipping companies reaped benefits as well. Transiting the canal drastically shortened the time that it took cargo vessels from New York, America's largest trading hub, to steam to East Asia. It also reversed the longstanding advantage that British merchantmen had enjoyed for their own trade in Chinese ports north of Shanghai. New York now lay closer to North

China, measured by steaming miles, than did the major British seaport of Liverpool. Shorter distances cut costs and made U.S. shippers more competitive.[8]

So profound was the turnabout in U.S. foreign policy and maritime strategy that Yale University professor Nicholas Spykman—arguably history's foremost scholar of geopolitics—claimed that digging the Panama Canal "had the effect of turning the whole of the United States around on its axis and giving it direct access to the Pacific Ocean."[9] The canal transformed American nautical culture, both mercantile and naval, and simplified the task of enforcing a benign status quo in the Western Hemisphere. The United States, a country accustomed to looking eastward toward Europe, now looked southward as well in search of prosperity and foreign policy clout.

The chasm between political ends and military means of which Lippmann had warned set up an eventual contest between the United States and imperial Japan in the Pacific Ocean. That contest ended in 1945, with the United States standing atop the regional and world orders and once again determined to lock in a status quo hospitable to its purposes. Then came the protracted Cold War with the Soviet Union and its allies. That forty-four-year struggle drew to a close in 1991, with the United States again bestriding the global order. This time, however, Washington faced no near-term challenger comparable to the Soviet Union. Only after the turn of the twenty-first century did Communist China come to pose such a challenge. How the new contest will play out remains to be seen.

Almost from the United States' inception, whenever the government has regarded a geopolitical situation as favorable, it has regarded itself as the trustee of the status quo. Its strategies for making good on that outlook have alternated between effective and ineffective, but the goal has remained a constant at least since the debut of the Monroe Doctrine in 1823. As Prussian soldier-philosopher Carl von Clausewitz saw it, a status quo strategy is a strategy of "negative aim." Strategists want to preserve what is in case anyone should try to snatch it away, but they have no "positive aims"—meaning they have no desire to take something from others. This has important implications for American strategists tasked with defending the international system as it exists today.

Second, the United States has long championed maintaining an "open door" for foreign commerce. In other words, it wants ready access to important trading regions for American firms and advocates free access for other countries as a matter of reciprocity. Diplomats dubbed this the Open Door policy starting in the McKinley years, when it appeared that the imperial powers, which had taken to asserting "spheres of interest" in China, might abridge or completely annul treaty rights in their spheres and in the process shut U.S. businesses out of the China trade. If that were to happen, the diplomats warned, prosperity would suffer all over the world. Accordingly, in 1899 Secretary of State John Hay circulated a diplomatic note among the European capitals and Tokyo entreating other governments not to erect tariff or nontariff barriers in their trading zones, but instead to leave the door ajar for businesses from all nations to trade openly—without giving preferential treatment to firms from their own home countries.[10]

Except for the years of the Great Depression, which began in the late 1920s, the Open Door policy became a staple of U.S. diplomacy. After World War II the United States went on to spearhead the foundation of multinational institutions such as the World Bank; the International Monetary Fund, which governs financial and economic relations among nations; and the General Agreement on Tariffs and Trade, which later became the World Trade Organization.[11] Such bodies consolidated the liberal international system of trade and commerce, and with it the beneficial postwar status quo won by American and Allied arms. Assuring the free flow of goods and services between industry and customers looking to satisfy their wants and needs doubtless will remain central to U.S. grand strategy—and to U.S. maritime strategy, itself a genre of grand strategy. American naval strategist Alfred Thayer Mahan declared that the purpose of a sea-oriented grand strategy like America's is access—commercial access, diplomatic access, and military access, in descending order of importance.[12] To Mahan, commerce is king. Diplomatic access facilitates it. Military access is necessary only insofar as it enables the other forms of access.[13] The Open Door, then, appears solidly moored, both in sea-power theory and in American strategic traditions. U.S. strategists should think in terms of access while remaining wary of hostile attempts to deny access—as they have for over a century.

Third, since the United States metamorphosed into the crusader state described by Walter McDougall, it has practiced a form of geopolitical balancing in important "rimlands," or coastal zones—primarily those that encircle the Eurasian supercontinent.[14] Spykman does an admirable job explicating the rimlands strategy. He observes that the Old World surrounds the New geographically. As a result, a hostile power or alliance could reach out across the Pacific or Atlantic and do Americans harm in their own hemisphere. This presents little problem so long as the Western European and East Asian (and today South Asian) rimlands remain fragmented among competing power centers.[15] But if some antagonist managed to unify one or more of the rimlands under its dominion, it would gain access to the hefty inventory of economic and military resources that has been accumulated in Eurasia.

Forestalling this nightmare scenario warranted throwing America's weight onto the scales through a forward diplomatic, economic, and military strategy. Spykman beseeched Washington to balance the ambitions of any would-be hegemon, be it Nazi Germany or imperial Japan or the Soviet Union.[16] Sadly, Spykman died during World War II, but he would instantly grasp the logic underlying the United States' postwar system of alliances, economic outreach, and forward military deployments. These are his rimlands strategy made manifest.

Fourth, and closely related, the United States aspires to command what Spykman terms the "girdle of marginal seas" washing against the rimlands.[17] If hemispheric defense is no defense at all, as he maintained, and if a forward strategy in the rimlands is the United States' surest security guarantee, then U.S. forces must be able to reach the rimlands across the sea, overcoming resistance from a regional opponent. This is practical reality not just for the United States but for any globe-spanning sea power. Great Britain made itself the world's dominant maritime hegemon for centuries because its Royal Navy could seize control of the Mediterranean Sea, South China Sea, Persian Gulf, and other seas bordering the Eurasian perimeter. The same dynamic holds for the United States today. It is hard for any force to shape events in the rimlands if it cannot get there. Hence the U.S. Navy has stationed fleets or squadrons in or adjacent to these expanses since 1945.

And fifth, the United States is an alliance builder and manager. It must be. It has no strategic position in Western Europe, East Asia, or South Asia without access to friendly soil. North America lies too far away from the rimlands to project power there on a sustained basis. U.S. forces could radiate power into the rimlands without access to seaports and bases and the logistical support they provide, but only in an intermittent and sporadic fashion. The great lesson of World War I, the collapse of the postwar settlement, and World War II was that America must never again disengage from Eurasian affairs lest the ensuing power vacuum bring on a third world war. After 1945 it helped rebuild allies and vanquished enemies alike, constructing an array of new alliances around the Eurasian periphery. Washington used these alliances to compete successfully against the Soviet empire for over forty years and kept them in place after the Soviet Union collapsed in 1991. The United States will continue tending its international fellowships during the coming age of strategic competition against China and Russia.

American grand strategy, then, weaves together defensive and offensive strands. As noted before, a status quo strategy is a strategy of negative aim, and thus the United States sees itself as the chief conservator of the international order as it currently stands. But it pursues its negative aim through active, outward-looking, offensively oriented methods—stationing forces in many countries to accomplish its goals of keeping the door open for commerce, diplomacy, and military endeavors and preventing a domineering hostile power from gaining control of the rimlands. And it must field maritime forces powerful enough to control the marginal seas. After all, maritime command is about sinking or blockading enemy naval forces—operations that are intensely offensive in outlook.

U.S. grand strategy, then, envisions playing strategic defense through tactical and operational offense. Would-be strategists must refine virtues of thought, temperament, and deed that are suited to help America preside over the liberal world order—and rule the sea—indefinitely.

MAKE BELIEVERS OF OTHERS TO DETER, COERCE, AND REASSURE

An offensive mindset is not the same thing as bloodlust. Strategic competitors, including contemporary America, try to get their way without fighting. A successful competitor prevails by swaying others rather than defeating them. In crude terms, the leadership can attempt to modify opinion through one of three ways—*deterrence*, or persuading an opponent not to do something that it would like to do; *coercion*, convincing an opponent to do something that it would prefer not to; or *reassurance*, convincing allies or friends that it can and will keep its commitments to them. The same basic principles apply to all three modes of forceful persuasion.

In particular scholars have dedicated thought and energy to probing the dynamics of deterrence. This comes as little surprise. Since the advent of the atomic age in 1945, after all, deterrence has been a matter of life and death for civilizations. The literature on it is vast, coming from such famed thinkers as the late American economist Thomas C. Schelling.[18] Strategic leaders, however, may profit most from a pithy formula compiled by former secretary of state Henry A. Kissinger. Kissinger's formula is workmanlike and user-friendly for those entrusted with devising and prosecuting operations aimed at deterring antagonists—whether in the nuclear or the conventional realm.

Kissinger writes that deterrence takes place not on some battleground where armies fight to a verdict of arms, but in the minds of prospective aggressors. The problem is that leaders of U.S. adversaries might contemplate taking some course of action that friendly leaders deem unacceptable. Deterrence means making that course of action "seem less attractive than all possible alternatives."[19] Convincing an opponent that aggression is the worst of all options, he maintains, "requires a combination of power, the will to use it, and the assessment of these by the potential aggressor."[20] He cautions, however, that "deterrence is a product of those factors and not a sum. If any one of them is zero, deterrence fails."[21]

The first two elements of deterrence are straightforward. For Kissinger, strength is a compound of physical power and willpower. So it is for Clausewitz, who describes a combatant's power as "the product of two inseparable factors," namely the martial means at its disposal and the leadership's resolve to use those means to obtain its goals.[22] A brawny contestant is armed with a keen-edged sword and is prepared to draw and swing it. The third element is trickier. It involves conveying a persuasive message to hostile leaders. "The assessment of these by the potential aggressor" is Kissinger's oblique way of referring to belief. It is one thing to *be* strong, but a contestant also has to convince others that it *is* strong. Deterrence should hold if strategic leaders convince the aggressor's leadership that they possess the power to carry out their deterrent threat and are irrevocably committed to doing so.

In other words, they make believers out of would-be aggressors. It is worth restating the coda to Kissinger's function: deterrence is a product of *multiplying* power, willpower, and belief, not of *adding* them. Multiplying the largest number by zero yields zero. Willpower accomplishes little without any power to deploy. All the physical power in the world is impotent if its wielder is too irresolute to use it. All the power and resolve in the world mean nothing if the target audience disbelieves in either ingredient of strength. It might defy the deterrent threat out of miscommunication, simple error, or recklessness. In similar fashion a contender hoping to coerce a rival into doing something must make a believer out of that rival. Otherwise the coercive threat will fall flat.

Kissinger hints at, but does not elaborate fully on, the reciprocal to deterrence and coercion—namely reassurance. Reassurance is designed not to dishearten, but to give heart by projecting an image of strength. Power combined with resolve reassures allies or friends even as it intimidates antagonists. All three modes of armed persuasion draw on the logic that people and societies accommodate themselves to realities of power. If one government makes a commitment to another, and if it displays the power and determination to follow through on that commitment, it will make a believer out of that government and the larger society over which it presides. Recipients of a pledge from a strong and resolute partner develop confidence in the pledge. They feel little need to accommodate a strong but malicious power out of self-preservation. Deterrence and reassurance, then, are commonly parallel endeavors, the one designed to cow antagonists, the other designed to embolden friends.

These endeavors bear some resemblance to trash-talking in sports. Think about it. In the weeks and days leading up to a boxing match, each pugilist tries to intimidate the other, inspire his own fans, and enrage his opponent's fans by boasting about his prowess while mocking his opponent for supposed feebleness. The opponent repays insult with insult. Spectators bicker about the probable outcome. Talking trash, in other words, means playing up one's own capability and commitment while deprecating the opponent's in order to influence others. The contenders harvest public-relations gain and advertising dollars—much as commanders and policymakers try to harvest strategic and political gain from portraying their forces as superior. Strategic leaders must make a habit of thinking of military forces as political implements for molding opinion among government officials and decision-makers who matter.

HARNESS THE IDEA OF FIGHTING

Peacetime statecraft is combative. At the risk of sounding Orwellian, it behooves strategic leaders to don a warlike visage to prosecute a peacetime competition. Peace is not war, but it often comes close and employs similar tools and methods. Accordingly, strategic practitioners must habituate themselves not just to forging implements of war but also to using them to shape opinion in a world where competitors jockey constantly to advance their geopolitical purposes—sometimes in inimical ways—while refraining from the overt use of arms. This is why chapter 2 warned military officialdom against deluding itself into believing that everlasting peace is at hand—or, as in the case of the U.S. sea services following the Cold War, that prevailing in a major struggle obviates basic functions such as the need to fight for maritime mastery. It does not. A new peer rival will come along sooner or later.

A lull in strategic competition may number among the fruits of victory, and often does. Yet, victory never abolishes competition altogether. Some philosophers and writers affirm that a measure of fatalism is healthy. Foresight should be tinged with anxiety, to recall Robert Kaplan's phrase (profiled in chapter 2). In book 1 of Plato's dialogue on the *Laws*, the Athenian philosopher proclaimed that "every State is, by a law of nature, engaged perpetually in an informal war with every other state."[23] Mao Zedong's foreign minister, Zhou Enlai, was just as bloody-minded. Zhou insisted that "all diplomacy is a continuation of war by other means."[24] Or, as the late University of Reading strategy professor Colin Gray put it tartly, "history reminds those willing to be reminded that bad times always return, and that every war-free period is actually an interwar era."[25]

Lest the martial overtones to this discussion ring too loudly, it is important not to take this ultracompetitive attitude to extremes. Peacetime diplomacy is not invariably about brinksmanship. Much depends on who the players are in a given international interaction. Ideally, diplomacy is about comporting oneself with tact and fellowship while radiating confidence in one's ability to manage events by force should relations sour. Students of strategy generally picture international interactions as playing out somewhere along a continuum. At the placid extreme lies peacetime diplomacy, a mode of intercourse in which the threat of armed force plays no part. Relations among the United States, Mexico, and Canada fall into this category. North American international relations are quarrelsome on occasion, but today it is virtually unthinkable that North Americans might rattle sabers at one another over immigration or trade, let alone actually take up the sword. In tranquil times such as these, governments reach agreements through negotiations, advancing national purposes through compromise at the bargaining table.

But the times are not always so serene or relations so cordial. Peacetime strategic competition ensues when strategic actors pursue incompatible aims and have recourse to arms. As chapter 2 maintained, strategic competition resembles an armed debate. Since competitors do not trade blows in peacetime, each tries to project an image of economic and martial vigor, convincing audiences that are able to influence the outcome of the competition that it *would* prevail if some dispute were to escalate to an exchange of blows. Competitive logic is simple and rooted in human nature. In all likelihood Henry Kissinger would concur with World War II general George S. Patton, who admonished the Third Army in 1944 that people love a winner and refuse to tolerate a loser.[26] As it is with individuals, so it is with groups. Individuals, societies, and governments take the measure of strategic competitors and rally to whichever party they estimate would triumph in combat.

In other words, it is natural to side with those deemed muscular and resolute. The magnetic quality to which Patton alluded bestows political influence on the contender that earns a reputation for power and resolve. The nonaligned are drawn to such a contender while edging away from a likely loser lest they entangle their fortunes with it and have to share the wages of defeat. A reputation for success attracts friends. Failure repels them.

Clausewitz, too, tenders the case for husbanding a bleak worldview. He takes a penetrating view of the relationship between force and statecraft, seeming to declare that war invariably involves violence: "Essentially war is fighting, for fighting is the only effective principle in the manifold activities generally designated as war. Fighting, in turn, is a trial of moral and physical forces through the medium of the latter."[27] Such passages earned Clausewitz his reputation as a theorist who espouses unleashing concentrated force to batter antagonists into submission. He counsels commanders to rain "blow after blow" on enemy legions, all "in the same direction: the victor . . . must strike with all his strength and not just against a fraction of the enemy's."[28] This is unambiguous and bareknuckles stuff.

Or so it seems. As a rule, Clausewitzian ideas are more subtle than they first appear. The Prussian master took delight in issuing an absolute, or "ideal," statement about martial affairs and then showing why reality almost always falls short of the absolute. That is true of his algorithm for overpowering force. Warfare seldom means pounding away until enemy forces capitulate or collapse. Sometimes pragmatic reasons prevent a combatant from concentrating all of its power to deliver a massive blow. There may be physical or political barriers to assembling its entire force at a scene of action. Usually, though, Clausewitz says, it is policy that "converts the overwhelmingly destructive element of war into a mere instrument. It changes the terrible battle-sword that a man needs both hands and his entire strength to wield, and with which he strikes home once and no more, into a light, handy rapier—sometimes just a foil for the exchange of thrusts, feints and parries."[29]

What does Clausewitz mean by this? Policymakers often blanch at the investment in time, lives, and resources that a complete battlefield victory could cost. The likely returns may not justify the expense or effort in the eyes of the leadership or its constituents. Or ethical or moral constraints might hold back the means deployed. Allies might prevail on the leadership to exercise restraint. In short, countless factors could intervene in the process, attenuating the pressure a combatant exerts against its foe.

Clausewitz admits that such factors generally do intrude, but he takes his case even further, implying that competitors can engage in *warlike* interactions that fall short of military engagement. He defines "combat" in an intriguing and counterintuitive way. For him, the term is not a synonym for "fighting," as it is normally used. Instead, fighting is that subset of combat during which arms actually are used. Clausewitz allows for a host of combat interactions when violence is threatened but not actually used. If competitors have the "idea" of fighting in mind when they interact, he writes, then they are engaging in combat: "Combat is the only effective force in war; its aim is to destroy the enemy's forces as a means to a further end. That holds good *even if no actual fighting occurs*, because the outcome rests on the assumption that if it came to fighting, the enemy would be destroyed" [italics mine].[30]

This is the key insight. If combat may be "far removed" from "the brute discharge of hatred and enmity of a physical encounter," as Clausewitz maintains, then there is no reason that combat cannot transpire in times of tense peace.[31] After all, the outcome of a peacetime show of force rests on encouraging influential audiences to conclude that one's antagonist would be destroyed as a fighting force should the encounter come to blows.

In a real sense, then, peacetime military and naval diplomacy is a nonshooting war intended to mold perceptions. Clausewitz holds that fighting is a trial of moral and physical forces through the medium of physical force; therefore, it is reasonable to construe peacetime "combat" as a trial of moral and physical forces through the medium of moral forces—of morale, in other words. It involves displaying formidable physical forces to sway opinion, dispiriting opponents while giving heart to allies and friends. The theory is that if one contender places its adversary in what looks like an impossible position, others will flock to that contender's standard, or at least prove pliant, while distancing themselves from the adversary. Commanders and their political masters should keep the idea of fighting first and foremost in their minds when framing diplomacy. If they do, they may not need to fight.

Cultivating an austere Clausewitzian mindset will predispose overseers of strategy to think about how military movements will impress audiences whose members are able to influence the outcome of an encounter, regardless of whether those audiences are friends, potential foes, or bystanders. Thus attuned, they can orchestrate operations to advance the war for perceptual advantage. In modern experience, that is where Clausewitz meets Kissinger—helping strategic practitioners ponder power, resolve, and belief. In a word, competition is spectacle.

CAST A SHADOW ACROSS THE SEA

Transpose these insights to the maritime realm. Maritime strategy masters Alfred Thayer Mahan and Julian Corbett say little about shaping opinion, although Corbett does make building and breaking alliances part of his "active defense" strategy, a strategy by which a weaker nautical contender bulks up its forces over time while simultaneously enfeebling the military strength of its foe.[32] Wooing new allies to one's cause while splitting hostile alliances and coalitions skews the aggregate balance in a favorable direction.

Still, Mahan and Corbett concerned themselves mainly with wartime strategy. Peacetime competition is an armed conversation for which the idea of fighting supplies the subtext. Contenders deploy forces in concert with rhetoric to make statements and rebuttals about relative power and weakness. In Kissingerian fashion, the conversation revolves around deterrence, coercion, and reassurance. Like boxers talking smack, protagonists in strategic competition conduct a virtual contest of arms in which each tries to convince others that it is stronger, if not invincible. For instance, a fleet exercise is a statement about seaborne fighting power. That statement is expressed in steel and in the words that senior leaders use to explain their purposes. Strategic competition is interactive. The opponent may reply by staging maneuvers of its own, hoping to persuade influential spectators that its fleet would emerge triumphant from a high-seas trial of arms.

Unlike Mahan and Corbett, American strategist Edward Luttwak places great weight on using peacetime force deployments to mold opinion. Luttwak terms this politico-military process "armed suasion" or, in a saltwater setting, "naval suasion." As he describes it, armed suasion "defines all reactions, political or tactical, elicited by all parties—allies, adversaries, or neutrals—to the existence, display, manipulation, or symbolic use of any instrument of military power, whether or not such reactions reflect any deliberate intent of the deploying party. 'Naval suasion' refers to effects evoked by sea-based or sea-related forces."[33] Brandishing naval forces can persuade other parties to take or desist from taking some action depending on political leaders' wishes. It also can have unintended political impact.

Naval vessels are especially well suited for strategic competition because warships perform double duty. They render nonmilitary service in peacetime—by succoring stricken countries after natural disasters or policing the sea for lawbreakers, for example. Yet they can shift into combat mode almost instantly after receiving orders from on high—and others know it. Thus, as Luttwak puts it, naval suasion casts a "shadow" across calculations in foreign capitals. The threat of naval force "impinges on the freedom of action of adversaries, because the capabilities perceived can be activated at any time, while the formulation of the intent to use them can be both silent and immediate."[34] The longer and darker the shadow that maritime operations cast, the greater its political effect. Foreign governments cannot disregard it when deliberating about policy or strategy.

Luttwak points to a perverse aspect of naval suasion: battle is the final arbiter of who is stronger and who is weaker, but no one fights battles in peacetime. If strategic competition is a war of perceptions rather than one of gun or missile salvos, then whichever contender most observers believe would have won a battle "wins" a peacetime test of strength. As a rule, though, the spectators are unschooled in military matters. Few civilian officials these days undergo military service. Ordinary people concern themselves chiefly with making a living and tending to their families, not with arcane matters such as sea combat. In short, the audiences for naval suasion are ill-qualified to judge which fleet would get the better of the other in action—yet their perceptions count all the same. In fact, Luttwak postulates that the lesser force may triumph in a virtual test of arms if it *looks* beefier than the opponent's. It will prevail if it exudes more "sex appeal."[35] And sex appeal sells in power politics as in everyday life.

In other words, not just pageantry but ship design accounts for the attractiveness of a naval force. During the late Cold War, American shipwrights took to installing vertical launch systems (VLS) on board Navy destroyers and cruisers. In essence, vertical launchers are missile silos embedded in a ship's decks. VLS represents a technological upgrade from old-style missile launchers, in large part because it simplifies machinery and procedures for weapons handling. Yet it is unobtrusive from a visual standpoint, sitting flush with the deck. Flat panels are unlikely to impress people who are untutored on naval architecture. By contrast, Soviet Navy vessels were characteristically festooned with highly visible launchers, guns, and sensors. A Soviet ship could make a deep impression politically even when it was technologically inferior to an American warship. It inspired awe!

But there still is more to suasion. Luttwak might have added that how well its crew presents a ship or aircraft helps mold impressions of competence, and so contributes to peacetime naval suasion. While Soviet vessels looked imposing in terms of the equipment and weapons they carried, inspecting them close up showed evidence of failings in professionalism, seamanship, and élan within the Soviet navy. Simple oversights such as rust on a ship's hull transmit the image that slovenly practices are the rule. A navy unmindful of small details probably will not do big things right either. A crew oblivious to routine upkeep seldom acquits itself well in battle. Sloppy shiphandling constitutes another symptom of a troubled force, detracting from impressions that are valuable for naval suasion. The spate of groundings and collisions that beset the U.S. Navy in 2017 tarnished its image as a globe-spanning hegemon. A major fire gutted a major amphibious warship at its moorings in 2020, adding to the aura of malaise. Such incidents have significant diplomatic implications.

It seems, then, that the art and science of naval statecraft involves fashioning warlike implements in sufficient numbers and capability to win battles and then displaying them so impressively in peace that they never have to be used in battle. If a competitor's fleet overshadows its antagonist, it stands a good chance of deterring or compelling that antagonist while lending comfort to friends. And the role of habit in armed debate? Few individual strategic practitioners command the full portfolio of Aristotelian traits and habits in the right proportions to excel in the freeform milieu of peacetime maritime strategy. Senior commanders and civilian leaders must be alert to the bewildering variety of interactions they face—in part so they can augment their personal leadership repertoires, in part so they can recruit teams that together muster the right stuff to thrive amid competitive times.

BRANDISH THE INTERAGENCY BIG STICK

Sizing and configuring a naval force is crucial to making the desired impression on audiences whose members are able to influence the outcome of a strategic competition. It is worth reiterating, however, that the twenty-first century is increasingly an age of joint and interagency sea power. Any implement able to shape events at sea is an implement of sea power, whether it is a ground-based air force, long-range army artillery, or an embassy headed by an ambassador who is seasoned in bluewater affairs. This is doubly true now that technology has endowed armaments with unprecedented range and precision, enabling them to strike at fleets far out at sea. Properly understood, sea power even includes not-strictly-military components such as coast guards and mercantile shipping.

Policymakers and commanders have many instruments at their disposal to shape opinion and reap political gain. There is plainly more to sea power—and to naval suasion—than battle fleets or even navies. Nowadays naval suasion is merely armed suasion with a seaward bent. It is important, however, not to exaggerate the novelty of maritime operations in today's brave new world. Corbett observes that astute practitioners have long believed that the "function of the fleet" is to contribute to maritime strategy in its broadest sense as well as to naval strategy narrowly construed. The fleet's function is

> part of what is called the higher or major strategy, and [bears] much the same relation to naval strategy as minor strategy does to tactics. For naval strategy, which is commonly and conveniently confined to the movements of the fleet in a theater of war, is really a form of minor strategy; and while tactics are concerned with the arena of a battle, and minor strategy with the arena of a campaign, so the study of the functions of the fleet is concerned with the *whole arena of an international struggle*. [italics mine][36]

The word *struggle* is a telling one. It connotes long-term strategic competition as well as open war. Corbett entreats naval practitioners to free themselves from a cramped view of their profession that lays inordinate stress on decisive battles waged for command of the sea. He accuses naval historians in particular of allowing themselves to be bewitched by the drama of naval battles such as Trafalgar or Tsushima Strait. Such events seldom transpire, yet obsessing over them obscures much else that fleets do.

Corbett argues that to apply a palliative for myopia, naval officialdom must strive for "wider vision" that keeps before its eyes "not merely the enemy's fleets or the great routes of commerce, or the command of the sea, but also the relations of naval policy and action to the whole area of diplomatic and military effort."[37] They must think of maritime strategy as a grand strategy. It is worth restating his formula, as reviewed in chapter 2: "The function of the fleet, the object for which it was always employed, has been threefold: firstly, to support or obstruct diplomatic effort; secondly, to protect or destroy commerce; and thirdly, to further or hinder military operations ashore."[38] This discourse does not negate Mahan's doctrine that commercial, diplomatic, and military access—in that order of importance—constitutes both the goal and an engine of maritime strategy (surveyed in chapter 2). But it does widen the scope of our understanding of maritime strategy beyond what Mahan taught. Commerce may be king, as Mahan maintains; it is not everything.

To execute this roster of functions, strategic leaders must learn how to meld the fleet into a single policy implement with fellow armed services and their country's diplomatic and economic elements of power. Like Corbett, contemporary British scholars such as Ken Booth and Geoffrey Till take an expansive view of sea power, accentuating navies' diplomatic and constabulary roles as well as their better-known role as a military executor of foreign policy and guardian of the sea lanes.[39] Thinking of sea power in holistic terms constitutes a worthy habit of mind.

Consider a historical example. Decades before Edward Luttwak coined the phrase *armed suasion*, its logic underwrote President Theodore Roosevelt's "big stick" doctrine in politics and diplomacy. T. R. invoked West African folkways to elucidate his formula for merging strategy with diplomacy. He quoted the proverb "speak softly and carry a big stick; you will go far" in a variety of contexts, both domestic and foreign.[40] For him, brandishing America's overpowering military might while conducting diplomacy with tact and humor bolstered the United States' chances of getting its way in strategic competition. Positioning the republic as the probable victor in any clash should render foreign leaders pliant. Speaking softly—taking care not to humiliate them, especially in public—made it easier for them to acquiesce in American policies. They could assent without losing face before their constituents.

So circumspect was big-stick diplomacy that President Roosevelt managed to deploy virtually the whole U.S. Navy battle fleet to the Caribbean Sea to deter a European effort to seize territory in Venezuela in contravention of the Monroe Doctrine. The Navy expedition took place in 1902; not until 2002 did historians prove conclusively that it had happened.[41] Bombast had no place in his approach.

Big-stick diplomacy reached its apogee during the 1907–1909 world cruise of the U.S. Navy's Great White Fleet, or battle fleet. Roosevelt ballyhooed the voyage as his "most important service" to the cause of peace.[42] The fleet circumnavigated the globe to put potential foes, imperial Japan in particular, on notice that America would not tolerate troublemaking at its expense. The Imperial Japanese Navy could not expect to defeat a U.S. Navy that was weary from operating far from home the way it had crushed the Russian navy piecemeal during the Russo-Japanese War of 1904–1905 a few years before. The Great White Fleet's grand tour showcased Navy fighting ships' power, the proficiency of their crews, and Washington's willingness to deploy naval might to deter or reassure. Best of all, T. R. insisted that the Great White Fleet had deterred Japan without damaging amicable relations across the Pacific Ocean.

Luttwak gently dissents from T. R.'s doctrine of the big stick. Or rather, he suggests that specific situations may warrant a different approach. "To speak softly while carrying a big stick may be less effective as a deterrent than to make a firm, overt commitment to use a rather smaller stick," he says.[43] All fleet movements have a "latent" potential for suasion because senior leadership could order the fleet's combat power activated at any time and other countries know it. That is how a fleet casts a shadow. Yet, Luttwak cautions against letting efforts at deterrence remain latent, or tacit, warning that doing so permits "wide scope for miscalculation" while actually weakening deterrence because "no rigid commitment to implement retaliation obtains."[44] A clear commitment backed by credible force stands a better chance at deterring than does a softly spoken—and therefore ambiguous—commitment backed by overwhelming force that adversaries believe may never be used. The message may not get through even if the fleet manages to overawe foreign audiences for whom the warning is intended.

Luttwak also points to a kind of virtual naval diplomacy exercised by oceangoing hegemons. Political leaders and senior commanders need not dispatch a massive naval contingent to a scene to demonstrate capability, he writes. *If* they enjoy a reputation for deploying forces under the circumstances that they say they will, and *if* the rival that is being deterred or coerced can harbor no doubt that an overwhelming force will be massed on the scene if its leadership defies the deterrent or coercive threat, then the hegemon can get by with a token display of force. The hegemon's leadership often can make do with a single "symbolic" ship, which acts more as a token of commitment than as a viable battle force.[45]

During their imperial heyday British leaders became adept at naval symbolism. "So long as the Royal Navy had a globally superior fleet in the North Sea or anywhere else," Luttwak affirms, "a single frigate could effectively impose the will of H.M. Government on recalcitrant coastal states the world over, since the flag it flew was the portent of potentially overwhelming *naval* force. And this was force that could always be brought to bear if the symbolic frigate was denied its due. . . . the symbolic ship derived its powers from the combat capabilities of the Royal Navy's battle fleet, and its symbolic power was proportional to genuine naval power."[46]

In Peace, Win Friends and Overawe Opponents • **103**

Strategic leaders, then, can get by with a lightweight or even a symbolic "stick," provided that the opponents whom they have targeted for deterrence or coercion know for sure that they will face the fleet's combined might if they balk. The leadership must have a big stick somewhere in the vicinity, but it might be doing other things beyond the horizon. The prospect of eventual naval action yields immediate political benefits if the leadership wields naval forces adroitly.

BEWARE OF THE SMALL STICK

Naval diplomacy is no longer an exclusive preserve of navies, however, or even of shore-based arms of military power that support fleets riding the waves. It is possible to put non-naval and nonmilitary ships to work as implements of sea power, advancing a contender's ambitions at sea bit by bit, over time, without resort to open war. In recent decades, U.S. rivals such as the People's Republic of China and the Russian Federation have raised such low-grade uses of sea power to a high art. The big stick is a battle fleet, but Beijing and Moscow prefer to swing a small stick, getting their way by increments so long as they remain patient. As a result, U.S. commanders must habituate themselves to a form of sea power that is largely alien to their experience.

Americans may not practice what I have taken to calling "small-stick diplomacy" themselves, but they must acquaint themselves with it so they know how to cope with it when others do.[47] By studying this subtle but hard-to-beat method of maritime operations, they may glean insights useful for U.S. and allied endeavors. In contemporary parlance, commentators dub forceful measures that stop short of war "gray-zone operations." Dwellers in the gray zone—the twilight zone where peace blurs into war—brandish a small stick when it suffices. As Hal Brands puts it, this shadowy technique

> is best understood as activity that is coercive and aggressive in nature, but that is deliberately designed to remain below the threshold of conventional military conflict and open interstate war. Gray zone approaches

are mostly the province of revisionist powers—those actors that seek to modify some aspect of the existing international environment—and the goal is to reap gains, whether territorial or otherwise, that are normally associated with victory in war. Yet gray zone approaches are meant to achieve those gains *without* escalating to overt warfare, *without* crossing established red-lines, and thus *without* exposing the practitioner to the penalties and risks that such escalation might bring.[48]

Gray-zone strategy may be an unusual mode of strategy, but it is a mode that is solidly grounded in the strategic canon. Gen. Helmuth von Moltke the Elder, the Prussian army chief of staff credited with a string of limited military victories (1864–1871) that helped unite Germany, riffed on Clausewitz, opining that "the tactical defense is the stronger, the strategic offensive the more effective form" of warfare.[49] What did he mean by that? Suppose one combatant covets a parcel of territory. Its army should catch the foe unawares, seize the ground, and hold it through tactical defense. It can then defy the foe to undo a done deal at steep cost and hazard to itself. Julian Corbett imports Moltke's ground-warfare insight into the maritime sphere:

> [T]his form of war presupposes that we are able by superior readiness or mobility or by being more conveniently situated to establish ourselves in the territorial object before our opponent can gather strength to prevent us. This done, we have the initiative, and the enemy ... must conform to our opening by endeavoring to turn us out. We are in a position to meet his attack on ground of our own choice and to avail ourselves of such opportunities of counterattack as his distant and therefore exhausting offensive movements are likely to offer.[50]

In other words, it is easier to take something that is lightly guarded or unguarded and hold it than it is to wrest an object from an entrenched opponent determined to keep it. An old saying holds that possession is nine-tenths of the law. By Moltke's and Corbett's lights, a similar truism holds for tactics and operations: an innate advantage goes to the defender. The combatant forced into tactical offense surrenders the initiative, fights on terrain that favors its adversary, and may wear itself out while trying to regain what it yielded through neglect.

In a sense, small-stick diplomacy, which is a politico-military strategy for times of uneasy peace, is even harder to defeat than the wartime variant Moltke prescribes, even though it operates by the same logic of merging strategic offense with tactical defense. Think about it. Moltke and Corbett accent the practical difficulty of taking back some object seized by an enemy on the battlefield, but they slight the political and psychological dimensions. Victors care a great deal about what they have won through force of arms, or else they would never have made the attempt. Success bucks up morale, bestowing a psychological advantage on them alongside military advantages such as controlling the battleground or setting the pace of action. By contrast, the defender's opponents are apt to blanch at the cost of retaking the object, measured in lives, hardware, and treasure. The cost threatens to exceed what the object is worth to the leadership. Rational cost-benefit calculations may prompt attackers to stand down, leaving those prosecuting strategic offense through tactical defense holding the disputed ground or object.

Similar dynamics permeate the gray zone. The stakes appear small when contenders square off over a reef in the South China Sea, to name a gray zone that has dominated headlines for more than a decade, and indeed the stakes are small in each individual encounter. But the sum of many small results can be large. A case in point: in 2012 ships from China's maritime law-enforcement services (later consolidated into the China Coast Guard) and maritime militia (an irregular fighting force embedded within the fishing fleet) occupied Scarborough Shoal, a ring of rocks and undersea reefs about 120 nautical miles west of the Philippine island of Palawan. First the Philippine navy appeared on site to oppose the unlawful

Chinese seizure. Then cutters from the Philippine coast guard took the navy's place. But what chance did either Philippine force stand?[51]

The answer: slight. The standoff at Scarborough verged on a no-win situation for Philippine leaders. Manila would have looked like the bully had Philippine warships sought to evict purportedly civilian Chinese ships from the shoal. At the same time the lopsided mismatch between the two contenders would have made it a laughingstock. The China Coast Guard is far more powerful than the various Southeast Asian coast guards. Indeed, it outguns the Philippine navy, whose flagship at the time was an old, retired, mostly disarmed cutter donated by the U.S. Coast Guard. As a result, Manila faced an acute quandary. It could insist on its rights and risk losing an unwinnable fight over a shoal that was important to Philippine citizens yet appeared trivial to potential foreign supporters. Or it could accept reality and forfeit its maritime rights.

Washington, too, faced a tricky diplomatic plight. If U.S. leaders had dispatched major warships to the embattled zone to uphold their ally's rights, America would have looked like a bully making a fuss over very little. And they would have appeared imprudent in the extreme, putting weighty U.S. priorities in jeopardy for little apparent reason. The intimate U.S.-China economic and diplomatic relationship would stand in peril over what some Western commentators took to calling "a pile of rocks"—in other words, a disputed object of negligible value.[52] Observers of such leanings insist that the meager stakes in the South China Sea do not warrant running the risk of armed conflict—or indeed much risk at all. They do not matter.

Yet Beijing disagreed about the stakes, even as it commanded a preponderance of physical power on the scene. Islands, rocks, and atolls mean a great deal to Chinese maritime strategy—as became obvious in 2014, when reporters revealed that engineers had taken to manufacturing artificial islands out of Chinese-held features in the region. Beijing ultimately installed military bases on the islands that were capable of hosting ships, aircraft, and armaments. In 2019, to his credit, Gen.

Joseph Dunford, USMC, then chairman of the Joint Chiefs of Staff, rejected efforts to downplay the importance of the Spratly and Paracel islands, asserting that the islands are "not a pile of rocks . . . and what is at stake [there] and elsewhere where there are territorial claims, is the rule of law, international laws, norms, and standards."[53]

Indeed, Beijing was not just wrenching reefs or atolls from its neighbors. The island-building campaign was part of its effort to claim "indisputable sovereignty"—state ownership, in effect, much as governments own land territory—over the South China Sea. It was manufacturing island redoubts to assert control over adjacent waters and skies, including massive swaths of "exclusive economic zones," offshore areas apportioned to Southeast Asian coastal states under the law of the sea. Freedom of the sea is a compelling interest for any seafaring people, yet China was chipping away at it by increments.

General Dunford was right. But a picture is worth a thousand words. Appealing to abstract-seeming concepts like international law and freedom makes a tough sell when photographs show an armed standoff over rocks that—as at Scarborough—barely break the water's surface. Beijing crafted an ingenious dilemma for its rivals.

Now let us classify small-stick diplomacy as a mode of strategy. First, think back to J. C. Wylie's famous dichotomy between sequential and cumulative operations, profiled in brief in the foreword. If sequential operations are successful, the country conducting them can deliver a clear, unambiguous victory by pounding away at the enemy repeatedly until it succumbs. But cumulative operations—numerous small-scale tactical encounters that do not take place in sequence, either in time or on the map—can produce big results as well. A series of minor triumphs can add up to major gains, albeit piecemeal rather than through repeated heavy punches. In the Chinese case, seizing an individual feature in the South China Sea makes little difference in itself. But seizing many features, improving them, and emplacing weaponry on them allows Beijing to lay claim to the vast majority of that body of water, challenging the fundamental legal precept that no one owns the sea (with very narrow exceptions set forth by treaty). Small-stick diplomacy is a quintessential cumulative strategy—and it aims at a decisive outcome.

Second, because the stakes are small in any individual standoff, neither party wants to escalate to hot war. Yet one side—the side waging strategic offense and tactical defense in Moltke's sense—cares more fervently about its aims than the other. Accordingly, it invests more heavily in getting its way and accepts more risk. And if it happens to goad a rival contender into firing the first shot, so much the better. That contender will bear the blame for initiating hostilities over what appears to be a minor point of contention. The aggressor stands to reap a propaganda windfall from the aggrieved party. This is a passive-aggressive mode of statecraft: it shifts the burden onto the victim.

Finally, practitioners of small-stick diplomacy substitute physical bulk for firepower. The big stick is the navy, while composite fleets of coast guard cutters, merchantmen, fishing vessels, or even—potentially—pleasure craft are the small stick. The latter are the nonmilitary implement of choice for some ambitious coastal states. In the South China Sea, the fishing fleet, crewed in part by maritime militiamen, constitutes the vanguard of Chinese sea power. Fishing vessels ply their trade in contested waters, guarded by the China Coast Guard. The fishing ground may lie within a neighboring state's exclusive economic zone, waters allocated to coastal states for harvesting natural riches from the water and seabed. If a Southeast Asian state's coast guard and navy are too weak to expel the Chinese flotilla, then China is left holding the contested sea area. Beijing chisels away at its neighbor's sovereign rights while lending credence to its own claims to sovereignty—however unfounded its claims may be from a legal standpoint.

There is another variant of small-stick diplomacy that some Chinese thinkers dub a "cabbage strategy." If Beijing covets an island or rock occupied by others, it can deploy unarmed or lightly armed ships in large numbers to stage a de facto blockade of that bit of dry land. Vessels surround it to levy pressure on its occupants and fend off relief and resupply efforts from outside. Or, if Beijing wants to defend something of its own—such as a platform unlawfully exploring for hydrocarbons within Vietnam's exclusive economic zone—it can harness the same approach to erect a defensive perimeter.[54]

Just as the layers of a cabbage encase and protect its core, so a cabbage strategy encases disputed objects with concentric layers of hulls and defies anyone to peel back the layers—and in the process brand itself an aggressor while risking defeat. A 2013 editorial in China's official news service, Xinhua, turned to "noted military expert" Zhang Zhaozhong to explain how a cabbage strategy works. Such a strategy can be encapsulated in "just one word, which is squeezing," Zhang says.[55] His explanation is worth quoting at length:

> For every measure there is a countermeasure. You send fishing ships. . . . If you send fishing vessels to resupply, then we will use fishing vessels to keep them out; if your coast guard sends supplies, then we will send marine surveillance to keep them out. If your [navy] ships hurry over, we will use naval vessels to keep them out. There is nothing to be afraid of, and we must stick it out to the end. The cabbage strategy of which I have spoken many times is to surround [the contested feature] layer by layer, and make them unable to enter.[56]

With its surfeit of marine power relative to Southeast Asian maritime forces, then, Beijing has the option to escalate in a controlled manner, laying siege to and squeezing opponents while keeping a damper on the dispute. No rival competitor enjoys such an option. Zhang also alludes to the final aspect of Chinese small-stick diplomacy—the fact that nonmilitary Chinese forces can summon overbearing support from the People's Liberation Army Navy (PLA Navy, the formal name for the Chinese navy) should things go wrong. Helmuth von Moltke and Julian Corbett would instantly grasp the logic underwriting Beijing's gray-zone offensive.

Much as observers knew that Edward Luttwak's lonely symbolic frigate had the combined might of the Royal Navy standing behind it, Southeast Asians know that the PLA Navy stands behind the coast guard and commercial craft as their backstop. The navy remains over the horizon, allaying impressions that Beijing is bullying the weak. The small stick's big-stick retinue makes its presence felt all the same. Small wonder that China's opponents seem daunted by problems intrinsic to the gray zone.

How should countries cope with small-stick diplomacy, which enables an aggressor to use a trifling degree of armed force in increments to achieve a major diplomatic effect? By imitation, for one thing. Adversaries are on to something in the gray zone. It is worth studying their methods, learning from them, and pressing them into service as the opportunity arises. Strategists should accustom themselves to thinking about sea power in holistic terms. Nonmilitary shipping is an instrument of sea power just as an aircraft carrier is. For example, the United States could try to institute multinational coast guard units in the South China Sea, merging U.S. Coast Guard personnel or units into patrols to show that America has skin in the game of safeguarding maritime freedom.

By building the habit of thinking holistically and imaginatively, strategic leaders will attune themselves to hunt for ways to drive antagonists out of the gray zone. Zhang Zhaozhong hints at one method: fielding a regionwide force roughly symmetrical to China's, and thereby granting China's rivals the option to escalate when Beijing does. Such a force would put the onus on Communist China's leadership to escalate out of the gray zone, and bear the blame for open conflict. Or it could de-escalate below the gray zone, postponing aggression while resuming routine peacetime interchange. Either way freedom-loving societies would have progressed toward preserving the liberal order at sea.

PEER INTO THE MURKY ARENA

Clearly, the armed conversation that is peacetime strategic competition takes place in a shadowland where inventive competitors use ships, planes, and munitions to project images of power and weakness to accompany their rhetoric. A force that earns a reputation for professionalism strengthens the hand of national leaders when they deal with others. A force with a reputation for material or human foibles weakens the negotiating position of national leaders. Having forged tools of sea power, strategic leaders display those tools to deter or coerce prospective antagonists and conciliate or reassure allies and friends, old and new. The principal Aristotelian habit valuable for peacetime competition is to think in these broad terms, beyond everyday concerns such as perfecting or maintaining a piece of equipment, learning the latest tactics, or managing a budget. Every one of these routine functions is crucial—but in peacetime it is crucial chiefly for how it helps a force or society burnish its reputation for nautical prowess relative to others.

It is hard to see how strategic leaders could be guilty of an excess of thinking about physical implements as political implements useful for molding opinion. Impressions count for a great deal in peacetime strategic competition. Seafarers should regard themselves and their services as political creatures and conduct themselves accordingly—as a matter of habit.

4

IN WAR, FIGHT FOR A BETTER STATE OF PEACE

Waging war requires that strategic leaders rebalance their bundle of habits, adjusting the proportions to fit the strategic situation around them. As chapter 2 showed, fabricating the rudiments of military power is a huge part of peacetime strategy. Foreseeing what the future holds and what type of force is suited to it is far from easy. Still, force design and building are fairly static endeavors. Chapter 3 showed that peacetime strategy also involves brandishing military implements skillfully enough to sway opinion among audiences whose views can affect a protagonist's strategic fortunes. Influencing opinion is a more dynamic and diffuse enterprise than fitting out ships or aircraft, administering a program, or overseeing a bureaucracy. Just as building a force is more science than art, using that force to deter or coerce opponents and hearten allies and friends is more art than science. Greek philosopher Aristotle's brand of prudence—practical wisdom aimed at accomplishing one's goals while taking heed of one's limits—is at a premium.

The outbreak of war takes dynamism to an altogether different level. At its most basic, war is an act of violent statecraft. American strategist Alfred Thayer Mahan defines it as "statesmanship directing arms."[1] War exhibits a dual nature. It differs sharply from peacetime strategic competition in that statesmen and commanders now add force to their armory of policy implements—alongside diplomacy, economics, and information (or rhetoric, as Aristotle would call it). The armed debate about

In War, Fight for a Better State of Peace • **113**

which side is stronger and which is weaker is no longer hypothetical once the parties take up arms. In taking up arms, the combatants seek to prove it. Each uses physical force to get its way against a recalcitrant antagonist that reciprocates in hopes of doing the same.[2]

Combatants thus submit the arguments and retorts that they lodged during their peacetime debate to the test of battle, which becomes the final and unsparing judge. This time, the verdict of arms—not the opinion of key audiences—entitles the victor to strategic and political gain. Sometimes battle yields a resounding result. A Battle of Trafalgar, Tsushima Strait, or Leyte Gulf leaves little doubt about relative power. In a good many cases the result is less conclusive. Sometimes the objectively weaker contender prevails. Chinese leader Mao Zedong, for instance, built his reputation on devising strategy that enabled his Red Army to win a civil war against the substantially stronger Chinese Nationalists.

Considering how violence transforms the strategic environment, it comes as little surprise that somewhat different habits of mind and passion help strategic leaders flourish in wartime (as opposed to peacetime competition). It also helps explain why some leaders thrive in one phase of competition yet flounder in another. Individuals' gifts vary. Not every soldier, mariner, or aviator is fit to excel in every mode of international interplay or on every level of strategy. The gifted few who do excel belong among the greats of diplomatic and military history.

British soldier and military theorist B. H. Liddell Hart would counsel that in one profound sense the metamorphosis from peacetime to wartime competition is *not* that sweeping. The purposes of grand strategy persist from peacetime competition into armed strife and thence into peacemaking and postwar peace enforcement. War is about amending the peace, not fighting battles for their own sake.

It is easy to lose sight of that. It may be necessary to pummel a foe into submission to bring about the "better state of peace" that ultimately is the goal of grand strategy as it is properly understood.[3] But wartime victory need not be the endgame and preferably will *not* be. Liddell Hart would caution executors of strategy to keep their craving for battlefield triumphs and renown subservient to their pursuit of a beneficial and durable postwar order. They must subdue their passions, keeping their gaze fixed on the nation's political and economic weal. Achieving strategic success might mean *tempering* actions on the battlefield, and thus stopping short of what purely military logic dictates. It could mean embracing courses of action that appear to contravene military logic yet make strategic sense.

It takes self-discipline to concentrate on postwar well-being amid the din of warfare. This chapter explores how violence transforms the setting and modifies the repertoire of habits that strategic leaders should inculcate. Making war demands range. To excel at it, strategic leaders must accustom themselves to thinking beyond tactics and battlefield operations—and even beyond the strictly military arena.

MASTER YOURSELF TO UNLOCK MARTIAL VIRTUE

As Prussian military strategist Carl von Clausewitz teaches, commanders at all levels of the military hierarchy should strive to attain the status of "military genius." Readers should consult book 1, chapter 3 of *On War*, titled "On Military Genius" (covered in more detail later), evaluate it against the case set forth here, and draw their own conclusions about priorities. For Clausewitz, genius is a compound of intellect and temperament. He catalogs indices of strategic fitness that qualify an aspirant as a genius. Much of what he says is beyond dispute, but I would frame things in somewhat different terms. Like Aristotle, Clausewitz seems to give physical and moral courage top priority among the virtues. Without a doubt, courage is pivotal, but I believe that self-mastery—mastery not just of fear but of human frailty of all sorts, both in intellect and in character—stands above it. This chapter explains why.

MASTER YOUR PASSIONS

Start with passion. Human beings are passionate creatures. Emotion poses special challenges during war. A clash of arms fires human passions—chiefly dark ones. It is hard to keep human reason in charge in a climate that is chronically hostile to reason. Clausewitz labels "primordial violence, hatred, and enmity" as primal and even "blind" forces in human affairs.[4] In other words, strategic deliberation and action take place in a combustible psychological atmosphere. Clausewitz pleads with senior commanders and their political superiors to manage their feelings, keeping reason supreme. Superimposing rationality on a climate that is inimical to it constitutes the essence of generalship and martial statecraft.

Losing one's composure dethrones virtue of all types, while keeping rational faculties in charge in impassioned times enables other virtues to flourish. That is why I consider self-mastery the virtue that rules them all. Self-mastery is chiefly, though not wholly, a virtue of temperament. Classical philosophers place great weight on it. In his dialogue on the *Laws*, for instance, Aristotle's teacher, Plato, has the Spartan citizen Clinias inform an Athenian interlocutor that "individually . . . each man is his own enemy."[5] Clinias holds that "the victory over self is of all victories the first and best while self-defeat is of all defeats at once the worst and most shameful."[6] Exactly. Mastering passions helps strategic leaders resist vices such as hubris and despair. It improves their ability to discern the excess and deficiency of other traits and strike the golden mean, attaining virtue while banishing vice.

Governing one's own passions is a timeless task. Strategic leaders should learn to tame their passions throughout the spectrum of human interactions, not just warfare. Nevertheless, self-restraint is most pressing in wartime, when the surroundings summon forth powerful emotions and losing control has direct—and deleterious—impact on tactical, operational, and strategic success. This is why self-mastery belongs in this chapter rather than the chapters on peacetime strategy. It is the virtue that unlocks all others—helping war leaders cope with countless factors that tend to deflect affairs of state from a strictly rational course.

Clausewitz does pay tribute to self-control. He portrays it as related and subordinate to "strength of will," a rubric under which it keeps company with such attributes as energy, presence of mind, and endurance. He maintains that it takes indomitable willpower to navigate a warlike landscape (or seascape) where danger, physical toil and suffering, and chance and uncertainty make up the topography. We simply differ on its importance relative to other worthwhile qualities.

Consider again what the ancients say about self-mastery. Clausewitz demonstrates that controlling oneself is important; the Stoic Roman philosopher Seneca explains one way to do it. In particular, he dwells on how to govern anger. Subduing anger is both critical and difficult because it is the "most hideous and frenzied of all the emotions," Seneca writes.[7] It is the hardest passion to tame because it is so intense. The warrior who masters it can master less molten emotions. And why not? Other passions "have in them some element of peace and calm," while anger is "wholly violent."[8] Seneca implores readers to regard it as a form of "temporary madness."[9] It is "devoid of self-control" and "closed to reason and counsel."[10] He beholds the martial impact of anger as well as its lunacy. The bitter fruits of warfare fueled by anger include "the downfall and destruction of cities and whole nations," infernos that make "great stretches of the country glow with hostile flame," and wastelands ravaged by armies and left "without a single dweller."[11]

This is bleak stuff. To counter it, Seneca offers practical advice, namely that people master anger by refusing to let it grip them in the first place. "It is easier to exclude harmful passions than to rule them," he declares, "and to deny them admittance than, after they have been admitted, to control them; for when they have established themselves in possession, they are stronger than their ruler and do not permit themselves to be restrained or reduced."[12] Reason, "to whom the reins of power have been entrusted, remains mistress only so long as she is kept apart from the passions."[13] Fellow adherents to the Stoic school of philosophy, most famously the Roman emperor Marcus Aurelius, likewise championed the virtue of self-restraint.

Stoics did not espouse suppressing emotion altogether, as is commonly reputed. They freely conceded that external stimuli, such as the deeds of others and the workings of fate, could kindle fear, rage, spite, or other passions in the most level-headed person. Stoics advocated *regulating* one's reactions when some event

In War, Fight for a Better State of Peace • **117**

or deed—say, hostile military action—introduced an accelerant for strong passions into the surroundings and threatened to set loose baleful consequences. Seneca describes an emotional cycle that people must interrupt to remain in control of themselves. An external stimulus generates automatic and largely unavoidable impressions. The passions that it rouses could spiral out of control through an action-reaction cycle, engendering worst-case thinking and rash actions if not kept in check. Accordingly, Seneca advises Stoics to refuse to give in to their initial reactions.[14] They should put what contemporary psychologists term "cognitive distance" between themselves and traumas that afflict them. Without that measure of detachment catastrophic thinking could sweep them into deeds that they come to rue.[15]

Now, it is possible to argue, as I would, that in their zeal to mute emotional excess Stoics such as Seneca and Marcus carry their advocacy of self-rule to excess. They seem to say that self-mastery is an all-or-nothing proposition. Rampant passion lies at one extreme, while total self-control lies at the other extreme and ought to be the goal. That sounds counter-Aristotelian. Indeed, classical Greek philosophers, Socrates in particular, seem to contradict the Stoic worldview in part. Socratic thinkers take a more dynamic view of the problem of self-rule.

Plato relays Socrates' views as usual. In his dialogue *Phaedrus*, for instance, Plato has Socrates fashion the "figure," or allegory, of a charioteer driving a pair of winged horses. The goal of the human charioteer is to coax the team to soar above a bank of clouds, where divine or absolute knowledge is visible.[16] But there is a problem, Plato says. One of the steeds is "noble and of noble breed," a "lover of honor and modesty and temperance, and [a] follower of true glory," while its mate is "ignoble and of ignoble breed," a balky beast given to "insolence and pride, shag-eared and deaf, hardly yielding to whip and spur."[17] The charioteer represents a human being's reason, the noble horse lofty human passions, and the ignoble horse base or dishonorable passions.

Yoking unlike beasts to the same goal proves trying for even the finest driver. Socrates' charioteer is "troubled indeed by the steeds" and finds it difficult to glimpse true wisdom.[18] Drivers lacking sufficient dexterity fare worse. Seldom, if ever, do they surge above the clouds and catch sight of perfect knowledge. It eludes them. The dynamism of Socrates' allegory and its accent on both uplifting and toxic passions set it apart from the Stoic view—a view that feels static, suggests that human sentiments are uniformly harmful, and implies that the choice is between ungovernable passion and no passion at all. The Socratic account seems more resonant with everyday life.

But does classical wisdom hold true for the profession of arms? The answer is, it depends on *which* classical wisdom. In all likelihood Clausewitz would dissent partwise from Stoic methods while inclining to Socrates. Clausewitz agrees wholeheartedly that regulating one's passions is important. He is adamant about keeping feelings subservient to reason, even amid the impassioned climate of warfare. In fact, he proclaims that self-control "is itself an emotion."[19] It "serves to balance the passionate feelings in strong characters without destroying them, and it is this balance alone that assures the dominance of the intellect."[20] A robust, self-regulated character, then, is not an emotionless character; it "is one *that will not be unbalanced by the most powerful emotions*."[21] It has emotional ballast as well as the stamina to cope with stressful circumstances over time.

Like Socrates' charioteer, soldiers who master themselves, harnessing feelings and freeing their intellect, stand the best chance of achieving excellence. Keeping sentiment within bounds is a central function of strategic leadership, particularly among commanders who take the field. After all, soldiers bestriding the battlefield encounter the gravest personal perils and are buffeted by sentiments that are hard to resist. Exerting self-rule is at once uniquely important and uniquely tough for them.

Many denizens of diplomatic and military history failed to curb their appetites and passions and came to grief. Consider another example from antiquity. Plutarch illumines the life of Alcibiades, a Greek general and a favorite son of classical Athens. Alcibiades was given to riotous excess in his quest for pleasure and personal renown. He was prone to what Plutarch, drawing from Thucydides' chronicle of the Peloponnesian War (431–404 BC), brands "lawless self-indulgence."[22]

Boston College professor Robert K. Faulkner proposes a "formula" for greatness in statecraft, deeming it an alloy of "allegedly superior character" and "allegedly superior political wisdom."[23] In Faulkner's judgment Alcibiades fell grievously short in character and temperament. He was supremely gifted with political and strategic wisdom, yet he exhibited "unbounded ambition, unbounded, at least, by the restraints moral and political of an Aristotelian gentleman-statesman."[24] Such a figure poses dangers. Faulkner warns that free republics—an Athens of antiquity, or an America of the present day—may need the talents of an Alcibiades, yet find it all but impossible to curtail the ambitions of an Alcibiades. The public implications could be profound.

There is little doubt about Alcibiades' brilliance at arms. During the Peloponnesian War, he managed to sojourn in all of the major warring societies, from his native Athens to oligarchic Sparta to monarchic Persia and back to Athens, before going into exile. The leaderships of all three states listened to and heeded his counsel. Their receptiveness to his message testifies to his political and military acumen. He singlehandedly shaped the course of the conflict.

Alcibiades measures up admirably by Faulkner's standard for political wisdom, yet his vices played a major part in Athens' defeat and ruin during the Peloponnesian War. According to Plutarch, personal profligacy was not Alcibiades' worst vice; his lust for honor and fame was. He gave in to pique when he felt slighted. For instance, he slandered his rival Nicias in the Athenian assembly when Athenians lauded Nicias, not Alcibiades, for bringing peace—actually more of a truce, dubbed the "Peace of Nicias"—in the Peloponnesian War. Alcibiades reached out to Spartan ambassadors out of spite, wooing them "wholly away from the influence of Nicias" to discredit him.[25] Yet he enthralled fellow citizens despite such petty intrigues. Reports Plutarch,

> his voluntary contributions of money, his support of public exhibitions, his unsurpassed munificence toward the city, the glory of his ancestry, the power

of his eloquence, the comeliness and vigor of his person, together with his experience and prowess in war, made the Athenians lenient and tolerant towards everything else.[26]

Athenians may have been culpable in part for Alcibiades' excesses. They excused his antics, declining to hold him accountable. No popular opprobrium gave him an incentive to govern his ambition or passions. As Plutarch and Thucydides allege, he was susceptible to flattery and favor and prone to wantonness. He was possessed of a poisonous mix of vice and virtue.

Ultimately, Athenians' tolerance ran out. Consider another episode from Alcibiades' checkered life. In 415 BC he cajoled the Athenian assembly into endorsing an invasion of Sicily, one of the breadbaskets of the Mediterranean world. The assembly appointed him co-commander of the expeditionary force yet, as Plutarch notes, it recalled him from command on apparently trumped-up charges of desecrating "sacred images" during a "drunken revel."[27] Rather than submit, Alcibiades fled to Sparta, Athens' archfoe. Spartans made him welcome and solicited his advice. Indeed, he authored some of their best strategic maneuvers of the war. Rather than lay low and husband his good fortune, however, Alcibiades seduced the wife of King Agis and earned that monarch's undying enmity. With that, Alcibiades' appetites overwhelmed his judgment—obliging him to leave Sparta to save his skin.

At times Alcibiades' dearth of self-mastery marred his strategic counsel—his intellectual virtue, in other words—as well as his personal life. He proposed plans for conquest that would have far outstripped the resources even of Athens, the foremost maritime empire of the age. As Plutarch reported, Alcibiades "counseled the Athenians to assert dominion on land" as well as at sea. They should cast off the strategy of their "first citizen," Pericles, who had recommended that they stay on the defensive on land in order to conserve finite resources for naval exploits.[28] Alcibiades wanted to do it all—hence his lust for Sicily. Athenians had long coveted the island, which could make their import-dependent city self-sufficient. But it was Alcibiades "who finally fanned this desire of theirs into flame."[29] Rather than recommend modest measures, he exhorted them to sail to the island "with a great armament" and "subdue it utterly" while cherishing "great hopes" for the outcome.[30]

Yet Alcibiades entertained still greater hopes. For him, subduing Sicily was just the first stage in a grandiose scheme aimed at dominion over the Mediterranean basin as a whole. Plutarch recounts how Alcibiades "regarded Sicily as a mere beginning" and not the "end of an expedition."[31] The island occupied a central geographic location, offering a springboard for further conquests. While Nicias sought in vain to dissuade the assembly from the venture, "Alcibiades was dreaming of Carthage and Libya, and, after winning these, of at once encompassing Italy and Peloponnesus," the Greek peninsula where antagonist Sparta lay.[32] In other words, he wanted to launch a fresh campaign whose goals had few evident limits. And he wanted to start before the city resolved its prolonged struggle with Sparta—a struggle that already threatened to exhaust the Athenian treasury. Alcibiades' strategy was folly, but it made little difference in the end: during its misadventure, Athens lost its entire expeditionary army and fleet. The city no longer had the means to attempt such a scheme.

Vainglory fueled Alcibiades' imprudence at the same time that oratory rendered his imprudent appeals persuasive. Hence the peril that Faulkner detects in larger-than-life figures. In effect Alcibiades helped convince the assembly to commit the city's entire expeditionary force to an assault it could have forgone. Betting everything on a discretionary undertaking is dangerous business. Yet, so inspiring was Alcibiades' appeal that the assembly assented joyfully when Nicias deliberately inflated the number of triremes—triple-decker galleys, the core of ancient battle fleets—that the expedition would demand. Nicias hoped the assembly would balk at the expense. Instead they voted to fund even more ships! So beguiled were Athenians that they later doubled down again (after Alcibiades had fled), dispatching yet another relief force when the situation deteriorated in Sicily. When the Sicilian expedition perished, the city lost the long arm of its foreign policy.

Granted, it would be wrong to lay *all* of the blame for Sicily at Alcibiades' feet. The assembly and commanders mishandled the expedition in almost every way conceivable. Recalling Alcibiades, who had been the venture's mastermind and one of its three generals, was a particularly glaring misstep. Athenians were fighting an enemy, the city-state of Syracuse, that was defending its own home ground and was a beneficiary of inspired leadership and Spartan help. The combination of self-inflicted troubles and capable opponents proved too much to overcome. In the end, concludes Thucydides, the Athenians "were beaten at all points and altogether . . . they were destroyed . . . with a total destruction, their fleet, their army—everything was destroyed, and few out of many returned home. Such were the events in Sicily."[33] One of history's worst military cataclysms, nevertheless, had its origins in a single man's inability to contain his ambitions and thirst for glory.

Nor was Alcibiades an anomaly. Clausewitz warns that the desire for honor lashes sovereigns and generals onward, sometimes into foolhardy courses of action: "Military honor and the renown of an army and its generals are factors that operate invisibly, but they constantly permeate all military activity."[34] The climate pervading strategy, then, tends to produce warriors who are gripped by an inordinate love of acclaim. Strategists must train themselves not to let their longing for fame seduce them into reckless exploits. Alcibiades is an archetype of how not to comport oneself.

Some major figures succeed in governing themselves, and thereby unlock their political and strategic talents. A few paragons of self-mastery grace the annals of diplomatic and military history. Faulkner contrasts Alcibiades with George Washington, who numbered among this exclusive cohort. Washington was impelled by the same passions that impel any soldier. He had a volcanic temper, but he tamed it. He craved martial glory, but he subordinated his craving to the public good. He had a proclivity for decisive Clausewitzian battlefield engagements—he longed to give the British redcoats a "fatal Stab"—but after a string of early defeats he grudgingly accepted that his Continental Army was the weaker contender and that he had to find more roundabout ways to win.³⁵ By subduing his desires, he advanced the cause of an independent American republic. By Faulkner's measure of character, he was the counter-Alcibiades.

Faulkner goes through an extended discourse about the exact nature of Washington's virtue. Rather than ascribe it to public-spiritedness descended from classical traditions of statecraft or to Enlightenment philosophy or to twentieth-century scholars' emphasis on the American founders' private interests, Faulkner maintains that Washington fashioned a type of enlightened self-interest for the modern era. In effect, Washington converted the desire for honor, of which Alcibiades was one of history's most notable exemplars, into "a passion for enduring superiority," complemented by "image making calculated to make oneself attractive and memorable."³⁶ He struck a bargain with contemporaries and posterity: he would supply Americans with private and public benefits in return for an immortal reputation. Lasting fame was his reward for honorable, self-restrained conduct.

Faulkner cites an episode from John Marshall's *Life of George Washington* to help prove his case. In mid-1777 word reached General Washington that a Royal Navy fleet was sailing toward the national capital at Philadelphia at the same time that a redcoat army was making its way south along the Hudson River toward the New York capital at Albany. Washington determined that the British ground expedition was a real expedition rather than a feint to siphon Continental Army forces away from defending Philadelphia. (In reality, both British forces were supposed to converge on Albany, but they diverged owing to a miscommunication within the British command.) He also determined that the Continental Army's prime goal should be to stymie the British advance down the Hudson.³⁷ Had the British expedition succeeded, New England would have been isolated from colonies to the south, with the river forming a barrier. Philadelphia was expendable by contrast with an entire region.

In Marshall's telling, Washington's actions constituted a parable. An Alcibiades might have gathered resources to his southern force in hopes of personally leading troops to victory outside Philadelphia and cementing his reputation for generalship—or, in Washington's case, recouping a reputation sullied by repeated tactical defeats spanning 1776. As Marshall reports, however, Washington sent letters pleading with state governors to dispatch militia units to New York. He dispatched some of his ablest militia commanders to the north, along with three New England regular brigades, a regiment of riflemen, and three New York militia regiments. Having designated the Hudson campaign as the priority effort, he allocated resources accordingly—and contented himself with heading a secondary effort in Pennsylvania. The cause came first.

While Washington doubtless coveted the glory that comes with personal command of a triumphant army, writes Marshall, he refused to let the "false glare" of fame "dazzle his eyes, or conceal from his view the superior public advantage" of turning back the northern army and keeping the enemy from using the Hudson to cut off New England from the rest of the colonies.[38] Washington's southern force fought several minor and ultimately unsuccessful engagements around Philadelphia, which the redcoats soon occupied. But the northern army won a signal victory at the Battle of Saratoga that fall. Saratoga paved the way for an alliance with France and thus for eventual victory in the Revolutionary War—albeit after four more years of bitter fighting and privation.

Washington's self-discipline not only paid off in operational and strategic terms, helping him set and enforce priorities among combat theaters, but it also produced long-term benefits for his newly formed country. It is a rare battlefield commander who excels at statesmanship during the transition from war to peace and beyond. Washington's contemporaries likened him to Cincinnatus, the Roman general to whom the Senate awarded dictatorial power on two occasions to quell a mortal danger to the state. In Cincinnatus' case, the victorious military leader discharged his duty, relinquished his extraordinary powers immediately after, and returned to his farm.[39] Similarly, after the Revolutionary War, Washington made a great show of stepping down from military command, and he refused pleas that he become monarch of the United States. In so doing he established self-denying traditions that have served the republic well for more than two centuries.

Plaudits from an unlikely source confirm Washington's standing as a founder and leader. After the Revolutionary War, the American painter Benjamin West informed Britain's King George III that the general was planning to surrender his military post and return to Mount Vernon, his family plantation. The king reportedly told West: "If he does that, he will be the greatest man in the world."[40] Alcibiades was a superb tactician who yielded to his baser impulses. Although Washington was an indifferent tactical commander, he wielded force to great effect as a strategic leader, and as a political leader he helped the republic find its bearings. He kept the covenant with Americans about which Faulkner writes—and earned the undying acclaim for which he had yearned.

In sum, Alcibiades is an example of passion not fully tamed by reason, while Washington mastered his passions and accomplished big things. Aspirants to leadership in the Aristotelian mold should model their habits on Washington while shunning Alcibiades.

MANAGE COMMUNAL PASSIONS

Self-mastery is essential for groups of people as well as individuals. Societies are subject to passion, and their passions have direct strategic and political implications. Societies can be enthusiastic or apathetic about a war effort. If popular sentiment approaches extremes of fervor or apathy, it could spur political leaders into rash actions or drain momentum from their policies. Clausewitz goes a step further than Socrates, and much further than the Stoics. As recounted earlier in this chapter, in Plato's tale of the charioteer seeking enlightenment, Socrates regards the surly horse—his metaphor for base passions—as a malefactor to be tamed. This may be true for individuals in daily life. But Clausewitz insists that some quotient of forceful passion—*including destructive urges such as malice and fear*—is not just praiseworthy but essential to prevail in a trial of arms. Ignoble impulses have something invaluable to contribute to any war effort.

Emotion is a psychological propellant. Without it the martial machinery sputters and stalls. An excess of fuel sends the machine hurtling into overdrive, with unknowable but probably baneful repercussions. Officialdom is the regulator of communal passions. Senior officials meter out psychological fuel at the proper rate through public communication and so control the mix of positive and negative emotions. Adept strategic communicators deploy rhetoric in concert with other forms of messaging to inflame, damp, or sustain popular ardor as battlefield circumstances warrant.

But war, like everyday life, is not entirely about passion. It is about tapping passion while keeping the rational (and thus dispassionate) calculus firmly in control. Chapter 1 reviewed the three dominant tendencies, or constituent factors, that make up any society at war.[41] The three elements, Clausewitz argues, are "primordial violence, hatred, and enmity, which are to be regarded as a blind natural force"; the "play of chance and probability within which the creative spirit is free to roam"; and war's "element of subordination, as an instrument of policy, which makes it subject to reason alone."[42] Portraying a people this way is quite different from Aristotle's conception of city-states with distinctive regimes or ways of life. It conveys the dynamism and complexity of peoples under arms.

These three elements combine and interact to make a warring society "a paradoxical trinity," and an innately unstable one at that.[43] Gusty passions are "mainly" found among the populace, Clausewitz writes, and they "must already be inherent" among ordinary folk if the leadership hopes to turn them to strategic benefit.[44] Any society needs popular fervor to impel warlike endeavors, yet the populace also can demand too much out of an endeavor—prodding the leadership into rash and perhaps self-defeating actions. Clausewitz implies that the most eloquent orator cannot conjure strong feelings from nothing. Strategic leaders can only harness latent passions—not create them. They are like social engineers. They must manage the three elements—passion, chance and creativity, and rationality—maintaining "a balance between these three tendencies, like an object suspended between three magnets."[45] The physics metaphor is well chosen. Physicists observe that keeping a ferrous object suspended among three magnets is a nonlinear, intrinsically erratic process. It is impossible unless operators constantly adjust each electromagnet's polarity to keep the mass steady and on center.[46] For Clausewitz there is no stable balance among the elements of a warring society.

Wise strategic leaders thus devote constant attention and labor to keeping the elements of society in balance and directed toward the leadership's war aims. Dexterity is at a premium. Subduing one's personal passions and impulses while tapping the energy that flows from collective passion makes leadership thoughtful yet forceful. In Aristotelian terms, the effort governs relations between the rational and nonrational elements of the soul and has implications for both intellectual and moral virtue. Those who make a habit of managing themselves and their societies tend to prosper amid martial strife.

TRAIN THE "INNER EYE," STOKE THE "INWARD FIRE"

Clausewitz has sage advice for the aspiring strategic leader: make yourself a genius! Far from being a mere platitude, however, Clausewitz's inquiry into military genius represents a primer on wartime leadership. By *genius* he means that military leaders must school their martial intuition and character, making leadership a reflex. He also considers strategy more an art than a science, even though important aspects of it—logistics and weapons design, for example—lend themselves to quantitatively rich scientific methods. Like artistic endeavors, military strategy inhabits the realm of chance, where guesswork and flashes of inspiration make all the difference. Genius, he says, is a compound of intellect and temperament. It is also an array of gifts. Taken together, he observes, a "harmonious combination of elements" constitutes "the essence of military genius."[47]

Clausewitz goes on to survey qualities indispensable for virtuosos. Like Aristotle, he lists courage as the first virtue for military leaders. Courage comes in two varieties. The first is "courage in the face of personal danger," whether that courage is innate to the individual or is fired by such "positive motives as ambition, patriotism, or enthusiasm of any kind."[48] The second is "courage to accept responsibility, either before the tribunal of some outside power or before the court of one's own conscience."[49] But there is far more to genius than courage. Because war is enveloped in "a fog of greater or lesser uncertainty," generalship demands "an intellect that, even in the darkest hour, retains some glimmerings of the inner light which leads to truth."[50] Having glimpsed the light through the fog, the general must exhibit "the courage to follow this faint light wherever it may lead."[51] In short, the adroit strategic leader needs an "inward eye" to sight courses of action obscured by the fractal nature of war, along with the "inward fire" to rouse the army to great feats of arms in pursuit of the leader's strategic vision.[52]

Finally, Clausewitz touches briefly on a few affiliated virtues. The general needs sufficient "presence of mind" to navigate the "climate of war"—a climate made up of "danger, exertion, uncertainty, and chance."[53] "Staunchness" is the willpower to withstand a single heavy blow, while "endurance" refers to staying power during protracted hardship. The former flows from powerful emotion, while the latter stems from intelligence. Clausewitz concludes that "history and posterity reserve the name of 'genius' for those who have excelled in the highest positions—as commanders-in-chief—since here the demands for intellectual and moral powers are vastly greater. . . . On that level strategy and policy coalesce: the commander-in-chief is simultaneously a statesman" with a firm grasp of how military operations advance policy aims, and a warrior with a firm grasp of national policy.[54] A supreme commander constitutes the interface between policy and strategy.

Military genius, then, is a composite of the intuition to select a course of action, the gumption to see that course of action through in the face of physical or moral hazard, and prudence lest the army exceed its capability and come to grief. Still, Clausewitzian ideas are not sacred writ. Whether only supreme commanders qualify for the label *genius* is open to debate. In all likelihood, Liddell Hart would approve. For him a genius needs range as well as the proper grand-strategic perspective. Chinese general Sun Tzu, with his emphasis on handling armies on the battlefield, might well demur. Regardless of who merits the honorific, Clausewitz sets a worthy standard for military officers and officials to strive toward over the course of a career as they ascend the ranks.

This bundle of characteristics bestows advantages aplenty on strategic leaders. To name just a few, it should help them sense the rhythms of combat and avoid either overshooting their resources or halting the effort before it achieves all it could. It should help them combine cumulative actions with sequential ones to grind down antagonists and land heavy blows. It should help them turn geography to advantage, much as Sparta's King Leonidas defended a narrow passage at the Battle of Thermopylae (480 BC) against an overbearing Persian host, or as Korea's sixteenth-century admiral Yi Sun-sin defended a narrow maritime defile against a Japanese navy that boasted overwhelmingly superior numbers at the Battle of Myeongyang (AD 1597). Great figures such as Leonidas and Yi made terrain their ally and triumphed despite what looked like insuperable odds. Studying their exploits for insight repays the effort many times over.

Strategic artistry, then, should be the goal for all strategic leaders. Natural geniuses can hone their leadership traits to an even finer edge through conscious effort, while those not so gifted can aspire to self-made genius through study, reflection, and conscious habituation. Leaders are made as well as born.

INTERPRET AND REINTERPRET
THE NATURE OF THE WAR

Self-rule also helps strategic leaders school their intellect. Geniuses know that they stand little chance of getting what they want out of an enterprise unless they understand what the enterprise is all about. To stand any chance of achieving strategic and political aims amid the dynamism and complexity of war, the war's overseers must grapple with its nature, Clausewitz declares. "The first, the supreme, the most far-reaching act of judgment that the statesman and commander have to make is to establish by that test the kind of war on which they are embarking; neither mistaking it for, nor trying to turn it into, something that is alien to its nature," he writes.

"This is the first of all strategic questions and the most comprehensive."[55] It should be second nature to pay the nature of the war close scrutiny and revisit the appraisal regularly to ensure it remains accurate.

War marks a change of state in competitive interactions. As chapter 3 demonstrated, competitors can advance their purposes by increments in peacetime by tapping diplomacy, economic policy, and nonviolent displays of military force. They try to burnish national well-being through cumulative methods reminiscent of those of the American strategic theorist Adm. J. C. Wylie.[56] No individual endeavor garners outright success by itself. Piecemeal or intermittent advances that are unrelated to one another in time or space may add up to cumulative progress. Diplomatic outreach might win over a new friend or ally; so could a humanitarian or disaster relief operation. Strategic advantage comes little by little through efforts at different times and places.

As the foreword showed, actually going to war injects what Wylie calls a sequential element into the competition.[57] For Clausewitz sequential campaigning means striking at some critical "center of gravity" to knock the foe off balance, then landing "blow after blow" in the same direction until the foe capitulates or can no longer resist.[58] Campaigning takes on a linear character. Each engagement depends on the last and prepares the ground for the next until a combatant reaches its strategic and political goal (or something, such as enemy action, interrupts the sequence). Once the goal is in hand and the time for peacemaking has come, relations between rivals revert to their cumulative state. This phase change has implications for strategic leadership. Actually pummeling a foe warrants somewhat different habits of mind, sentiment, and deed than does designing forces for a hypothetical future engagement, moving them around on the map to swing opinion in peacetime strategic competition, or making peace after the guns fall silent in armed conflict.

There are many ways to classify wars. Sometimes combatants take up arms for limited political aims, such as seizing a parcel of territory or repulsing aggression. Sometimes they aspire to unlimited goals, such as ousting a hostile government

In War, Fight for a Better State of Peace • 131

and replacing it with one more to their liking. Sometimes they devote a fraction of their martial means to an endeavor. Other times they fling all available resources into it. Some wars are global in scale, rage on for years, and are fought by alliances for the highest of stakes. Others are regional in scope, aim at modest stakes, and may or may not involve alliances. Internal wars constitute a special case. By definition they take place within a single state, and so remain confined in geographic scope. Within that confined area, however, the contenders set unlimited goals. They fight to the finish to determine who will rule. Victory in internal war commonly entails eradicating domestic foes' political—or even physical—existence.[59]

The physical setting also matters a great deal. Clausewitz's insights bear on wars of all kinds, but he appraised the discipline of strategy through the lens of ground warfare between contiguous European states. After all, he served with massed armies, seeking to use land engagements for the purpose of wars against revolutionary and Napoleonic France. In the maritime domain, fleets contend for mastery of important waters in order to support diplomacy, levy economic and military pressure on their enemies, and project power ashore. Today air forces vie for command of the sky, which confers on them the power to bombard targets on the surface for tactical or strategic effect. In internal wars, insurgents wage a contest for political legitimacy against incumbent rulers. Besides the various categories of diplomatic, economic, and military interactions, the existence of continental, maritime, air, and insurgent varieties of military strategy puts a premium on somewhat different habits.

Making sense of all this is pivotal to strategic success. Sun Tzu takes a "pentagonal" approach to evaluating how well one force stacks up to another on likely battlegrounds.[60] He sets "five fundamental factors" as parameters for analyzing a conflict: the general's "moral influence" on the army, which molds its fighting spirit; weather; terrain; command; and doctrine.[61] How well each contender rates by the metrics of moral influence, command, and doctrine indicates who holds the tactical, operational, and strategic advantage in general terms. Factoring in weather and terrain suggests how the armies will fare against each other on a specific battleground during a specific season of the year. Candid appraisal of the army's strong suits and weaknesses helps the wise general redress its shortcomings while reaping maximum advantage from its strengths.

Clausewitz takes a drastically different approach to assessing the nature of a particular war. He focuses on military resources, starting from the commonsense claim that the more one contender demands from its enemy, the stiffer a fight the enemy will put up. The more resistance the army is likely to encounter, the more resources its leadership must summon to overpower that resistance. To "discover" the scale and type of resources needed to prevail in a fight, Clausewitz says, "we must first examine our own political aim and that of the enemy."[62] Elsewhere in *On War* he maintains that the "political object" or goal drives everything for any rational combatant. The cost-benefit calculus resembles the one that a prospective buyer undertakes before making a major purchase in everyday civilian life. How much buyers want something—a car, a house—determines how big a price they are prepared to pay for it. Similarly, how badly political leaders and their constituents want their political goal determines how much they spend on it.

That brings us to Clausewitz's central idea. According to him, war waged by a rational combatant is "not an act of senseless passion but is controlled by its political object."[63] Sensible passion combined with objective analysis sets a goal's worth. In turn, "the value of this object must determine the sacrifices to be made for it in *magnitude* and also in *duration*."[64] By magnitude he means the rate at which a contender expends resources, measured in lives, national treasure, and military hardware, to attain the political object. By duration he means how long the contender keeps up the expenditure. Just as in elementary physics, multiplying the rate by the time reveals the total amount of something—in this case the cost of achieving the political goal. Or, to go back to the commercial analogy broached above, waging war is like buying a car or house on an installment plan. Magnitude is the amount of each periodic payment, while duration is the number of payments stretched across a set amount of time. The buyer can multiply the one by the other to calculate the total price. This simple function helps a combatant's leadership gauge whether the aim is worth the expense. If not, the combatant should forgo the attempt to obtain it.

The key difference between warfare and shopping is that cost-benefit calculations are neither fixed nor eternal for Clausewitz. The amount of each installment and the number of payments both may fluctuate. A contestant also has the option of canceling the transaction if it stops caring enough to pay the price. If the "expenditure of effort" comes to exceed "the value of the political object," Clausewitz warns, "the object must be renounced and peace must follow."[65] It could be that previous calculations underestimated the magnitude of the effort or how long it would take. It could be that the enemy deliberately drove up the cost or dragged out the war to make it more expensive. It could be that the leadership or larger society stopped treasuring the goal and was loath to pay the requisite price for it. Or the contestant might have acquired another commitment that took precedence. Strategic leaders must make a habit of keeping cost-benefit logic uppermost in mind and revisiting their calculations regularly to make sure fighting on still makes sense. They must also estimate what the opponent wants, how much the opponent wants it, and how hard the opponent will fight for it.

For Clausewitz, the second step in appraising the nature of the war is to "gauge the strength and situation of the opposing state."[66] This is the familiar process of "net assessment" that intelligence services use to evaluate the belligerents' geography, economic and industrial prowess, and military means—forecasting the physical might that each can bring to bear within the constraints imposed by its geographic position.[67] Clausewitz's third step is to "gauge the character and abilities of its government and people and do the same in regard to our own."[68] In other words, the leadership must take stock of each combatant's paradoxical trinity (described previously), assessing how its government, people, and military relate to one another in an environment made up of turbulent passions, chance and creativity, and efforts to keep warfare subservient to rational control. In Aristotelian parlance, they should study the hostile power's regime, meaning not just its governing arrangements but its way of life. These three steps provide a rough guide to the combatants' power relative to each other.

But war does not unfold in a vacuum. It has an impact on the belligerents' allies and partners, the inhabitants of the region where the war takes place, and potentially the international community at large. Accordingly, Clausewitz writes, there is a fourth step to sizing up the nature of a war: "We must evaluate the political sympathies of other states and the effect the war may have on them."[69] Operations could drive wedges into alliances or coalitions—or bring them together. Allies or coalition partners could desert one combatant or join another depending on how the fighting progresses. The war could draw international censure, isolating one or more combatants. Strategic leaders should take account of potential fallout from their actions when plotting strategy and operations.

None of this is easy. Clausewitz declares that collecting and assessing data in bulk "clearly calls for the intuition of a genius" and laments that Sir Isaac Newton "himself would quail before the algebraic problems it could pose."[70] Take an example: the Korean War of 1950–1953.[71] Classifying the nature of the Korean War seems straightforward. Communist North Korea invaded the U.S.-backed South with the unlimited aim of destroying the Southern government in Seoul and unifying the peninsula under Northern rule. President Harry Truman prevailed on the United Nations Security Council to authorize a UN expedition to restore international peace and security. This translated into the limited aim of repulsing aggression and restoring the South Korean government. Fighting seesawed up and down the peninsula for a year or so of a war of movement, followed by two years of bloody stalemate while the parties dickered over where the border between the Koreas would be drawn. They agreed on an armistice in 1953, putting a halt to the fighting if not to the legal state of war.

The straightforward nature of the conflict is deceptive, however. The war appears to be a regional one, in which North Korea sought unlimited aims and South Korea sought to deny it outright victory. But the months before the Northern invasion witnessed an insurgency and counterinsurgency in South Korea that claimed scores of thousands of lives. The Korean War originated not as an international war but as a civil war between communists based in the North and noncommunists in the South. The UN coalition briefly transformed it into a war for unlimited aims, namely unifying the peninsula under Seoul's leadership. The war took place during the aftermath of a global war, World War II, when East Asian powers were still sorting out the fate of Japan and the erstwhile Japanese Empire, of which the Korean Peninsula had formed a part. It erupted during the months after the civil war in neighboring China, when the new Chinese Communist regime was still mopping up remnants of the vanquished Nationalists. It was a theater unto itself in the burgeoning Cold War. The leading cold warriors, the Soviet Union, Communist China, and the United States, more or less usurped the Korean civil war, relegating Pyongyang and Seoul to secondary combatants on their own peninsula.

As simple wars go, the Korean War was remarkably intricate. Imagine being a strategic leader in a multifaceted, multilayered conflict that combined counterinsurgent warfare, a civil war, a regional war, and a global Cold War. The war testifies to the abiding wisdom found in the strategic canon. Sun Tzu's injunction to know oneself and know the enemy sounds like a truism, as does Clausewitz's template for net assessment. Yet truisms are hard to put into effect even in the simplest of wars. Strategic leaders must routinely recheck their estimate of the nature of the war to ensure that what they do fits the circumstances.

RESPECT THE FOE

The enemy is integral to the nature of the war, and the enemy is not a potted plant that will just stay put. It is an intelligent, determined, oftentimes ornery strategic agent whose leaders harbor ideas of their own about the course the war should take. It is hard to overstate the importance of affording the enemy the respect due any belligerent society. Sun Tzu appears to disparage antagonists' ingenuity and desire to win, claiming that his methods are foolproof: "If a general who heeds my strategy is employed, he is certain to win. Retain him! When one who refuses to listen to my strategy is employed, he is certain to be defeated. Dismiss him!"[72] This may be sales hype in part, as Sun Tzu evidently composed his tract in hopes of securing employment with sovereigns who read it. Clausewitz takes a gloomier view. His jaundice derives in part from the nature of war, an enterprise shrouded in a fog of uncertainty. Sun Tzu presupposes that a diligent general can amass perfect knowledge of the situation; Clausewitz brands intelligence reportage "unreliable and transient" during the thick of campaigning.[73] In other words, he regards gathering and analyzing information as crucial while at the same time admonishing commanders not to take information they receive at face value. This is a warning worth heeding even in today's high-tech age, with its deluge of data.

Clausewitz's dour view stems in part from the nature of interaction between combatants determined to get their way. Warlike pursuits are intrinsically unpredictable. Each contender tries to outcompete the other. That being the case, it is a fallacy of the first order to succumb to "scriptwriting."[74] Scriptwriting refers to the practice of compiling a theory of victory postulating how actions taken by friendly forces will bring about ultimate success, and assuming the foe will follow the part the scriptwriter—the strategist or war planner—assigns it. The problem is, every combatant draws up a theory of victory. It is nothing more than a chain of cause and effect positing, in essence, that if we do X, Y, and Z, these actions will yield strategic effects A, B, and C. Theory charts a combatant's roadway to success.[75]

The fallacy lies not in conceiving a theory of victory, but in assuming that the opponent will abide by it.[76] Warfare is not Hollywood. Actors on stage or screen are passive. They do what the writers and directors say if they want a paycheck. Commanders hold no such authority over defiant opponents. The antagonist has every incentive to go off-script, ruining the production while pursuing its own conflicting theory of victory. Clausewitz stresses how this perverse form of reciprocity works. War "is not the action of a living force upon a lifeless mass ... but always the collision of two living forces," he affirms. "So long as I have not overthrown my opponent I am bound to fear that he may overthrow me. Thus I am not in control: he dictates to me as much as I dictate to him."⁷⁷ The contenders trade move for countermove, deflecting operations from any predictable pathway. Sun Tzu seemingly downplays the likelihood of reversals of fortune and thus unwittingly encourages complacency among sovereigns and field commanders. The Clausewitzian view is the safer view. It enjoins those who make war to respect the foe while trying to impose their will on the foe.

Scriptwriting is the deficiency of respect for the enemy, while being awestruck by enemy prowess is the excess—and strategic leaders should err toward the excess. Slighting a living antagonist courts disaster.

SET, ENFORCE, AND SOMETIMES RETHINK PRIORITIES

Regulating personal and public passions, refining intuition, and paying the enemy due homage helps keep the rational calculus of war in charge, where the strategic canon says it belongs. If rationality reigns supreme, the scientific habit of mind predominates, notwithstanding myriad factors that threaten to displace rational faculties. A century ago Rear Adm. Bradley Fiske opined that "to be skillful in strategy," the strategist must have "its scientific principles firmly imprinted on his mind . . . [making] its practice so thoroughly familiar to his mental muscles that he can use strategy as a trained soldier uses his musket—automatically."⁷⁸ Aristotle would agree. Battlefield commanders must cultivate a regimen of intellectual habits to accompany self-rule of their passions.

Chapter 2 made the case that strategy at its most fundamental is about setting and enforcing priorities in a setting marked by competitive interaction. Contestants harbor many interests and desires. Unless they discipline their desires and interests, they risk frittering away finite resources trying to accomplish big things that lie beyond their means—or trying to accomplish everything, everywhere, at the same time. That way lies failure and perhaps ruin. Strategy means applying resources to top priorities while taking a self-denying attitude toward lesser interests and goals. Strategic leaders commonly have to postpone some worthwhile initiatives or cancel them altogether. Acknowledging this reality is crucial.

The giants of strategic theory advance somewhat different ideas about how to manage priorities in stride when the war is raging and its nature could be changing. When, if ever, is it advisable to divert resources from the main effort into a secondary theater or operation? Sun Tzu is a champion of secondary undertakings, while Clausewitz frowns on them. The Chinese master takes it for granted that any field commander should divide his host into "normal" and "extraordinary" forces (also translated as "direct" and "indirect" forces).[79] Doing so serves defensive and offensive purposes. The army "is certain to sustain the enemy's attack without suffering defeat" when the general wields normal and extraordinary forces nimbly, he maintains.[80] The normal force confronts the enemy while the extraordinary force strikes the enemy's flanks. In battle, then, the commander should "use the normal force to engage" and "the extraordinary to win."[81]

Nor is this division of labor fixed. Normal and extraordinary forces come in "limitless" combinations, Sun says.[82] He advises the wily general to take a fluid approach to managing the two components. For instance, the extraordinary force could launch a direct frontal engagement if its prospects appeared promising—in other words, if it found weakness. The secondary effort would become the primary. The extraordinary force would become the normal force, the erstwhile normal force would become the extraordinary force, and the focus of effort could shift back and forth as battlefield circumstances warranted. The general should combine and recombine forces as combat intuition indicates, disorienting the enemy army while assailing its weak spots.

It is worth noting, however, that Sun Tzu seems to countenance *tactical* division of forces and effort, not *strategic*. He envisions dividing forces while grappling with a single enemy army—a tactical venture. When Clausewitz frets about opening secondary efforts, he sounds diametrically at odds with Sun. But in reality Clausewitz seems worried less about dividing forces on a single battlefield than about dividing forces strategically. In fact, he instructs the general to divide the army into several columns in a bid to envelop the enemy tactically.[83] Such guidance would gladden the heart of Sun Tzu. What Clausewitz warns against is fragmenting the army between widely separated theaters of action, making it hard to reapportion resources to reinforce the main theater should things go badly there.

Clausewitz also worries about efficiency. Hammering away at the hostile center of gravity constitutes his chief concern. For him concerted effort is the swiftest and surest route to victory. Chapter 2 profiled Clausewitz's Three Rs—reward, risk, and resources. Strategic leaders should pass up any secondary theater or campaign that does not appear exceptionally fruitful. Even if an effort does promise rich rewards, however, the leadership should still forego it if subdividing the army risks failure in the primary theater, which by definition is what matters most. Only if the combatant enjoys decisively superior resources in the primary theater should it consider a secondary effort. This is a high standard to meet, and it embodies sound cost-benefit logic. To restate this doctrine, Clausewitz counsels against risking what matters most for the sake of something that is less important. Sun Tzu might well concur with those priorities.

Implicit in the Clausewitzian discourse about secondary commitments is that strategic leaders must muster the moral fortitude to wind down a commitment. Rerunning the calculus periodically might indicate that a secondary effort no longer offers exceptional reward or is consuming too many resources, and thus has come to entail an unacceptable risk to the primary theater. It has outlived its usefulness and has begun to pose dangers. But there is more to shutting down a venture than cost-benefit analysis. An element of passion, and thus of self-mastery, also comes into play. Economists decry the fallacy of "sunk costs."[84] To oversimplify, this is the habit of escalating commitment to a losing endeavor. In the martial sphere, a commander or statesman who has sunk resources into an endeavor is afraid to terminate it precisely because so much has been invested in it—in personal or national prestige as well as resources. Canceling it, strategic leaders fear, represents an admission of failure, if not malfeasance. There is an element of passion to rational calculations about priorities.

While such phrases as *sunk costs* would not be coined for millennia after his death, the life of Pyrrhus, the third century–BC king of Epirus, doubles as a parable on the wages of strategic indiscipline. Generalship is more than raw ability. Fellow soldiers esteemed Pyrrhus. Indeed, Plutarch recalls that Hannibal—himself rated among history's ablest captains—exalted Pyrrhus as "the foremost of all generals in experience and ability"—by implication even greater than Macedonian leader Alexander the Great.[85] Hannibal, who terrorized Rome for seventeen years on Italian soil, deemed himself third best after Scipio Africanus, who smashed Hannibal's army to close out Rome's second titanic war against Carthage.

And yet, despite Pyrrhus' battlefield genius, he never knew when to consolidate his gains or cut his losses. Win or lose in some campaign, Pyrrhus flung his army into a new theater or campaign, usually against the Roman Republic. Over time he bled his army and country dry through ceaseless soldiering. After clashing with Roman armies at the Battle of Asculum in 279 BC, he retorted to a comrade's congratulations: "If we are victorious in one more battle with the Romans, we shall be utterly ruined."[86] Much like Lord Charles Cornwallis, the British general, in the American South, Pyrrhus confronted a foe that could replenish its strength more readily than could his own host. Strategic victory went to the contestant that was better able to regenerate combat power.[87]

In Pyrrhus' case, the Roman legions that opposed him boasted superior reserve strength and could make up heavy losses, while Pyrrhus' army could not. Hence the phrase "Pyrrhic victory," shorthand for a tactical success that bankrupts one's resources and sets back the cause strategically and politically. American military strategist Edward Luttwak calls the tendency to overextend and subject oneself to defeat an ironic "reversal" of fortune.[88] Strategic leaders must attune themselves to the rhythms of the battlefield—doubly so when battlefield operations span multiple theaters. Otherwise commitments may outrun resources to catastrophic effect, as they did for King Pyrrhus.

Aristotelian strategists guard against the proclivity to double down. Boldness certainly is a virtue on the battlefield, while an overabundance of skepticism toward new undertakings could give rise to timid strategy and thus underperformance. The virtue to inculcate is introspection. Commanders and political chieftains must weigh the costs and perils of new efforts against the possibility of accomplishing great things at a stroke through secondary measures. Juxtaposing Clausewitzian insights against those of Sun Tzu enlightens us—as does investigating military history and biography.

CONFIGURE FORCES FOR THE PLACE, TIME, AND OPPONENT

It sounds like sheerest common sense: the art and science of battlefield strategy is to be stronger where it matters, when it matters, in order to overpower hostile forces. Clausewitz declares emphatically that "the best strategy is always to be very strong; first in general, and then at the decisive point."[89] Generating military power—making oneself very strong in general, as Clausewitz puts it—may not be the province of battlefield commanders. Applying military power at the scene of action is. Clausewitz counsels commanders that "there is no higher and simpler law of strategy than that of keeping one's forces concentrated. No force should ever be detached from the main body unless the need is definite and urgent"—hence Clausewitz's qualms toward secondary efforts.[90]

Mahan transposes the logic of local supremacy to the sea. He sketches a "broad formula" that holds that a fleet or fleet detachment "must be great enough to take the sea, and to fight, with reasonable chances of success, the largest force likely to be brought against it."[91] The Mahanian formula is no simple slide rule for calculating how many ships, planes, and armaments to assign. Comparing forces by the usual metrics—ship numbers, weapons range, seamanship and tactical proficiency, and the like—certainly is a critical part of assessing whether the fleet is powerful enough to duel a hostile force. But it is only part. How can a fleet commander estimate how much of their total force rival commanders are *likely* to commit to battle?

Answering this question demands more than technical or tactical acumen. It also demands that naval overseers make a habit of thinking in geopolitical terms. If a prospective foe cares a great deal about its goals—if it treasures the *political object* of the conflict, in Clausewitzian parlance—then it will devote a substantial amount of resources to the endeavor for a considerable time. Its leadership believes that the prospective payback justifies generous investment. If the enemy cares little about its political aims or has commitments to attend to elsewhere, it will dedicate a smaller share of its maritime forces to battle. Whatever fraction the enemy assigns, factoring in the value of the object, the likely opportunity costs of risking an encounter, and so forth, yields the fraction of hostile forces that is likely to appear on the scene of battle. That fraction—not the enemy force as a whole—becomes the benchmark for adequacy when calculating the size and shape of a naval deployment. It indicates how much is enough.

There is no substitute for studying opponents and gauging what they prize—and are willing to fight hard for—in world affairs. The Mahanian formula likewise applies to ground and air forces. As a matter of routine, commanders must take account of politics and risk alongside physical and human measures of sufficiency. They should look to Clausewitz and Mahan when deciding on what forces to array.

KEEP UP WITH THE TIMES

Managing change is demanding by any measure. As chapter 2 pointed out, Niccolò Machiavelli portrays initiating something, managing transitions, and bringing things to a satisfactory end as the most grueling tests of statecraft. Unexpected developments come fast and furious in times of war. Change results from the interplay among the multitude of factors cataloged by Clausewitz and Sun Tzu. The masters of strategy urge combatants to impose change on one another, bolstering their chances of outdoing the enemy. As noted before, Sun Tzu counsels generals to combine and recombine normal and extraordinary forces in fluid ways. In so doing they avoid setting foreseeable patterns in their handling of battlefield operations. They render themselves genuinely unpredictable.

But Sun Tzu wanted generals to go beyond deceit. He asserts that "those skilled at making the enemy move do so by creating a situation to which he must conform."[92] They take charge of the surroundings and prevent the enemy from keeping up with changing times. The late American military strategist John R. Boyd would agree with Sun Tzu. A former Air Force fighter pilot who became one of the twentieth century's keenest military thinkers, Colonel Boyd urged tacticians and strategists to observe the surroundings, orient themselves to them, decide what to do, and act—all with a speed and dexterity that are superior to the opponent's. In fact, he insisted it was possible not merely to take charge of the surroundings but to change them abruptly—disorienting the opponent and leaving its leadership out of touch with the situation. Boyd termed his approach "fast transients."[93] For Boyd and Sun Tzu alike, a marked advantage goes to the contestant that is nimbler and more solidly keyed to the strategic and operational setting.

How should the military cope with transient circumstances, whether they arise from the nature of warfare or deliberate action by the foe? By tending to individual excellence and institutional culture. Individuals should reach for the Clausewitzian ideal of military genius, schooling their intuition and associated traits. Top leaders must go further than self-development, nurturing a corporate culture that is not merely hospitable to adaptation but that generously rewards it. Chapter 2 lavished attention on the importance of culture. An ethos that is centered on technical excellence and combat prowess helps a force make maximum use of the implements provided to it. It also imbues service members with fighting traditions and ways of thinking about the profession of arms. A supple, adaptive culture results.

To assess their culture and renovate it if necessary, contemporary American seafarers can profit by consulting British and French naval history once again. During the age of sail Great Britain constructed an empire on which the sun never set and laid the keels for an oceangoing Royal Navy to police it. British strategists excelled at forging an imperial trident. But how to use it in action? Political and naval leaders fostered an offensive mindset by which mariners and their political overseers accepted risk when questing for big things. Or as Mahan puts it, British naval policy spurred seafarers to assert themselves "at all risks upon the sea."[94] The "keynote to England's naval policy" was that "the nation that would rule upon the sea must always attack."⁹⁵ British maritime culture was founded on energy, daring, and enterprise. A venturesome institution positions itself to manage and thrive from change.

The French leadership conspicuously declined to embrace entrepreneurial precepts, preferring conservative and defensively minded tactics and strategy. As a consequence, France underperformed at sea despite often fielding a fine navy competently led. Adm. Pierre-Charles Villeneuve, the French commander vanquished at Trafalgar, complained that the "system of defensive war prescribed by the French government" enfeebled his navy. Defensive methods "penetrated our habits," he recalled; the conservative approach, "so to say, weakened our arms and paralyzed our self-reliance."⁹⁶ Defeat often resulted from this cultural mismatch. Comparing the French experience to that of the British prompted Mahan to conclude: "More important even than the size of the navy is the question of its institutions, favoring a healthful spirit and activity."⁹⁷ Senior leaders habituate their institutions to attitudes and practices they deem desirable, and regard cultural upkeep as integral to their duty.

The Mahanian view did not go undisputed even in his time. It is possible to take a culture that is premised on derring-do to excess. British historian Julian Corbett applauded the Royal Navy's offensive culture, but denied that operational offense was the proper course of action at all times and places. In fact, he argued that it could prove downright dangerous if pursued mindlessly. As chapter 2 pointed out, Corbett angered the Royal Navy old guard on more than one occasion, for instance by lampooning maxims such as *the enemy's coast is our frontier*. To him, making offense a fetish, not a mere preference, smacked of hubris. And a prideful service risks paying a severe penalty in war.

Corbett was no defeatist, nor was he overcautious or defensive-minded in the French tradition. He wanted to win. He merely acknowledged the stark reality that no military force reigns supreme everywhere on the map (or nautical chart) at all times. Sometimes it will be locally inferior and forced to await reinforcements. In the meantime, Corbett said, commanders should institute measures to redress the force imbalance. They can mass existing forces or construct new ones. They can search out new allies or splinter enemy alliances. Or they can launch small-scale attacks to chip away at enemy superiority and confound enemy aims until such time as they reverse the imbalance and can go on offense.

As chapter 3 pointed out, Corbett terms his restless approach *active defense*, yet pronounces offense to be the soul of it. U.S. Adm. Chester Nimitz was a practitioner of active defense par excellence, using the battered remnants of the prewar U.S. Pacific Fleet to make things rough on the Imperial Japanese Navy until shipyards back in the United States could rivet together a new battle fleet. American active defense reached its zenith at the Battle of Midway, which halted the Japanese strategic advance and made counteroffensive operations thinkable for the first time. Corbett's supple way of thinking, predicated on blending defensive methods with offensive ones to eventually accomplish strategically offensive aims, is worth codifying in any fighting institution's culture.

A Corbettian culture boasts the dynamism to cope with transients or even turn them to advantage, as John Boyd might say. As chapter 2 contended, furthermore, top leadership should encourage productive discord at all times in order to counteract groupthink. The clash of ideas remains at a premium in wartime. It reveals the full array of options to decision-makers while highlighting likely costs, benefits, risks, and trade-offs inherent in any course of action. It helps them resist such scourges as scriptwriting, memes, and martial sloganeering. And it keeps them humble and grounded in reality—virtues worth making second nature. Cultural stewardship does not cease when fighting breaks out.

ENJOY A TRIUMPH, REJECT TRIUMPHALISM . . . AND GET READY

What if success graces one's tactics, operations, and strategy? It is one thing to relish a martial triumph, but rejecting *triumphalism* is an indispensable habit of mind. After all, Bernard Brodie cautions posterity not to read too much into major battles. They seldom come along, so the sample size is small. It is hazardous in the extreme to extrapolate too much from few data points. Plus, technology and the strategic setting have a way of changing in between major engagements—giving comparisons an apples-and-oranges quality. Nor, in most cases, is a particular outcome fated. Alter a few variables, and an engagement could have produced radically different results—and analysts would then draw radically different lessons with the same degree of confidence.[98]

Clausewitz warns sternly that strategy resembles cutting cards in a casino. He hints that even masterful strategists seldom manage to skew the odds more than about 60–40 in their favor.[99] Failure is always an option. That being the case, a bleak if not fatalistic attitude befits those embarking on martial enterprises. Prideful commanders overextend themselves, mistakes are legion, and ironic reversals of fortune are commonplace. The humble may not inherit the earth in strategy—but a measure of humility improves their chances of prospering. The masters of strategy would advise them not to preen about past success or let it lull them into believing that future success is preordained. It is not. They should rededicate themselves to honing excellence at the profession of arms, and get ready for the next test.

IN VICTORY, CONSTRUCT A BETTER PEACE

Drawing war to a successful close and extracting strategic and political results from it demands a kind of grand-strategic alchemy. It is one thing to win on the battlefield, quite another to erect a favorable and durable peace on the substructure of victory. A peace settlement in which the defeated acquiesce is vastly preferable to one that has to be enforced at gunpoint. Devising such a settlement is a job for diplomats backed by armed force. It is a blunder of the first order to think that armed force stops playing a role in politics when the guns fall silent. As pointed out time and again, Clausewitz maintains that the value of the political object governs the magnitude and duration of the effort that go into attaining it. What Clausewitz does not say is that the victor must care enough about the peace to keep investing resources of substantial magnitude afterward—and to sustain the investment for as long as it hopes the postwar order will endure. That usually is a long time.

Since the leadership presumably hopes to make its wartime gains permanent, in fact, postwar peace enforcement will last for an open-ended duration—driving up the costs of peace. To comply with Clausewitzian logic, therefore, political and military leaders must keep the magnitude of the effort manageable while persuading influential stakeholders—their own populace in particular—that they must continue caring about their gains even after the drama of war fades. They cannot take these gains for granted. If stakeholders keep cherishing what their arms achieved, and if keeping the peace is not too expensive, then the cost-benefit relationship may hold—and the peace along with it. How to keep the magnitude down? Strategic leaders must make it their goal to craft a settlement whereby the defeated assent in their defeat, even if grudgingly, rather than mount a new assault on the system later. Preserving the peace is easy and inexpensive when no one challenges it.

This explains why the greats of diplomacy and statecraft commonly assume a mild stance toward defeated foes once they have victory in hand. Charity was integral to Marcus Aurelius' worldview, for instance. The Roman emperor refused to exact vengeance even on those who rebelled against his rule. Canadian author Donald J. Robertson retells how Marcus took the family of Avidius Cassius, a pretender who had taken the field against the emperor, under his protection after Cassius' downfall and death. According to Robertson, Marcus "wished to be able to say that only those slain *during* the rebellion had died as a result of it: there were to be no witch hunts or acts of revenge afterward."[100]

The combination of martial prowess and mercy shown by Marcus is an archetype of what Machiavelli calls cruelty "well used." Harsh methods such as warfare can succeed, he says, if "done at a stroke" and then "not persisted in but . . . turned to as much utility" for the targeted populace as possible.[101] Cruelty used promiscuously leaves enmity festering that could subvert the peace. For Machiavelli, cruelty is well used when meted out quickly and sparingly against a narrow range of targets. Machiavellian practices cauterize the wound. People soon reconcile themselves to a select use of cruelty, especially if a Marcus Aurelius is in charge and abstains from new affronts. Peace prevails.

British prime minister Winston Churchill fashioned his own motto to convey the proper attitude toward martial affairs of state: "in war: resolution; in defeat: defiance; in victory: magnanimity; in peace: good will."[102] Such sentiments are a common refrain among those, like Churchill and Marcus, who manage to transmute wartime results into a better state of peace. Ideally, practitioners of peacemaking should strive to outdo Liddell Hart's dictum that grand strategy is about improving ambient conditions *for oneself*. A genuinely secure peace is agreeable to *everyone*, including the defeated. In the optimal case the loser sincerely endorses the peace settlement. But even if the defeated resign themselves to the new normal only sullenly, policing it will prove far less burdensome for the victor—and so politically acceptable to its government and people. The victor's stamina holds.

Apart from their moral worth as a guide to peacemaking, then, magnanimity and goodwill are expedients that carry enormous practical import. The architects of peace following the French Revolutionary and Napoleonic Wars approximated the ideal. Owing to their diplomatic handiwork, writes former secretary of state Henry A. Kissinger, "there was not only a physical equilibrium, but a moral one" after Napoleon's overthrow at Waterloo.[103] In other words, instituting a balance of power "reduces the opportunities for using force," convincing the defeated that no fresh challenge will succeed.[104] Meanwhile "a shared sense of justice reduces the desire to use force." The vanquished accept the new system as the way to manage international disputes. A postwar order "which is not considered just will be challenged sooner or later," Kissinger concludes.[105] The erstwhile combatants readmitted post-Napoleonic France to the fraternity of nations while fashioning a balance of power to oppose the ambitions of a new Napoleon. The peace that they negotiated at the Congress of Vienna lasted for almost a century, from 1815 until the guns of August rang out in 1914.

In a sense, then, peacemakers should regard themselves as founders. They should strive to found a new order that is amenable to all while at the same time supplying the physical power to counterbalance against future challengers. And, just as they did during the prewar and wartime phases, strategic leaders should steep themselves and their institutions in habits fit for the times and surroundings.

MONITOR THE NATURE OF THE PEACE

Keeping abreast of the nature of the political and strategic setting is an evergreen habit for strategic leaders. Strategy reverts to Wylie's cumulative state once the fighting ceases. There is no using armed force to bludgeon opponents in sequential fashion. Strategic leaders are back to flourishing armaments to win influence and cow potential opponents. Progress comes by increments. Habits congenial to the postwar world resemble those from the prewar world, except the war will have altered that world, perhaps imperceptibly in the case of a minor regional skirmish, perhaps fundamentally in the case of a system-shattering world war or a global cold war. To make sense of the new normal, there is no substitute for seeking tirelessly to know oneself, know potential allies, friends, and enemies, and know the surroundings. Consulting the masterworks of strategy and history remains the starting point for wisdom.

PREPARE FOR WAR AGAIN

And last, no matter how smashing a triumph they achieve, strategic leaders should never allow themselves to be gulled into thinking peace is perpetual. They should hope for lasting peace and do their utmost to bring it about, but they should not expect it. Chapter 2 reprimanded the U.S. Navy and Marine Corps for talking themselves into believing that naval history had ended along with the Soviet navy's demise in 1991, and that they could assume they would never again have to fight for maritime command. They more or less stopped practicing skills for sea warfare and improving their sensor and weapons technology. They exited from history just as China made its return to naval history for the first time since the Imperial Japanese Navy crushed the Qing dynasty's Northern Fleet off the Korean coast in 1895. Nor did Russia ever give up on being a naval power of note despite the economic mayhem that postponed its quest following the Soviet collapse. American complacency granted these prospective foes a strategic opportunity. They availed themselves of that opportunity with verve, closing the gap between their armed forces and the U.S. military. Whether America can regain its edge remains to be seen.

The upshot is that no victory is forever. Strategic leaders must refuse to believe that prevailing in one round of competition puts an end to competition altogether or repeals the major functions that armed forces perform. Fatalistic habits of mind and sentiment constitute the best antidote for postwar hubris, just as they do for hubris when striding onto the field of battle. Humility is central to the habits of highly effective strategists—no matter what the state of international relations happens to be.

TAKE OWNERSHIP

In the end, officers and officials must take charge of their destiny as strategists. They should regard self-improvement as an Aristotelian affair. The first teacher makes a sure guide to training their reflexes. Self-mastery, introspection, inquisitiveness, skepticism, and fatalism are innate qualities they should nurture. In turn, these habits of mind and character will help them take the right perspective on strategy, keep ends and means in alignment, manage risk and change, and revivify the ethos within institutions they superintend. Let's make the U.S. sea services a Lyceum for strategy.

NOTES

PREFACE: AN UNDISCIPLINED STUDY

1. Richard Feynman to J. M. Szabados, November 30, 1965, in Richard P. Feynman and Michelle Feynman, *Perfectly Reasonable Deviations from the Beaten Track: Letters of Richard P. Feynman* (New York: Basic Books, 2004), 206.
2. Feynman to Szabados, November 30, 1965, in Feynman, *Perfectly Reasonable Deviations from the Beaten Track*, 206.
3. Carl von Clausewitz, *On War*, trans., intro. Peter Paret and Michael Howard (Princeton: Princeton University Press, 1976), 177.
4. B. H. Liddell Hart, *Strategy*, 2d ed., rev. (1954; repr., New York: Meridian, 1991), 321–22.
5. Liddell Hart, *Strategy*, 321–22.
6. J. C. Wylie, *Military Strategy: A General Theory of Power Control*, intro. John B. Hattendorf (1967; repr., Annapolis: Naval Institute Press, 2014), 14.
7. Typical of the genre is Mark R. McNeilly, *Sun Tzu and the Art of Business: Six Strategic Principles for Managers*, rev. ed. (New York: Oxford University Press, 2011).
8. The classic account is Kenneth N. Waltz, *Man, the State, and War: A Theoretical Analysis* (New York: Columbia University Press, 1959).
9. John Keegan, *The Face of Battle* (New York: Viking, 1976), 23.

CHAPTER 1. PURSUE THE GOOD LIFE IN STRATEGY

1. Stephen R. Covey, *The 7 Habits of Highly Effective People: Restoring the Character Ethic* (1989; repr., New York: Free Press, 2004), 18–32.
2. James Clear, *Atomic Habits: An Easy & Proven Way to Build Good Habits & Break Bad Ones* (New York: Avery, 2018).
3. Covey, *The 7 Habits of Highly Effective People*, 46.
4. Ralph Waldo Emerson, "History," in *Ralph Waldo Emerson: Essays and Journals*, intro. Lewis Mumford (Garden City: Doubleday, 1968), 71–72.

5. Emerson, "History," 72.
6. Nor is it a peculiarly Western insight. While Confucius and Aristotle saw human nature in somewhat different terms, the Eastern and Western titans both preached the value of virtue. "Confucius," *Stanford Encyclopedia of Philosophy*, March 31, 2020, https://plato.stanford.edu/entries/confucius/#VirtCharForm. The philosopher Bryan Van Norden acknowledges their differences while nonetheless depicting both as purveyors of "virtue ethics." Bryan W. Van Norden, *Virtue Ethics and Consequentialism in Early Chinese Philosophy* (Cambridge, UK: Cambridge University Press, 2007).
7. Carnes Lord, "Aristotle," in Leo Strauss and Joseph Cropsey, eds., *History of Political Philosophy* (Chicago: University of Chicago Press, 1987), 118, 122; *Aristotle's Politics*, trans., intro. Carnes Lord, 2d ed. (Chicago: University of Chicago Press, 2013), xvi.
8. "Aristotle," *Stanford Encyclopedia of Philosophy*, July 29, 2015, https://plato.stanford.edu/entries/aristotle/; J. L. Ackrill, *Aristotle the Philosopher* (Oxford: Oxford University Press, 1981).
9. Lord, "Aristotle," 120.
10. Historian Arthur Herman traces the influence of Plato, the prototypical "deductive" thinker, and Aristotle, who touts the value of everyday experience, on Western society. His work is worth perusing as an aid to self-knowledge. Knowing whether one inclines toward Platonic or Aristotelian thinking could help the strategist guard against blind spots—and thus improve the making and execution of strategy and operations. Arthur Herman, *The Cave and the Light: Plato versus Aristotle, and the Struggle for the Soul of Western Civilization* (New York: Random House, 2014).
11. In a similar vein, the late professor Michael Handel notes that someone can be Clausewitzian without ever reading the works of Carl von Clausewitz. After all, much of what he wrote was applied common sense. He was as much a codifier as an originator of strategic insight. Michael I. Handel, *Masters of War: Classical Strategic Thought*, 3d ed. (London: Frank Cass, 2001), 11.

12. Lord, "Aristotle," 119.
13. Lord, "Aristotle," 119.
14. Lord, "Aristotle," 119.
15. *Aristotle's Art of Rhetoric*, trans., intro. Robert C. Bartlett (Chicago: University of Chicago Press, 2019), 22.
16. *Aristotle's Nicomachean Ethics*, trans., intro. Robert C. Bartlett and Susan D. Collins (Chicago: University of Chicago Press, 2011), 23–25.
17. Bartlett and Collins, *Aristotle's Nicomachean Ethics*, 23–25.
18. Bartlett and Collins, *Aristotle's Nicomachean Ethics*, 23–25.
19. Bartlett and Collins, *Aristotle's Nicomachean Ethics*, 23–25.
20. Bartlett and Collins, *Aristotle's Nicomachean Ethics*, 23–25.
21. Bartlett and Collins, *Aristotle's Nicomachean Ethics*, 25–26.
22. Bartlett and Collins, *Aristotle's Nicomachean Ethics*, 25–26.
23. Bartlett and Collins, *Aristotle's Nicomachean Ethics*, 25–26.
24. Bartlett and Collins, *Aristotle's Nicomachean Ethics*, 25–26.
25. Clausewitz, *On War*, 141.
26. Lord, "Aristotle," 125.
27. Bartlett and Collins, *Aristotle's Nicomachean Ethics*, 28.
28. Bartlett and Collins, *Aristotle's Nicomachean Ethics*, 28.
29. Bartlett and Collins, *Aristotle's Nicomachean Ethics*, 28–29.
30. Bartlett and Collins, *Aristotle's Nicomachean Ethics*, 28–29.
31. Theodore Roosevelt, *An Autobiography* (New York: Macmillan, 1913), 60.
32. Jordan Ellenberg, *How Not to Be Wrong: The Power of Mathematical Thinking* (New York: Penguin, 2014), 20–24.
33. Pausanias, *Description of Greece*, trans. W. H. S. Jones, 4 v. (1935; repr., Cambridge, MA: Harvard University Press, 1961), vol. 4, 507.
34. See for instance *The Landmark Herodotus*, ed. Robert B. Strassler (New York: Penguin, 2009), 466, 554–55, 558, 572.
35. Lord, *Aristotle's Politics*, 2d ed., viii.
36. Aristotle, *The Politics*, trans., intro. Carnes Lord, 1st ed. (Chicago: University of Chicago Press, 1984), 35.
37. Bartlett and Collins, *Aristotle's Nicomachean Ethics*, 27.
38. Lord, "Aristotle," 134–37.
39. Lord, *Aristotle's Politics*, 2d ed., 63.
40. Lord, *Aristotle's Politics*, 2d ed., 73.
41. Lord, *Aristotle's Politics*, 2d ed., 73–74.

42. Lord, *Aristotle's Politics*, 2d ed., 67.
43. Strassler, *Landmark Herodotus*, 224.
44. The translation comes from Harvey Mansfield, "Democracy in Trump's America: Political Lessons from an Unlikely Comparison," *City Journal*, September 1, 2019, https://www.city-journal.org/democracy-trump-tocqueville.
45. Shahram Heshmat, "Satisficing vs. Maximizing," *Psychology Today*, June 13, 2015, https://www.psychologytoday.com/us/blog/science-choice/201506/satisficing-vs-maximizing.
46. Clausewitz, *On War*, 88–89.
47. Clausewitz, *On War*, 111.
48. Clausewitz, *On War*, 88–89.
49. Lord, *Aristotle's Politics*, 2d ed., 45.
50. Lord, *Aristotle's Politics*, 2d ed., 73.
51. William James, *The Principles of Psychology*, 2 v. (New York: Henry Holt, 1890), vol. 1, 105.
52. James, *Principles of Psychology*, vol. 1, 103.
53. James, *Principles of Psychology*, vol. 1, 104.
54. James, *Principles of Psychology*, vol. 1, 105.
55. James, *Principles of Psychology*, vol. 1, 106.
56. James, *Principles of Psychology*, vol. 1, 121–22.
57. James, *Principles of Psychology*, vol. 1, 121–22.
58. James, *Principles of Psychology*, vol. 1, 112.
59. James, *Principles of Psychology*, vol. 1, 114.
60. James, *Principles of Psychology*, vol. 1, 122.
61. William Manchester, *Disturber of the Peace: The Life of H. L. Mencken* (New York: Harper, 1950), 50.
62. James, *Principles of Psychology*, vol. 1, 120.
63. James, *Principles of Psychology*, vol. 1, 121.
64. James, *Principles of Psychology*, vol. 1, 121.
65. James, *Principles of Psychology*, vol. 1, 121.
66. James, *Principles of Psychology*, vol. 1, 121.
67. James, *Principles of Psychology*, vol. 1, 122.
68. James, *Principles of Psychology*, vol. 1, 123.
69. James, *Principles of Psychology*, vol. 1, 123.
70. James, *Principles of Psychology*, vol. 1, 123.
71. James, *Principles of Psychology*, vol. 1, 123.
72. James, *Principles of Psychology*, vol. 1, 124.
73. James, *Principles of Psychology*, vol. 1, 126.

74. Clausewitz, *On War*, 131–32.
75. Clausewitz, *On War*, 131–32.
76. Sun Tzu, *The Art of War*, trans. Samuel B. Griffith (Oxford: Oxford University Press, 1963), 63.
77. B. H. Liddell Hart, *Strategy* 2d., rev. (1954; repr., New York, Meridian, 1991), 338.
78. Clausewitz, *On War*, 609.

CHAPTER 2. IN PEACE, PREPARE FOR WAR

1. Sun Tzu, *The Art of War*, trans. Samuel B. Griffith (Oxford: Oxford University Press, 1963), 77.
2. Carl von Clausewitz, *On War*, ed., trans. Peter Paret and Michael Howard (Princeton: Princeton University Press, 1976), 91.
3. Alfred Thayer Mahan, *The Problem of Asia* (Boston: Little, Brown, 1900), 29–30, 33.
4. Alfred Thayer Mahan, *The Influence of Sea Power upon History, 1660–1783* (1890; repr., Boston: Little, Brown, 1905), 22–23.
5. Craig L. Symonds, *World War II at Sea: A Global History* (Oxford: Oxford University Press, 2018), 179.
6. Clausewitz, *On War*, 131–32.
7. Clausewitz, *On War*, 131–32.
8. Clausewitz, *On War*, 131–32.
9. Mahan, *Influence of Sea Power upon History*, 26.
10. Margaret Tuttle Sprout, "Mahan: Evangelist of Sea Power," in Edward Mead Earle, ed., *Makers of Modern Strategy: From Machiavelli to Hitler* (Princeton: Princeton University Press, 1943), 415–45.
11. John Keegan, *The American Civil War* (New York: Knopf, 2009), 242.
12. Mahan, *Influence of Sea Power upon History*, vii, 70.
13. Mahan, *Influence of Sea Power upon History*, 71.
14. Mahan, *Influence of Sea Power upon History*, 71.
15. Mahan, *Influence of Sea Power upon History*, 71–72.
16. Mahan, *Influence of Sea Power upon History*, 72–73.
17. Mahan, *Influence of Sea Power upon History*, 73.
18. Mahan, *Influence of Sea Power upon History*, 73.
19. Mahan, *Influence of Sea Power upon History*, 73–74.

20. Evidently this is a case of minds running in parallel, as Professor Rodrigue reports being unfamiliar with Mahan's writings. Exchange of correspondence between the author and Jean-Paul Rodrigue, July 31, 2018.
21. Jean-Paul Rodrigue, "The Geography of Global Supply Chains," *Journal of Supply Chain Management* 48, no. 3 (July 2012): 15–23. See also John-Paul Rodrigue, ed., *The Geography of Transport Systems*, 4th ed. (London: Routledge, 2017).
22. Mahan, *Influence of Sea Power upon History*, 25.
23. Mahan, *Influence of Sea Power upon History*, 29–35.
24. Mahan, *Influence of Sea Power upon History*, 35–44.
25. Alfred Thayer Mahan, *The Interest of America in Sea Power, Present and Future* (Boston: Little, Brown, 1897), 271–314.
26. Mahan, *Influence of Sea Power upon History*, 33.
27. Mahan, *Influence of Sea Power upon History*, 44–49.
28. Mahan, *Influence of Sea Power upon History*, 44.
29. Mahan, *Influence of Sea Power upon History*, 44.
30. Mahan, *Influence of Sea Power upon History*, 49.
31. Mahan, *Influence of Sea Power upon History*, 46.
32. Mahan, *Influence of Sea Power upon History*, 48.
33. Mahan, *Influence of Sea Power upon History*, 50–58.
34. Mahan, *Influence of Sea Power upon History*, 51.
35. Mahan, *Influence of Sea Power upon History*, 51.
36. Mahan, *Influence of Sea Power upon History*, 53.
37. Wolfgang Wegener, *The Naval Strategy of the World War*, trans., intro. Holger H. Herwig (1929; repr., Annapolis: Naval Institute Press, 1989), 95–97.
38. Mahan, *Influence of Sea Power upon History*, 82.
39. Mahan, *Influence of Sea Power upon History*, 58–89.
40. Mahan, *Influence of Sea Power upon History*, 58.
41. Mahan, *Influence of Sea Power upon History*, 58.
42. Mahan, *Influence of Sea Power upon History*, 58–59.
43. Winston Churchill, *The Second World War* (New York: Houghton Mifflin, 1950), vol. 3, *The Grand Alliance*, 299.
44. Alfred Thayer Mahan, *The Life of Nelson, the Embodiment of the Sea Power of Great Britain* (Boston: Little, Brown, 1899).
45. Alfred Thayer Mahan, *Retrospect & Prospect: Studies in International Relations, Naval and Political* (Boston: Little, Brown, 1902), 19.

46. Mahan, *Retrospect & Prospect*, 19.
47. Diogenes Laertius, *The Lives and Opinions of Eminent Philosophers*, trans. C. D. Yonge (London: George Bell and Sons, 1905), 259–318.
48. Morgenthau sketches "six principles of political realism" in his classic *Politics among Nations*. Hans J. Morgenthau, *Politics among Nations: The Struggle for Power and Peace*, 5th ed., rev. (New York: Knopf, 1978), 4–15.
49. Dwight D. Eisenhower, "Address at the Second Assembly of the World Council of Churches," Evanston, Illinois, August 19, 1954, American Presidency Project Website, University of California-Santa Barbara, https://www.presidency.ucsb.edu/documents/address-the-second-assembly-the-world-council-churches-evanston-illinois.
50. *Atomic Habits* author James Clear provides a succinct rundown on this decisionmaking tool. James Clear, "How to Be More Productive and Eliminate Time Wasting Activities by Using the 'Eisenhower Box,'" https://jamesclear.com/eisenhower-box.
51. Clausewitz, *On War*, 595–96.
52. Clausewitz, *On War*, 618.
53. A common way to vet a course of action is by estimating such factors as its risks, rewards, costs, opportunity costs, feasibility, and acceptability, not to mention what an opponent may do.
54. *Seneca: Selected Philosophical Writings*, trans., intro. Brad Inman (Oxford: Oxford University Press, 2007), 25.
55. B. H. Liddell Hart, *Strategy*, 2d., rev. (1954; repr., New York: Meridian, 1991), 322.
56. Liddell Hart, *Strategy*, 338.
57. Julian S. Corbett, *England in the Seven Years' War: A Study in Combined Strategy*, 2d ed. (London: Longmans, Green, 1918), vol. 2, 376.
58. Corbett, *England in the Seven Years' War*, vol. 1, 8–9.
59. Frank McLynn, *1759: The Year Britain Became Master of the World* (New York: Atlantic, 2004).
60. Mahan, *Influence of Sea Power upon History*, 524.
61. Mahan, *Influence of Sea Power upon History*, 527–28.
62. Mahan, *Influence of Sea Power upon History*, 338–39.
63. Mahan, *Influence of Sea Power upon History*, 78.

64. Mahan, *Influence of Sea Power upon History*, 514–17.
65. Russell F. Weigley, *The American Way of War* (Bloomington: Indiana University Press, 1973), 21.
66. Mahan, *Influence of Sea Power upon History*, 387–91, 485–501.
67. Herbert Richmond, *Statesmen and Sea Power* (Oxford: Clarendon, 1946), 156–57.
68. Richmond, *Statesmen and Sea Power*, 158–59.
69. Richmond, *Statesmen and Sea Power*, 159.
70. Christopher Nelson, "Fleet Tactics Returns—A Conversation with Authors Wayne Hughes and Bob Girrier," Center for International Maritime Security Website, July 30, 2018, http://cimsec.org/fleet-tactics-returns-a-conversation-with-authors-wayne-hughes-and-bob-girrier/37040.
71. Theodore Roosevelt, "Message of the President to the Senate and the House of Representatives," December 3, 1907, in U.S. Department of State, *Foreign Relations of the United States, 1907* (Washington: Government Printing Office, 1908), lvi–lvii.
72. Julian S. Corbett, *Some Principles of Maritime Strategy*, intro. Eric J. Grove (1911; repr., Annapolis: Naval Institute Press, 1988), 16.
73. Corbett, *England in the Seven Years' War*, vol. 1, v.
74. Corbett, *Some Principles of Maritime Strategy*, 16.
75. Corbett, *England in the Seven Years' War*, vol. 1, 6.
76. Corbett, *England in the Seven Years' War*, vol. 1, 3–4.
77. Daniel W. Drezner, Ronald R. Krebs, and Randall Schweller, "The End of Grand Strategy: America Must Think Small," *Foreign Affairs*, May/June 2020, https://www.foreignaffairs.com/articles/world/2020-04-13/end-grand-strategy.
78. *Public Papers of the Presidents of the United States: Dwight D. Eisenhower, 1957* (Washington, DC: National Archives and Records Service, 1958), 818.
79. *Public Papers of the Presidents of the United States: Dwight D. Eisenhower, 1957*, 818.
80. *Public Papers of the Presidents of the United States: Dwight D. Eisenhower, 1957*, 818.
81. Clausewitz, *On War*, 134.
82. Clausewitz, *On War*, 134.

83. Clausewitz, *On War*, 572–74.
84. Nassim Nicholas Taleb, *The Black Swan: The Impact of the Highly Improbable* (New York: Random House, 2007), for instance 9–14.
85. Mahan, *Retrospect & Prospect*, 10–17.
86. Taleb, *The Black Swan*, 9–14.
87. Robert D. Kaplan, "The Return of Ancient Times: Why the Warrior Politics of the Twenty-first Century Will Demand a Pagan Ethos," *Atlantic*, June 2000, https://www.theatlantic.com/magazine/archive/2000/06/the-return-of-ancient-times/378247/.
88. Plutarch was a Roman citizen of Greek birth. He lived from around AD 46 to around AD 119 Plutarch, "Themistocles," in *The Parallel Lives*, trans. Bernadotte Perrin, 11 v. (Cambridge, MA: Harvard University Press, 1914), vol. 2, 11.
89. Plutarch, "Themistocles," 11.
90. Plutarch, "Themistocles," 11.
91. Plutarch, "Themistocles," 11–13.
92. The Greek historian Herodotus chronicles the Persian Wars. See *The Landmark Herodotus: The Histories*, trans. Andrea L. Purvis, ed. Robert B. Strassler (New York: Pantheon, 2007), 425–722. A lively recent history of the Athenian navy comes from John R. Hale, *Lords of the Sea: The Epic Story of the Athenian Navy and the Birth of Democracy* (New York: Viking, 2009).
93. Plutarch, "Themistocles," 21.
94. The reference comes from Plato's *Republic*. See Malcolm Schofield, "The Noble Lie," in *The Cambridge Companion to Plato's* Republic, ed. G. R. F. Ferrari (Cambridge, UK: Cambridge University Press, 2007), 138–64.
95. Plutarch, "Themistocles," 13.
96. See for instance Niccolò Machiavelli, *Discourses on Livy*, trans. Harvey C. Mansfield and Nathan Tarcov (Chicago: University of Chicago Press, 1996), 28–33.
97. Plutarch, "Themistocles," 9.
98. Plutarch, "Fabius Maximus," in *The Parallel Lives*, trans. Bernadotte Perrin, 11 v. (Cambridge, MA: Harvard University Press, 1916), vol. 3, 119–97; B. H. Liddell Hart, *Greater Than Napoleon: Scipio Africanus* (Boston: Little, Brown, 1927).

99. Machiavelli, *Discourses on Livy*, 240.
100. Machiavelli, *Discourses on Livy*, 239.
101. Clausewitz, *On War*, 77.
102. Machiavelli, *Discourses on Livy*, 240.
103. David Miller, ed., *Popper Selections* (Princeton: Princeton University Press, 1985), 133–42; "Karl Popper," *Stanford Encyclopedia of Philosophy*, August 7, 2018, https://plato.stanford.edu/entries/popper/.
104. This account of Sims' gunfire revolution derives from Elting E. Morison, *Men, Machines, and Modern Times* (Cambridge, MA: MIT Press, 1966), 17–44.
105. Benjamin F. Armstrong, "Continuous-Aim Fire: Learning How to Shoot," *Naval History* 29, no. 2 (April 2015), https://www.usni.org/magazines/naval-history-magazine/2015/april/continuous-aim-fire-learning-how-shoot.
106. Corbett, *Some Principles of Maritime Strategy*, xxix.
107. Bernard Brodie, *Strategy in the Missile Age* (Santa Monica: RAND, 1959), 27.
108. Michael Howard, "Men Against Fire: Expectations of War in 1914," *International Security* 9, no. 1 (Summer 1984): 41–57.
109. Francis Fukuyama, "The End of History?" *National Interest* 16 (Summer 1989): 3–18; Francis Fukuyama, *The End of History and the Last Man* (New York: Free Press, 1992).
110. U.S. Navy and Marine Corps, "... From the Sea: Preparing the Naval Service for the 21st Century," September 1992, GlobalSecurity Website, https://www.globalsecurity.org/military/library/policy/navy/fts.htm.
111. Andrew Gordon, *The Rules of the Game: Jutland and British Naval Command* (1996; repr., Annapolis: Naval Institute Press, 2000), 155–92. See also James R. Holmes, "How 'The Rules of the Game' Can Help the U.S. Navy," *National Interest*, March 30, 2017, https://nationalinterest.org/feature/how-the-rules-the-game-can-help-the-us-navy-19953.
112. Gordon, *Rules of the Game*, 155–92.
113. Miller, *Popper Selections*, 118–19.
114. Miller, *Popper Selections*, 119.
115. While Professor Eliot Cohen of Johns Hopkins University evidently coined the phrase, I am indebted to my former

colleague Bradford Lee of the Naval War College, who has done most to develop and popularize it. Officials sometimes use the phrase "theory of success" to convey the same idea in a peacetime context. By that they mean there are no military victories in peacetime.
116. Plato, "The Apology," trans. Benjamin Jowett, in Charles W. Eliot, ed., *The Harvard Classics* (1909; repr., New York: Collier, 1937), 26.
117. Edmund Burke, *Reflections on the Revolution in France* (London: George Bell, 1897), 437.
118. Burke, *Reflections on the Revolution in France*, 437.
119. Thomas Paine, *The Rights of Man*, intro. Arthur Seldon (1791–1702; repr., London: Dent, 1915).
120. Andrew W. Marshall, *Long-Term Competition with the Soviets: A Framework for Analysis* (Santa Monica: RAND, 1972).
121. Around a decade ago a team of researchers, including myself, sought to update Marshall's concepts for contemporary times. See Thomas G. Mahnken, ed., *Competitive Strategies for the 21st Century: Theory, History, and Practice* (Stanford: Stanford University Press, 2012).
122. Hal Brands, "The Lost Art of Long-Term Competition," *Washington Quarterly* 41, no. 4 (Winter 2019): 36.
123. Carnes Lord, *The Modern Prince: What Leaders Need to Know Now* (New Haven: Yale University Press, 2003), 117–18.
124. Max Weber, *Economy and Society: An Outline of Interpretive Sociology*, ed. Guenther Roth and Claus Wittich, trans. Ephraim Fischoff et al., 3 v. (New York: Bedminster Press, 1968), 223.
125. Weber, *Economy and Society*, 973.
126. Weber, *Economy and Society*, 223.
127. Weber, *Economy and Society*, 987.
128. Weber, *Economy and Society*, 988.
129. Weber, *Economy and Society*, 988.
130. Weber, *Economy and Society*, 988.
131. Weber, *Economy and Society*, 989.
132. "Meme," Merriam-Webster Online, https://www.merriam-webster.com/dictionary/meme.
133. Richard Dawkins, *The Selfish Gene* (1976; repr., Oxford: Oxford University Press, 2006).

134. Mark A. Jordan, "What's in a Meme?" Richard Dawkins Foundation for Reason & Science, February 4, 2014, https://www.richarddawkins.net/2014/02/whats-in-a-meme/.
135. On bureaucratic culture, see for instance Weber, *Economy and Society*, 215–23, and Robert W. Komer, *Bureaucracy at War: U.S. Performance in the Vietnam Conflict* (Boulder: Westview, 1986), 17–18, 43–49.
136. Since the 1980s memes imported from the business world have swept the U.S. Navy periodically, going by such slogans as "Total Quality Leadership," "Lean Six Sigma," and "Just-in-Time Logistics."
137. Irving L. Janis, *Groupthink*, 2d ed. (Boston: Houghton Mifflin, 1982), 3, 9.
138. Janis, *Groupthink*, 9.
139. Janis, *Groupthink*, 268.
140. Lord, *The Modern Prince*, 116–24.
141. "Armed Forces: Denting the Featherbed," *Time*, April 21, 1961.
142. Henry L. Stimson and McGeorge Bundy, *On Active Service in Peace and War* (New York: Harper, 1948), 506.
143. Eric Hoffer, *The Ordeal of Change* (New York: Harper, 1952), 149.
144. Hoffer, *The Ordeal of Change*, 149.
145. Hoffer, *The Ordeal of Change*, 150.
146. Hoffer, *The Ordeal of Change*, 112–16.
147. Hoffer, *The Ordeal of Change*, 114.
148. Hoffer, *The Ordeal of Change*, 115.
149. Office of the Chief of Naval Operations, "Memorandum for the Secretary," November 12, 1940, Franklin Delano Roosevelt Library Website, http://docs.fdrlibrary.marist.edu/psf/box4/a48b01.html.
150. Thomas B. Buell, *Master of Sea Power: A Biography of Fleet Admiral Ernest J. King* (1980; repr., Annapolis: Naval Institute Press, 1995), 313–14.
151. John B. Hattendorf, "Introduction," in J. C. Wylie, *Military Strategy: A General Theory of Power Control*, intro. John B. Hattendorf (1967; repr., Annapolis: Naval Institute Press, 2014), xxii.

152. J. C. Wylie, *Military Strategy: A General Theory of Power Control*, intro. John B. Hattendorf (1967; repr., Annapolis: Naval Institute Press, 2014), 12.
153. Wylie, *Military Strategy*, 12–13.
154. Mao Zedong, "Problems of Strategy in China's Revolutionary War," in *Selected Works of Mao Zedong*, vol. 1 (Beijing: Foreign Languages Press, 1954), Marxists Internet Archive, https://www.marxists.org/reference/archive/mao/selected-works/volume-1/mswv1_12.htm.
155. William Manchester, *Disturber of the Peace: The Life of H. L. Mencken*, intro. Gerald W. Johnson (New York: Harper, 1951), 43.
156. Manchester, *Disturber of the Peace*, 43.
157. "The Feynman Technique: The Best Way to Learn Anything," FS Website, https://fs.blog/2012/04/feynman-technique/.

CHAPTER 3. IN PEACE, WIN FRIENDS AND OVERAWE OPPONENTS

1. Max Fisher, "16 Most Hair-Raising General Mattis Quotes," *Atlantic*, July 9, 2010, https://www.theatlantic.com/politics/archive/2010/07/16-most-hair-raising-general-mattis-quotes/340553/.
2. Hal Brands, "Barack Obama and the Dilemmas of American Grand Strategy," *Washington Quarterly* 39, no. 4 (Winter 2017): 101.
3. Walter McDougall, *Promised Land, Crusader State: The American Encounter with the World since 1776* (Boston: Houghton Mifflin, 1997).
4. Ruhl J. Bartlett, *The Record of American Diplomacy: Documents and Readings in the History of American Foreign Relations*, 4th ed. (New York: Knopf, 1964), 181–82.
5. The classic work on the subject is Dexter Perkins, *A History of the Monroe Doctrine*, 2d ed., rev. (Boston: Little, Brown, 1963).
6. McDougall, *Promised Land, Crusader State*.
7. Walter Lippmann, *Foreign Policy: Shield of the Republic* (Boston: Little, Brown, 1943), 42.
8. Nicholas J. Spykman, *The Geography of the Peace*, ed. Helen R. Nicholl, intro. Frederick Sherwood Dunn (New York: Harcourt, Brace, 1944), 23–24.

9. Spykman, *Geography of the Peace*, 23–24.
10. Secretary Hay's note and the responses it elicited are found in Bartlett, *Record of American Diplomacy*, 409–13.
11. "A Decade of American Foreign Policy 1941–1949: The Bretton Woods Agreements," Avalon Project, Yale Law School Website, https://avalon.law.yale.edu/20th_century/decad047.asp.
12. Alfred Thayer Mahan, *Retrospect & Prospect: Studies in International Relations, Naval and Political* (Boston: Little, Brown, 1902), 246.
13. For a detailed exploration of Mahan's writings see my *Brief Guide to Maritime Strategy* (Annapolis: Naval Institute Press, 2019). Chapter 1 reviews his ideas about grand strategy.
14. Spykman, *Geography of the Peace*, 40–41.
15. Spykman, *Geography of the Peace*, 45–61. See also Nicholas J. Spykman, *America's Strategy in World Politics: The United States and the Balance of Power* (New York: Harcourt, Brace, 1942), 446–72.
16. Spykman, *Geography of the Peace*, 45–61; Spykman, *America's Strategy in World Politics*, 446–72.
17. Spykman, *Geography of the Peace*, 35, 54–61.
18. See for instance Thomas C. Schelling, *Arms and Influence* (New Haven: Yale University Press, 1967).
19. In Clausewitzian parlance, deterrence is a strategy with a negative aim, to prevent a rival from taking something away, while coercion is a strategy with a positive aim, namely to induce a rival to give something up. Henry A. Kissinger, *The Necessity for Choice: Prospects of American Foreign Policy* (New York: Harper, 1961), 12; Carl von Clausewitz, *On War*, trans. Peter Paret and Michael Howard (Princeton: Princeton University Press, 1976), 94–98.
20. Kissinger, *Necessity for Choice*, 12.
21. Kissinger, *Necessity for Choice*, 12.
22. Clausewitz, *On War*, 77.
23. Plato, *Plato in Twelve Volumes*, 12 v., vols. 10–11 trans. R. G. Bury (Cambridge, MA: Harvard University Press, 1967), vol. 10, 7.
24. Zhou was applying a common Maoist axiom to the international realm. Mao proclaimed that "politics is war without

bloodshed while war is politics with bloodshed." Zhou Enlai, quoted in *Saturday Evening Post*, March 27, 1954; Mao Tsetung, "On Protracted War," May 1938, Marxists Internet Archive, https://www.marxists.org/reference/archive/mao/selected-works/volume-2/mswv2_09.htm.
25. Colin S. Gray, "History for Strategists: British Seapower as a Relevant Past," *Journal of Strategic Studies* 17, no. 1 (March 1994): 8.
26. Terry Brighton, *Patton, Montgomery, Rommel: Masters of War* (New York: Crown, 2009), 261.
27. Clausewitz, *On War*, 127.
28. Clausewitz, *On War*, 596.
29. Clausewitz, *On War*, 606.
30. Clausewitz, *On War*, 97.
31. Clausewitz, *On War*, 95.
32. Julian S. Corbett, *Some Principles of Maritime Strategy*, intro. Eric J. Grove (1911; repr., Annapolis: Naval Institute Press, 1988), 165.
33. Edward N. Luttwak, *The Political Uses of Sea Power* (Baltimore: Johns Hopkins University Press, 1974), 10–11.
34. Luttwak, *Political Uses of Sea Power*, 11.
35. Luttwak, *Political Uses of Sea Power*, 39, 43.
36. Julian S. Corbett, *England in the Seven Years' War: A Study in Combined Strategy*, 2d ed. (London: Longmans, Green, 1918), vol. 1, 1–2.
37. Corbett, *England in the Seven Years' War*, vol. 1, 5.
38. Corbett, *England in the Seven Years' War*, vol. 1, 6.
39. Ken Booth, *Navies and Foreign Policy* (New York: Crane, Russak, 1977); Geoffrey Till, *Seapower: A Guide for the Twenty-First Century*, 4th ed. (London: Routledge, 2018).
40. Theodore Roosevelt to Henry L. Sprague, January 16, 1900, in Theodore Roosevelt, *The Letters of Theodore Roosevelt*, ed. Elting Morison et al., 8 v. (Cambridge, MA: Harvard University Press, 1951–54), vol. 2, 1141.
41. Edmund Morris, "'A Matter of Extreme Urgency': Theodore Roosevelt, Wilhelm II, and the Venezuela Crisis of 1902," *Naval War College Review* 55, no. 2 (Spring 2002), https://digital-commons.usnwc.edu/cgi/viewcontent.cgi?article=2419&context=nwc-review.

42. For a review of T.R.'s use of the Great White Fleet for diplomatic effect, see James R. Holmes, "'A Striking Thing': Leadership, Strategic Communications, and Roosevelt's Great White Fleet," *Naval War College Review* 61, no. 1 (winter 2008): 51–67.
43. Luttwak, *Political Uses of Sea Power*, 11–12.
44. Luttwak, *Political Uses of Sea Power*, 12–13.
45. Luttwak, *Political Uses of Sea Power*, 28–34.
46. Luttwak, *Political Uses of Sea Power*.
47. James R. Holmes and Toshi Yoshihara, "Small-Stick Diplomacy in the South China Sea," *National Interest*, April 23, 2012, https://nationalinterest.org/commentary/small-stick-diplomacy-the-south-china-sea-6831.
48. Hal Brands, "Paradoxes of the Gray Zone," FPRI E-Note, February 5, 2016, http://www.fpri.org/article/2016/02/paradoxes-gray-zone/.
49. *Moltke on the Art of War: Selected Writings*, ed. Daniel J. Hughes, trans. Daniel J. Hughes and Harry Bell (Novato: Presidio, 1993), 68.
50. Corbett, *Some Principles of Maritime Strategy*, 73.
51. An excellent starting point for information about Scarborough Shoal and the rest of China's island-building campaign is: "China Island Tracker," Asia Maritime Transparency Initiative, Center for Strategic and International Studies Website, https://amti.csis.org/island-tracker/china/.
52. Robert Haddick, "Salami Slicing in the South China Sea," *Foreign Policy*, August 3, 2012, https://foreignpolicy.com/2012/08/03/salami-slicing-in-the-south-china-sea/. It is worth noting that the author is not describing contested islands as a "pile of rocks" himself. Rather, he is relaying how many commentators have scoffed at their importance over the years.
53. Adam Twardowski, "At Brookings, Gen. Joseph Dunford Comments on Threats from Russia, China, North Korea, and Beyond," Brookings Institution Website, June 4, 2019, https://www.brookings.edu/blog/order-from-chaos/2019/06/04/at-brookings-gen-joseph-dunford-comments-on-threats-from-russia-china-north-korea-and-beyond/.

54. In recent years China has staked its claim in contested waters by exploring for oil there, among other methods. It does what sovereigns do in order to reinforce impressions that it is sovereign in disputed waters. See Huong Le Thu, "China's Incursion into Vietnam's EEZ and Lessons from the Past," Asia Maritime Transparency Initiative, Center for Strategic and International Studies Website, August 8, 2019, https://amti.csis.org/chinas-incursion-into-vietnams-eez-and-lessons-from-the-past/.
55. "PRC Commentator Suggests 'Cabbage' Strategy on the Second Thomas Shoal," Beijing Xinhua Domestic Service, May 30, 2013, Open Source Center-CPP20130620671001.
56. "PRC Commentator Suggests 'Cabbage' Strategy," May 30, 2013.

CHAPTER 4. IN WAR, FIGHT FOR A BETTER STATE OF PEACE

1. Alfred Thayer Mahan, *The Influence of Sea Power upon the French Revolution and Empire*, 2 v. (Boston: Little, Brown, 1892), vol. 1, iv.
2. The classic definition comes from Clausewitz, who holds that "war is simply a continuation of political intercourse, with the addition of other means. We deliberately use the phrase 'with the addition of other means' because we also want to make it clear that war in itself does not suspend political intercourse or change it into something entirely different." Clausewitz is commonly misquoted as claiming that war is an extension of politics "*by* other means" (my emphasis), which implies that political interchange stops when the shooting starts. In other words, everything is about crushing the enemy by whatever means necessary. He takes pains to show that that is not the case. Carl von Clausewitz, *On War*, trans. Michael Howard and Peter Paret (Princeton: Princeton University Press, 1976), 605. For more on the consequences of misquoting *On War*, see James R. Holmes, "Everything You Know About Clausewitz Is Wrong," *Diplomat*, November 12, 2014, https://thediplomat.com/2014/11/everything-you-know-about-clausewitz-is-wrong/.
3. B. H. Liddell Hart, *Strategy*, 2d., rev. (1954; repr. New York: Meridian, 1991), 338.

4. Clausewitz, *On War*, 89.
5. *Plato in Twelve Volumes*, 12v., vols. 10–11 trans. R. G. Bury (Cambridge, MA: Harvard University Press, 1926), vol. 10, 9.
6. Bury, *Plato in Twelve Volumes*, vol. 10, 9–11.
7. *Seneca: Moral Essays*, trans. John W. Basore, 3 v. (Cambridge, MA: Harvard University Press, 1928), vol. 1, 107.
8. Basore, *Seneca: Moral Essays*, 107.
9. Basore, *Seneca: Moral Essays*, 107.
10. Basore, *Seneca: Moral Essays*, 107.
11. Basore, *Seneca: Moral Essays*, 107.
12. Basore, *Seneca: Moral Essays*, 125.
13. Basore, *Seneca: Moral Essays*, 125.
14. Basore, *Seneca: Moral Essays*, 171–75.
15. An excellent modern summary of Stoic thought comes from Donald Robertson, *How to Think Like a Roman Emperor: The Stoic Philosophy of Marcus Aurelius* (New York: St. Martin's, 2019), 64–66.
16. Plato, *Phaedrus*, trans. Benjamin Jowett, Internet Classics Archive, http://classics.mit.edu/Plato/phaedrus.html.
17. Plato, *Phaedrus*.
18. Plato, *Phaedrus*.
19. Clausewitz, *On War*, 106.
20. Clausewitz, *On War*, 106.
21. Clausewitz, *On War*, 106.
22. Plutarch, "The Life of Alcibiades," in *The Parallel Lives*, trans. Bernadotte Perrin, 11 v. (Cambridge, MA: Harvard University Press, 1916), vol. 4, 17.
23. Robert Faulkner, *The Case for Greatness: Honorable Ambition and Its Critics* (New Haven: Yale University Press, 2007), 177.
24. Faulkner, *The Case for Greatness*, 38.
25. Plutarch, "Alcibiades," 34–37.
26. Plutarch, "Alcibiades," 42.
27. Plutarch, "Alcibiades," 50.
28. Plutarch, "Alcibiades," 40.
29. Plutarch, "Alcibiades," 45.
30. Plutarch, "Alcibiades," 45.
31. Plutarch, "Alcibiades," 45.
32. Plutarch, "Alcibiades," 45.

33. *The Landmark Thucydides: A Comprehensive Guide to the Peloponnesian War*, ed. Robert B. Strassler, intro. Victor Davis Hanson (New York: Touchstone, 1996), 478. Thucydides' account of the Sicilian campaign comes in books 6 and 7.
34. Clausewitz, *On War*, 548–49.
35. Russell Weigley, *The American Way of War: A History of United States Military Strategy and Policy* (Bloomington: Indiana University Press, 1977), 3–39.
36. Faulkner, *The Case for Greatness*, 180–82.
37. Faulkner looks to Marshall's account because the author knew Washington, but he also contends that he could make the case for Washington's virtue just as well using modern accounts such as Joseph J. Ellis, *His Excellency: George Washington* (New York: Vintage, 2004). John Marshall, *The Life of George Washington*, 3 v. (Philadelphia: G. P. Wayne, 1804), vol. 3, 127–29; Faulkner, *The Case for Greatness*, 250.
38. Marshall, *Life of George Washington*, vol. 3, 129.
39. See for instance Livy, *The Early History of Rome*, trans. Aubrey de Sélincourt, intro. R. M. Ogilvie (1960; repr., New York: Penguin, 2002), 227–30.
40. As chronicled in Paul Johnson, *George Washington: The Founding Father* (New York: Atlas, 2005), 78.
41. Clausewitz, *On War*, 89.
42. Clausewitz, *On War*, 89.
43. Clausewitz, *On War*, 89.
44. Clausewitz, *On War*, 89.
45. Clausewitz, *On War*, 89.
46. Alan Beyerchen bridges between strategy and the natural sciences to make this point. See Alan Beyerchen, "Clausewitz, Nonlinearity, and the Unpredictability of War," *International Security* 17, no. 3 (Winter 1992–93): 69.
47. Clausewitz, *On War*, 100.
48. Clausewitz, *On War*, 100.
49. Clausewitz, *On War*, 100.
50. Clausewitz, *On War*, 101–2.
51. Clausewitz, *On War*, 102.
52. Clausewitz, *On War*, 102, 104.
53. Clausewitz, *On War*, 103.

54. Clausewitz, *On War*, 111.
55. Clausewitz, *On War*, 88–89.
56. J. C. Wylie, *Military Strategy: A General Theory of Power Control*, intro. John B. Hattendorf (1967; repr., Annapolis: Naval Institute Press, 2014), 22–26.
57. Wylie, *Military Strategy*, 22–26.
58. Clausewitz, *On War*, 596.
59. David Galula, *Counterinsurgency Warfare: Theory and Practice* (1964; repr., Westport: Praeger Security International, 2006).
60. I am indebted to my colleague and friend Professor Andrew Wilson for the phrase "pentagonal analysis."
61. Sun Tzu, *The Art of War*, trans. Samuel B. Griffith (Oxford: Oxford University Press, 1963), 61–66.
62. Clausewitz, *On War*, 585–86.
63. Clausewitz, *On War*, 92.
64. Clausewitz, *On War*, 92.
65. Clausewitz, *On War*, 92.
66. Clausewitz, *On War*, 585–86.
67. On the process, see Anthony Daniel Konecny, *Net Assessment: An Examination of the Process*, M.S. thesis, Naval Postgraduate School, 1988.
68. Clausewitz, *On War*, 585–86.
69. Clausewitz, *On War*, 585–86.
70. Clausewitz, *On War*, 585–86.
71. University of Georgia professor William Stueck presents a highly readable account of the war, accenting its civil war dimension. William Stueck, *Rethinking the Korean War: A New Diplomatic and Strategic History* (Princeton: Princeton University Press, 2004).
72. Sun Tzu, *Art of War*, 66.
73. Clausewitz, *On War*, 117.
74. The phrases *scriptwriting* and *mirror-imaging* are common parlance in strategic-studies programs. They are not my own invention. They both refer to making unwarranted assumptions about antagonists. Mirror-imaging refers to the practice of assuming everyone sees the world the same, and thus will interpret and respond to events the same way the strategist does. This is a recipe for self-imposed surprise.

75. Mark Morris, "AirSea Battle vs. Offshore Control: Which Has a Better Theory of Victory?" *War on the Rocks*, November 26, 2013, https://warontherocks.com/2013/11/airsea-battle-vs-offshore-control-which-has-a-better-theory-of-victory/.
76. J. Boone Bartholomees, "Theory of Victory," *Parameters* 32, no. 8 (Summer 2008): 25–36.
77. Clausewitz, *On War*, 77.
78. Bradley A. Fiske, *The Navy as a Fighting Machine* (New York: Scribner, 1916), 150.
79. Sun Tzu, *Art of War*, 91–92.
80. Sun Tzu, *Art of War*, 91.
81. Sun Tzu, *Art of War*, 137.
82. Sun Tzu, *Art of War*, 92.
83. Clausewitz, *On War*, 546–47.
84. Robert L. Leahy, "Letting Go of Sunk Costs," *Psychology Today*, September 24, 2014, https://www.psychologytoday.com/us/blog/anxiety-files/201409/letting-go-sunk-costs.
85. Plutarch, "Pyrrhus," in *The Parallel Lives*, trans. Bernadotte Perrin, 11v. (Cambridge, MA: Harvard University Press, 1920), 367.
86. Plutarch, "Pyrrhus," 417.
87. Here I am indebted to my friend and former teaching partner, Cdr. Kevin Delamer, who postulates that victory generally goes to the contender able to regenerate strength after the shock of battle.
88. Edward N. Luttwak, *Strategy: The Logic of War and Peace*, 2d ed. (Cambridge, MA: Harvard University Press, 2001), 3, 16–17, 20, 50, 147.
89. Clausewitz, *On War*, 204.
90. Clausewitz, *On War*, 204.
91. Alfred Thayer Mahan, *The Interest of America in Sea Power, Present and Future* (Boston: Little, Brown, 1897), 198.
92. Sun Tzu, *Art of War*, 93.
93. John R. Boyd, *A Discourse on Winning and Losing*, ed. Grant T. Hammond (Maxwell AFB: Air University Press, 2018), 20–21.
94. Alfred Thayer Mahan, *The Influence of Sea Power upon History, 1660–1783* (1890; repr., Boston: Little, Brown, 1905), 59.
95. Mahan, *Influence of Sea Power upon History*, 78–79.

96. Quoted in Mahan, *Influence of Sea Power upon History*, 80–81.
97. Mahan, *Influence of Sea Power upon History*, 82.
98. Bernard Brodie, *A Guide to Naval Strategy* (Princeton: Princeton University Press, 1944), 250–53.
99. He counsels: "Absolute, so-called mathematical, factors never find a firm basis in military calculations. . . . In the whole range of human activities, war most closely resembles a game of cards." Clausewitz, *On War*, 86.
100. Robertson, *How to Think Like a Roman Emperor*, 250.
101. Niccolò Machiavelli, *The Prince*, trans. Harvey Mansfield (Chicago: University of Chicago Press, 1998), 37–38.
102. Winston S. Churchill, *Their Finest Hour* (Boston: Houghton Mifflin, 1949), frontispiece.
103. Henry A. Kissinger, *Diplomacy* (New York: Simon & Schuster, 1994), 79.
104. Kissinger, *Diplomacy*, 79.
105. Kissinger, *Diplomacy*, 79.

INDEX

active defense strategy, 79, 95–96, 145
Adams, John Quincy, 83
adaptation. *See* change
Agis, King of Sparta, 120
air forces: joint operations and, 49–50; war involving, 131
Alcibiades: on conquest of Sicily, 120–21; lack of self-mastery of, 119–20; lawless self-indulgence of, 118; Washington compared with, 125
Alexander the Great, 140
alliance builder and manager, U.S. as, 88
allies, Clausewitz on nature of a war and, 134
American Independence, War of, 44, 46, 47
aristocracy, Aristotle on virtue and rule by, 12, 13
Aristotle: on balancing rational and nonrational elements of the soul, 127; Herman on Plato on strategy vs., 152n10; on human nature, 152n6; on importance of habit, 2; on individual virtue through habit, 6–10; joint operations and, 49; on organizational regimes, 15–16; on personal regimens, 19; philosophy of practical sciences and, 4–6; on political regimes and collective habits, 10–15; on priority setting, 137; on prudence, 112; on study of war, 21; on tailoring message to readers/listeners, 77; on virtues worth making second nature, 38
armed conflict, phase before, strategists and, 21
armed suasion, 96. *See also* naval suasion
army, Corbett on joint operations and, 49
Artemisium, Battle of (480 BC), 53
Arthashastra (Kautilya), viii
artillery ranges: continuous-aim firing and, 59–60; technology advances in, 47
Asculum, Battle of (279 BC), 140
Athens: Alcibiades and, 119–20, 121; classical, as "buoyant and even frivolous" epoch, 75; founding a navy in, 54
Atomic Habits (Clear), 1, 157n50
authoritative regimes or autocracies: Aristotle on virtue and rule by, 12; Hoffer on operational excellence and, 75; Machiavelli on republics vs., 55–56; Mahan on Colbert in France under, 29; national character or culture and, 34. *See also* Louis XIV of France

Bain, Alexander, 18–19
Beyerchen, Alan, 169n46
Bezos, Jeff, 9
big stick diplomacy, 99–103
biography, study of strategy and, 2–4
black swan metaphor, forecasting and, 51
Book of Five Rings (Musashi), viii
Booth, Ken, 100
Boyd, John R., 143, 145
Brands, Hal, 67, 82, 103–4

174 • Index

Britain: Battle of Bunker Hill as meme and, 70–71; French sea warfare with, 37; late eighteenth century naval policy, 42–45; seafaring work in great age of sail and, 33. *See also* Royal Navy

Brodie, Bernard, 61, 72, 145

builders of armed forces, strategic leaders as, 25

Bunker Hill, Battle of (1775), 70–71

Bureau of Ordnance, Sims on continuous-aim firing and, 60

bureaucracy (bureaucratic institutions): Hoffer on change in, 74–76; memes interfering with clash among ideas of, 70–71; as organizational administrative model, 68; as organizational regimes, 16; shortcomings of, 68–69. *See also* military institutions

Burke, Edmund, 65

cabbage strategy, as Chinese small-stick diplomacy, 108–9, 166–67n54

Canada, United States and Mexico and, 92

cards in a casino, cutting, Clausewitz on failure as an option and, 146, 172n99

Cassius, Avidius, 147

center of gravity, Clausewitz on enemy's, 40, 139

chance and creativity, Clausewitz on societies and, 14, 126, 133–34

change: habits and, 18–19; institutional leadership and, 73–74; managing, 142–45

character ethic, Covey on, 1

China, People's Republic of: active defense strategy of, 79; cabbage strategy, 108–9, 166–67n54; end of the Cold War and, 62–63, 149; geopolitical aspirations and cultural inventiveness of, 67, 161n121; gray-zone operations and, 105–7; joint forces of, 48–49; Korean War (1950–1953) and, 135; PLA Navy and gray-zone operations of, 109–10; small-stick diplomacy and, 103; U.S. foreign policy and, 85

Churchill, Winston, 148

Cincinnatus, statesmanship of, 124

Civil War, Mahan on population density and, 32–33

Clausewitz, Carl von: on assessing nature of a war, 132–33, 135; on components of societies, 14; on desire for honor, 122; on dividing forces, 138–39; Europeans relying on maxims attributed to, 61; on failure as option, 146; on fear of opponent, 57; on force and statecraft, 93–94; on forceful passion and war, 125–26; on forces for the place, time, and opponent, 141–42; framework for strategy of, ix; Handel on applied common sense of, 152n11; on intelligence reports of enemy, 136–37; on normal and extraordinary forces, 138; on peacekeeping resources, 146–47; on personal passions, 114–15; on principles, rules, or systems of war, 50–51; priority setting by, 40; on self-control, 115–16, 118; on self-education, 7; on sequential approach of preparation, 20; on sequential campaigning, 130; on status quo strategy, 85; on strength and situation of opponent, 133–34; on striving for military genius, 114; Sun Tzu's insights on priority setting and, 141; on understanding nature of war,

129–30; on war, 167n2; on winning a war, 24, 27
Clear, James, 1, 157n50
Clinias, 115
coalitions, Clausewitz on nature of a war and, 134
coercion, Kissinger on deterrence and, 89–90
Colbert, Jean-Baptiste, 28–29
Cold War, 62–63, 67, 85, 135. *See also* Soviet Union
combat, Clausewitz on idea of, 94–95
command, Sun Tzu's pentagonal approach to war and, 131
common sense, Aristotle on, 4, 5
communication, clarity of, during peacetime, 76–80
competition: force design and, 65–67. *See also* peacetime strategic competition
Confucius, 152n6
Congress: as audience, 76–77; strategic decisions and, 78–79
Congress of Vienna (1815), 148
Conolly, Richard L., 78
continuous-aim firing, Sims' use of, 59–60
Copernicus, Nicolaus, 58
Corbett, Julian: on active defense, 95–96, 145; on army and navy in plan of war, 49; on function of the fleet, 99–100; on gray-zone operations, 104, 105, 109; on operational offense at all times, 144–45; on orthodoxy in offensive operations, 60–61; on peace after Seven Years' War, 42
Cornwallis, Charles, at Yorktown, 45–46, 140
cost-benefit analysis, 133, 139, 147
courage: Aristotle on habituation and, 8–9; Clausewitz on types of, 127–28; mean between excess and deficiency and, 10
Covey, Stephen R., 1–2

critical thinking, on virtues, vices, and habits lists of others, 10
cruelty well used, Machiavelli on, 147
crusader state, United States as, 84, 87
culture: Mahan on sea power and, 37; Marshall on strategic framing and, 67, 161n121
cumulative operations: Wylie on, xiii–xiv, 107–8, 130. *See also* gray-zone operations
Cunningham, Browne, 36

Darwin, Charles, 70
Dawkins, Richard, 69–70, 71, 73
deficiency and excess, Aristotle on mean between, 8, 9–10
democracy, Aristotle on virtue and rule by, 12
demographics, Mahan on sea power and, 32–33
deterrence: Clausewitz on, 164n19; Kissinger on coercion and, 89–90; reassurance and, 91
devil's advocates, to counter groupthink, 73
diplomacy, defeated foes and, 147
diplomatic institutions, Mahan on sea power and, 36
doctrine, Sun Tzu's pentagonal approach to war and, 131
Dunford, Joseph, 107
duration, Clausewitz on nature of a war and, 132–33

education: Aristotle on forming virtue and, 7; Clausewitz on, 7–8
Eisenhower, Dwight D., 39–40, 50, 157n50
Elizabethan England, as "buoyant and even frivolous" epoch, 75
Ellenberg, Jordan S., 9
Emerson, Ralph Waldo, 2
emotion: as psychological propellant, 126. *See also* passions

"End of History, The" (Fukuyama), 62
ends: keeping ways and means in alignment with, 38–47; Wylie's definition of, x
endurance, Clausewitz on navigating climate of war and, 128
enemy respect, nature of war and, 135–37
English, plain, for communication, 79
enlightenment: Holmes sources of, vii
Enlightenment, as "buoyant and even frivolous" epoch, 75
Europe, Clausewitz on ground war in, 131
excess and deficiency, Aristotle on mean between, 8, 9–10
extent of territory, country's, 32
extraordinary forces, Sun Tzu on, 138

Fabius Maximus, "the Delayer," 55
fast transients, Boyd on imposing change and, 143
fatalism: ownership of destiny and, 150; peacetime strategic competition and, 92
Faulkner, Robert K., 119, 121, 122–23, 125, 169n37
Feynman, Richard P., vii, ix, 76, 79–80
Fiske, Bradley, 137
fleet exercises, seaborne fighting power and, 96
fog of war, Clausewitz on inner light leading through, 128
football, study of strategy in, 3–4
force design: competition and, 65; Marshall on opportunity costs and, 66
foreign policy: Monroe Doctrine on, 83–84; Panama Canal and, 84–85

foresight: anxious, as habit, 64–65; anxious, Kaplan on, 52, 56–57; anxious, peacetime strategic competition and, 92; Clausewitz on, 50–51; Eisenhower on, 50, 51; end of the Cold War and, 62–63; fealty to paradigms and, 61–62; Kuhn on paradigms and, 58, 59, 60; Machiavelli on republics and, 54–56; opposition to change and, 57–58; projecting the past and, 51–52; Themistocles and, 52–54; U.S. strategy and, 26. *See also* strategy
founders, peacemakers as, 148–49
France: British sea warfare with, 37; building up sea power and maritime culture in, 28–29; naval policy of defensive tactics and strategy, 144; peacemaking after Waterloo for, 148. *See also* Napoleonic Wars
Frederick the Great, ix
French Revolution, 45, 131, 148
". . . From the Sea" (U.S. Navy), 62, 64
Fukuyama, Francis, 62

general, Sun Tzu on moral influence of army's fighting spirit and, 131
genius, military: Clausewitz on, 114; Clausewitz on becoming, 127–29
geographic position, Mahan on sea power and, 31
George III, King, 125
Gerald R. Ford, 15
girdle of marginal seas, Spykman on, 87–88
global wars, 131
goals, vital vs. nonvital, 39–40
golden mean, Aristotles': between excess and deficiency, 9–10; in foresight, 54–56; in jointness, 49–50

good life in strategy: for ancient philosophers, 4–6; Aristotle on individual virtue through habit, 6–10; Aristotle on political regimes and collective habits and, 10–15; biographies depicting, 1–4; long view of, 22; for modern philosophers, 16–19; organizational regimes and, 15–16; phased approach to, 19–22
Gordon, Andrew, 63–64, 65
government: Aristotle on political regimes and, 11–12; Mahan on sea power and character of, 35–36. *See also* military institutions; political regimes
grand strategy: American, 82–89; Liddell Hart on, ix, 21
Grant, Ulysses S., 2
gray-zone operations: peacetime strategic competition and, 103–5; sequential and cumulative operations and, 107–8; in South China Sea, 105–7
Great Britain. *See* Britain
Great Depression, 25–26
Greek city-states: divine counsel sought by, 11; warfare and, 5–6
groupthink, 72, 73, 145
gumption, Clausewitz on military genius and, 128

habits: of anxious foresight, 64; armed debate and, 98; change and, 18–19; James on philosophy of, 16–17; of peacetime strategic competition, 111; reform over time of, 60–61. *See also* good life in strategy
Handel, Michael I., 152n11
Hannibal, 55, 140
Hay, John, 86
Herman, Arthur, 152n10
Herodotus, 13, 159n92
Hippocratic Oath, strategic, 16

Histories (Herodotus), 11
history, study of, rhetorical fluency and, 78
Hoffer, Eric, 74–76
humility: forecasting future trends and, 64; habits of highly effective strategists and, 150; rejecting triumphalism and, 146

Imperial Japanese Navy, 71, 101, 145, 149. *See also* Japan
Influence of Sea Power upon History, 1660–1783, The (Mahan), 27
insider language, problems with, 78–79
intellect (habits of the mind), Aristotle on, 38
intellectual virtue: Aristotle on moral virtue vs., 7; Clausewitz on, 7–8
internal wars, 131
introspection: ownership of destiny and, 150; priority setting and, 141. *See also* reflection
intuition: Clausewitz on military genius and, 128; refining, priority setting and, 137

Jackson, Lamar, 3
James, William, 16–17, 18–19
Janis, Irving, 72, 73
Japan: Battle of Tsushima Strait as meme and, 71; Korean War (1950–1953) and, 135; Pacific Ocean of United States and, 85. *See also* Imperial Japanese Navy
joint operations, 47–50
Jutland, Battle of (1916), 63

Kaplan, Robert, 52, 56, 92
Keegan, John, xii–xiii, 28
King, Ernest J., 77
kingship, Aristotle on virtue and rule by, 12

Kissinger, Henry A., 89–91, 93, 95, 96, 148
Korean War (1950–1953), 134–35, 170n71
Kuhn, Thomas, 58, 59, 60, 72

Laertius, Diogenes, 38
Laws (Plato's dialogue on), 92, 115
lee of previous triumph, Gordon on, 63–64
Leonidas, King of Sparta, 129
levels of analysis, Holmes's approach to, xii
Leyte Gulf, Battle of (1944), 64, 113
Liddell Hart, Basil H.: on grand strategy from peacetime to wartime, 113; grand strategy of, ix, 21; Mahan's vision compared with, 28; on military genius, 128; on peacemaking, 148; on postwar order, 113–14; on war preparations as about peace, 41–42
lies, Themistocles use of, 53–54
Life of George Washington (Marshall), 123–24
limited political wars, 130
Lippmann, Walter, 84
Lives and Opinions of Eminent Philosophers (Laertius), 38
Lord, Carnes, 4, 5, 8, 68, 73–74
Louis XIV of France ("Sun King"), 28–29, 36
Luttwak, Edward, 96, 101–2, 140
Lyceum, in Athens, Greece, 4

Machiavelli, Niccolò: on cruelty well used, 147; on habits and change, 18; on individual's inability to change, 57; on managing change, 142; on republics and change, 54–56; on subduing a bureaucratic organization, 73–74

magnets, Clausewitz on elements of war compared to, 126–27, 169n46
magnitude of sacrifices, Clausewitz on nature of a war and, 132–33
Mahan, Alfred Thayer: on British vs. French at Trafalgar, 144; on building parallel supply chains, 29–30; on chain of sea power, 28–29; on character of government and sea power, 35–36; on forces for the place, time, and opponent, 141; on historical trends and forecasting, 51; on maritime strategy in peace and war, 24; on national character, 34–35; on peacetime forces, 33–34; on peacetime preparations for war, 27–28; on sea-oriented grand strategy, 86; on shaping opinion, 95–98; on war, 112
Mahomes, Patrick, 3
Manchester, William, 17–18
Manila Bay, Battle of (1898), 59
Mao Zedong, 79, 113, 164–65n24
Marathon, Battle of (490 BC), 52
Marcus Aurelius, 116, 117, 147
Marine Corps, 62–63, 107, 149–50
Maritime Strategy, 82
Marshall, Andrew, 66
Marshall, John, 123–24
Mattis, James N., 82
maxims: paradigms, memes and, 72; paradigms of bureaucratic dysfunction and, 69–70
McClellan, George B., 3
McDougall, Walter, 83, 87
McKinley, William, 84, 86
McLynn, Frank, 43
measures or measurements, Wylie's definition of, xi
memes: of bureaucratic dysfunction, Dawkins on, 69–70; from business, U.S. Navy and,

162n136; military, examples of, 70–71; paradigms, maxims and, 72
Mencken, H. L., 17–18, 79
Mexico, United States and Canada and, 92
Microsoft, 15
Midway, Battle of, 26, 145
military institutions: challenging memes in, 73–74; groupthink in, 72–73; Mahan on sea power and, 36–37; peacetime design and care for, 68–76. *See also* bureaucracy
military power, in battlefield strategy, 141–42
Military Strategy (Wylie), 78–79
Miller, J. Roscoe, 39
mirror-imaging, use of term, 170n74
moderation, Aristotle on, 8
Moltke, Helmuth von, the Elder, 104, 105, 108, 109
Monroe, James, 83
Monroe Doctrine, 83, 85, 101
Montesquieu (Charles-Louis de Secondat), 13
moral courage, 41
moral virtue, 7–8
Morgenthau, Hans, 39–40, 157n48
Morison, Elting, 59, 60
Musashi, Miyamoto, viii
muscle memory, strategic way of mind and, 3
Myeongyang, Battle of (AD 1597), 129

Napoleon Bonaparte, ix
Napoleonic Wars, 45, 131, 148
national character, Mahan on sea power and, 34–35
National Defense Strategy, 82
National Military Strategy, 82
National Security Strategy, 82
natural resources, in North America vs. European nations, 27–28
naval power. See sea power
naval suasion: Corbett on function of the fleet and, 99–100; Luttwak on, 96–97; ship design and maintenance and, 97–98
Naval War College, 78
Navy, U.S.: as bureaucracy, 74; as communicators during World War II, 77; end of the Cold War and, 62–63, 149–50; first battle fleet of, 84; Great White Fleet's world cruise, 101; malign effects of previous triumphs for, 64; memes imported from business world and, 162n136
Nelson, Horatio, 37, 47
Nicias, 119, 121
Nimitz, Chester, 145
normal forces, Sun Tzu on, 138

offensive-mindedness, French sea warfare and, 37
oligarchy, Aristotle on virtue and rule by, 12
On War (Clausewitz), 7, 24, 114, 132
Open Door policy, U.S., 86–87
opportunity costs, Marshall on hardware investments and, 66
Ordeal of Change, The (Hoffer), 74
Oregon, 84
organizational regimes, Aristotle on, 15–16

Pacific Ocean, U.S.-Japanese contest over, 85
Panama Canal, 31, 32, 84–85
paradigms: bureaucratic dysfunction and, 69–70; dangers of fealty to, 61–62; Kuhn on anomalies to, 58, 59; Kuhn on shifts in, 60; maxims, memes, and, 72

paradoxical trinity, Clausewitz on, 14, 126, 133–34
passions: Clausewitz on societies and, 14, 126, 133–34; communal, mastering, 125–27; personal, mastering, war and, 114–25; priority setting and, 137; rethinking priorities and, 139
past, projecting the future on, 51–52
Patton, George S., 93
Peace of Nicias, Peloponnesian War (431–404 BC) and, 119
peacetime (peace): clear communication during, 76–80; competing through force design during, 65–67; constructing, close of war and, 146–49; design and care for institutions during, 68–76; exercising foresight during, 50–65; Mahan on forces needed during, 33–34; Mahan on preparations for war during, 27–28; monitoring the nature of, 149; thinking jointly during, 47–50; war as amending of, 113–14; war preparation during, 23–25. *See also* sea power
peacetime strategic competition: American grand strategy and, 82–89; big-stick diplomacy and, 99–103; deterrence, coercion, and reassurance and, 89–91; effects of, 110–11; idea of fighting and, 91–95; overview, 81–82; shaping opinion and, 95–98; small-stick diplomacy and, 103–10
Pellew, Edward, 33
Peloponnesian War (431–404 BC), 118, 119
People's Liberation Army Navy (PLA Navy), 109–10
Pericles, 120

Persia, Themistocles' preparations against, 52–53, 159n92
Phaedrus (Plato), 117
Philippines, 84, 105–6
physical conformation, country's, Mahan on sea power and, 32
pioneering spirit, American, change in military institutions and, 74–75
Pitt, William, the Elder, 43, 47
Pitt, William, the Younger, 46–47
"Plan DOG" memorandum, Stark's, 77
plan of action, Wylie's definition of, x
Plato, 53, 115, 152n10
Plutarch: on Alcibiades' hopes to dominate Mediterranean basin, 121; on Alcibiades' lust for honor and fame, 119–20; brief biography, 159n88; on Hannibal exalting Pyrrhus, 140; on lawless self-indulgence, 118; on Themistocles against Persians, 52, 53, 54
political goals: Clausewitz on forces for, 141–42; Clausewitz on nature of a war and, 132–33
political regimes: Aristotle on collective habits and, 10–15; Aristotle on combatants' power relative to each other, 133–34. *See also* government
politics: Aristotle on, 4–5, 6; realism in, Morgenthau on principles of, 157n48
polity, Aristotle on virtue and rule by, 12
Popper, Karl, 57, 64
population density, Mahan on sea power and, 32
power, Holmes on strategy and, xi
practical wisdom, Aristotle on, 4, 5
presence of mind, Clausewitz on navigating climate of war and, 128

Principles of Psychology (James), 16–17
priority setting, 39–41, 137–41, 157n50, 157n53
promised land, early United States as, 83–84
prudence, Clausewitz on military genius and, 128
psychology, of bureaucratic dysfunction, 69–70
purpose, Wylie's definition of, x
Pyrrhic victory, 140
Pyrrhus, king of Epirus, 139–40

rationality: Clausewitz on mastering personal passions and, 115; Clausewitz on societies and, 14, 126, 133–34; passion, war and, 126; priority setting and, 137
reassurance, peacetime strategic competition and, 89, 90–91
reflection: strategic, preparation through, 3. *See also* habits; introspection
Renaissance, as "buoyant and even frivolous" epoch, 75
repetition, strategic, preparation through, 3–4, 19
republics, Machiavelli on change and, 55–56
Retrospect & Prospect (Mahan), 51
revolt of the admirals, navy officials' communications and, 77–78
reward, risk, resources (Clausewitz's Three R's), 40, 139, 157n53
Rhetoric (Aristotle), 6, 77
Richmond, Herbert, 46–47
rimlands: geographic position and, 31; U.S.'s geopolitical balancing in, 87
Robertson, Donald J., 147
Rodrigue, Jean-Paul, 30, 156n20
Roosevelt, Franklin, 74
Roosevelt, Theodore, 9, 48, 60, 100–101
Royal Navy: Mahan on, after Seven Years' War, 43–45; malign effects of previous triumph for, 63; maritime culture of energy, daring, and enterprise and, 143–44; rimlands strategy of, 87–88; symbolic power of, 102. *See also* Britain
Russia (Russian Federation), 103, 149–50

Saintes, Battle of the (1782), 45, 46
Salamis, Battle of (480 BC), 53–54
Santiago, Battle of (1898), 59
Saratoga, Battle of (1777), 124
Schelling, Thomas C., 89
scientific method, Popper on, 57
Scipio Africanus, 55, 140
Scott, Percy M., 59
scriptwriting: as deficiency of respect for the enemy, 136–37; use of term, 170n74
sea power: failure to understand or explain, 78; France's need for, 28–29; Mahan on attributes of, 31–36; Mahan on components of, 29–30; nonmilitary shipping and, 110; as option for United States, 27–28; weapons technology and, 47–48
self-discipline, keeping ways and means in alignment with ends and, 38–39
self-improvement, James on change and, 18–19
Selfish Gene, The (Dawkins), 69–70
self-mastery: Alcibiades' lack of, 118, 119–20; Aristotle on, 6; collective or group, 125–27; ownership of destiny and, 150; rethinking priorities and, 139;

as virtue of temperament, 115. *See also* Stoics
Seneca, 41, 116, 117
senior-most military commanders, Clausewitz on political regimes and, 14
sequential approach, strategic habits and, 19–20
sequential operations: Wylie on, xiii–xiv, 107–8, 130. *See also* gray-zone operations
7 Habits of Highly Effective People, The (Covey), 1
Seven Years' War (1756–1763), 42, 43–45, 62
ship design, public perception of, 97–98
shore-based defenses, weapons technology and, 48
Sicily: Alcibiades on invasion of, 120, 121; Athenian assembly on, 122
Sims, William S., 59–60
Sino-Japanese War (1894–1895), 149
skepticism: of Aristotelian strategists, 140; of maxims, 61; ownership of destiny and, 150
small-stick diplomacy: China's cabbage strategy and, 108–9, 166–67n54; gray-zone operations and, 103–5; sequential and cumulative operations in, 107–8; in South China Sea, 105–7
societies, Clausewitz on components of, 14
Socrates, 65, 117–18, 125
South China Sea: China's island-building campaign in, 166n51; gray-zone operations in, 105–7, 166n52; sequential and cumulative operations in, 107–8
Soviet Union: appearance of Navy vessels of, 97–98; at end of Cold War, 62; Korean War (1950–1953) and, 135; Marshall on Russian way of war for, 67; Marshall on U.S. hardware investments vs., 66; U.S. foreign policy and, 85. *See also* Russia
Spain, Mahan on national character of, 34
Spanish-American War, 84
Sparta: Alcibiades and, 120; Aristotle on military oligarchy in, 12–13
Spirit of the Laws, The (Montesquieu), 13
Spruance, Raymond A., 2
Spykman, Nicholas, 31, 85, 87
Stark, Harold R., 77
statecraft, defeated foes and, 147
status quo strategy, U.S., 85–86, 88
staunchness, Clausewitz on navigating climate of war and, 128
stewardship: Aristotle on organizational regimes and, 15; cultural, 145; institutional, for strategic leaders, 76; of institutional culture, 68; Monroe Doctrine and, 83. *See also* military institutions
Stimson, Henry, 74
Stoics, 38, 116–17, 118, 125. *See also* Seneca
strategic leaders: Clausewitz on becoming, 127–29; Clausewitz on cost-benefit logic of, 133; institutional stewardship for, 76; managing passion, chance and creativity, and rationality, 126; ownership of destiny as, 150; triumphalism rejected by, 145–46; as warrior diplomats, 25
strategic leadership: habits associated with, vii, 21; self-mastery and, 118
strategic narrative: function of, 76–77; plain English for, 79

Index • **183**

strategy: Aristotle on practical sciences and, 5–6; Holmes' definition of, xi; Holmes' qualifiers and disclaimers on, xii; plainspoken language as habit and, 80; priority setting and, 137; as storytelling, 76–80; Sun Tzu on division of forces and effort and, 138; as theory of cause-and-effect, 58–59. *See also* good life in strategy
Strategy in the Missile Age (Brodie), 61
Structure of Scientific Revolutions, The (Kuhn), 58
Stueck, William, 170n71
subordination, as instrument of policy, Clausewitz on, 14, 126
Sun Tzu: on assessing nature of a war, 135; Clausewitzian insights on priority setting and, 141; on dividing forces, 138–39; on the enemy, 135–36, 137; on evaluating forces on likely battlegrounds, 131–32; on imposing change, 142–43; on military genius, 128; no discussion of raising a force by, 27; on study of war, 20–21; on winning without fighting, 23–24
sunk costs, rethinking priorities and, 139
supply chains: Mahan vs. economists on, 30–31; for maritime commerce and naval power, 27; parallel, Mahan on building, 29–30
Syracuse: Athenians fighting against, 122. *See also* Sicily

tactics, Sun Tzu on division of forces and effort and, 138
Taleb, Nassim Nicholas, 51
talking trash, foreign policy and, 91

technology: advances in, major engagements and, 145–46; weapons, advances in, 47–48
temperament: of Alcibiades, Faulkner on, 119; Clausewitz on genius and, 114, 127; habits of, 38; refinement of, 89; self-mastery and, 115
terrain, Sun Tzu's pentagonal approach to war and, 131–32
Themistocles, 52–54
Thermopylae, Battle of (480 BC), 129
Thucydides, 118, 120, 122
Till, Geoffrey, 100
trade reciprocity, Mahan on sea power and, 37
Trafalgar, Battle of (1805), 37, 63, 113, 144
trauma, jolting institutions out of obsolescent ways by, 73
triumphalism, rejecting, as habit of mind, 145–46
Truman, Harry, 134
Tryon, George, 63
Tsushima Strait, Battle of (1905), 71, 113
Two-Ocean Navy Act (1940), 25–26
tyranny, Aristotle on virtue and rule by, 12

United Nations Security Council coalition, Korean War (1950–1953) and, 134, 135
United States: countering China's small-stick diplomacy by, 110; end of the Cold War and, 62–63; gray-zone operations in South China Sea and, 106–7; Korean War (1950–1953) and, 135; Marshall on Soviet Union hardware investments vs., 66; Mexico and Canada and, 92; peacetime forces for, 34; sea power as option for, 27–28. *See also* Navy, U.S.

Van Norden, Bryan W., 152n6
vertical launch systems (VLS), Cold War and, 97–98
Victoria, HMS, 63
victory: constructing a better peace after, 146–49; strategic, regenerating combat power and, 140, 171n87; theory of, strategists on resources allotted and, 65; theory of, use of phrase, 160–61n115
Vietnam's exclusive economic zone, China's cabbage strategy and, 109, 166–67n54
Villeneuve, Pierre-Charles, 144
Vinson, Carl, 25, 26, 52
viral, memes going, adaptability of institutions and, 70
Virginia Capes, Battle of the (1781), 45
virtue: Aristotle on political regimes and collective habits and, 12, 14–15; individual, through habit, 6–10; practicing, as matter of routine, 2

war: classifications for, 130–31; Clausewitz on military genius for, 114; configuring forces for, 141–42; constructing a better peace in victory in, 146–49; definition of, Clausewitz on, 167n2; dominant tendencies during, 126; fashioning instruments of, 25–37; managing change and, 142–45; mastering communal passions and, 125–27; mastering personal passions and, 114–25; monitoring the nature of peace after, 149; nature of, interpreting and reinterpreting, 129–35; overview of peacetime strategy and, 112–14; preparing again for, 149–50; priority setting, enforcing, or rethinking, 137–41; rejecting triumphalism in, 145–46; respecting the foe during, 135–37; strategic leadership during, 21; training the inner eye or inward fire for, 127–29; winning without fighting, 23–25. *See also* gray-zone operations; victory
warrior diplomats, strategic leaders as, 25
Washington, George: Cincinnatus compared with, 124–25; as exemplar for American strategists, 2; Faulkner on self-mastery of, 122–23, 125, 169n37; two-pronged British attacks and, 123–24
Waterloo, peacemaking after, 148
weapons technology advances, 47
weather, Sun Tzu's pentagonal approach to war and, 131–32
Weber, Max, 68, 69, 70
Wegener, Wolfgang, 35
Weigley, Russell, 45
Wellington, Duke of, 18
West, Benjamin, 125
World War II, U.S. Two-Ocean Navy Act (1940) and, 25–26
Wylie, Joseph C.: generic definition of strategy by, x–xi; on insider language and communication, 78–79; on peace as cumulative state, 149; on rhetorical deficit among navy officials, 77–78; on sequential and cumulative operations, xiii–xiv, 107–8, 130

Yi Sun-sin, 129
Yorktown, Cornwallis' army at, 45–46

Zama, Battle of (202 BC), 55
Zeno of Citium, 38
Zhang Zhaozhong, 109, 110
Zhou Enlai, 92, 164–65n24

ABOUT THE AUTHOR

James R. Holmes is J. C. Wylie Chair of Maritime Strategy at the U.S. Naval War College and a former U.S. Navy engineering and gunnery officer. He formerly served on the faculty of the University of Georgia School of Public and International Affairs.

The Naval Institute Press is the book-publishing arm of the U.S. Naval Institute, a private, nonprofit, membership society for sea service professionals and others who share an interest in naval and maritime affairs. Established in 1873 at the U.S. Naval Academy in Annapolis, Maryland, where its offices remain today, the Naval Institute has members worldwide.

Members of the Naval Institute support the education programs of the society and receive the influential monthly magazine *Proceedings* or the colorful bimonthly magazine *Naval History* and discounts on fine nautical prints and on ship and aircraft photos. They also have access to the transcripts of the Institute's Oral History Program and get discounted admission to any of the Institute-sponsored seminars offered around the country.

The Naval Institute's book-publishing program, begun in 1898 with basic guides to naval practices, has broadened its scope to include books of more general interest. Now the Naval Institute Press publishes about seventy titles each year, ranging from how-to books on boating and navigation to battle histories, biographies, ship and aircraft guides, and novels. Institute members receive significant discounts on the Press' more than eight hundred books in print.

Full-time students are eligible for special half-price membership rates. Life memberships are also available.

For a free catalog describing Naval Institute Press books currently available, and for further information about joining the U.S. Naval Institute, please write to:

Member Services
U.S. Naval Institute
291 Wood Road
Annapolis, MD 21402-5034
Telephone: (800) 233-8764
Fax: (410) 571-1703
Web address: www.usni.org